D0054183

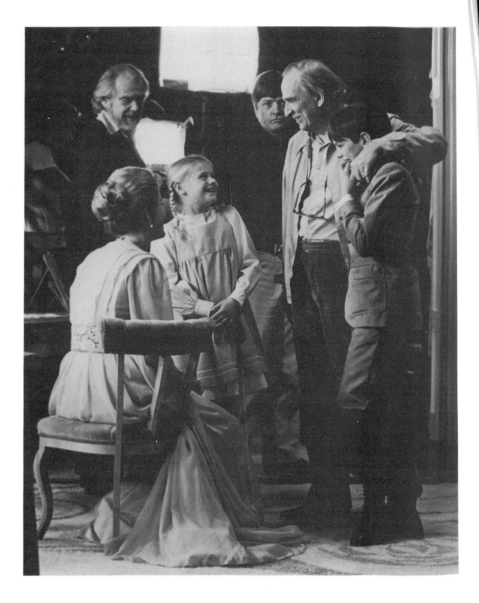

Frontispiece Ingmar Bergman and his young stars during the shooting of *Fanny and Alexander*.

Film and Video Editing

TR
899
C74
1995

Film and Video Editing

Second edition

Roger Crittenden

BLUEPRINT
An Imprint of Chapman & Hall

London · Glasgow · Weinheim · New York · Tokyo · Melbourne · Madras

3443147

WITHDRAWN
UNIVERSITY OF NEVADA LAS VEGAS
LIBRARY

Published by Blueprint, an imprint of Chapman & Hall, 2–6 Boundary Row, London SE1 8HN, UK

Chapman & Hall, 2–6 Boundary Row, London SE1 8HN, UK

Blackie Academic & Professional, Wester Cleddens Road, Bishopbriggs, Glasgow G64 2NZ, UK

Chapman & Hall GmbH, Pappelallee 3, 69469 Weinheim, Germany

Chapman & Hall USA, 115 Fifth Avenue, New York, NY 10003, USA

Chapman & Hall Japan, ITP-Japan, Kyowa Building, 3F, 2–2–1 Hirakawacho, Chiyoda-ku, Tokyo 102, Japan

Chapman & Hall Australia, 102 Dodds Street, South Melbourne, Victoria 3205, Australia

Chapman & Hall India, R. Seshadri, 32 Second Main Road, CIT East, Madras 600 035, India

First published in 1981 as *The Thames and Hudson Manual of Film Editing*, Thames and Hudson Ltd, London

Second edition 1995

© 1981 Thames and Hudson Ltd, 1995 Roger Crittenden

Typeset in 10/12 Palatino by WestKey Ltd, Falmouth, Cornwall

Printed in Great Britain by St Edmundsbury Press, Bury St Edmunds, Suffolk

ISBN 1 85713 011 1

Apart from any fair dealing for the purposes of research or private study, or criticism or review, as permitted under the UK Copyright Designs and Patents Act, 1988, this publication may not be reproduced, stored, or transmitted, in any form or by any means, without the prior permission in writing of the publishers, or in the case of reprographic reproduction only in accordance with the terms of the licences issued by the Copyright Licensing Agency in the UK, or in accordance with the terms of licences issued by the appropriate Reproduction Rights Organization outside the UK. Enquiries concerning reproduction outside the terms stated here should be sent to the publishers at the London address printed on this page.

The publisher makes no representation, express or implied, with regard to the accuracy of the information contained in this book and cannot accept any legal responsibility or liability for any errors or omissions that may be made.

The use of the terms his and man is not indicative of specific gender and should be taken to mean his/her and man/woman throughout, except in specific case examples.

A catalogue record for this book is available from the British Library

Library of Congress Catalog Card Number: 95-78842

∞ Printed on acid-free text paper, manufactured in accordance with ANSI/NISO Z39.48–1992 (Permanence of Paper).

Contents

Acknowledgements and thanks   viii
Introduction   ix

1 Historical perspective: how editing has evolved   **1**
    D. W. Griffith   2
    The Soviet cinema   4
    Eisenstein   5
    Robert Flaherty   8
    Buñuel and surrealism   9
    The coming of sound   10
    The silent comedians   10
    Persistence of vision   12
    The Moviola   12
    Sound pioneers   13
    Linear versus reflexive   13
    Deep focus   14
    Jean Renoir   14
    William Wyler   15
    Orson Welles   15
    Documentary   17
    Humphrey Jennings   17
    Jean Vigo   19
    Yasujiro Ozu   21
    After Welles   22
    Neo-realism   23
    Editors turned directors   24
    The New Wave   24
    The effect of television   29

Wide screen   29
Stereophonic sound   30
The small screen   30
Sons of poets   32
Recent trends   34

2 **Shooting with cutting in mind**   **36**
The shooting process   37
Identification and synchronization   39
Documentary shooting   45
The proper use of sound   49
Paperwork   50

3 **From cutting room to edit suite: the development of the
   technology**   **54**

4 **Editing procedure**   **64**
Checking your material for faults   65
Synchronizing the rushes   67
Coding the rushes   71
Logging   71
Transcribing or marking up the script   72
Viewing the sync rushes   72
Breaking down the film   75
Cutting   76
Video editing   78
Random access   79
The relationship between director and editor   81

5 **The language of editing: giving your material form and
   refining its meaning**   **83**
Reasons for cutting   87
Cutting and reaction: dramatic emphasis   90
Directors and editing – some examples   91
Cutting and the private-eye genre   102
Editing and genre   103
Form and content   107

6 **Sound in editing**   **108**
The effect of equipment   109
Working methods   109
Categories of sound   111
Dialogue   111
Post-synchronization (ADR)   112

Effects   114
Foley   114
Voice-over or narration   114
Music   117
Playback   121
Tracklaying   122
Dubbing charts   128
The mix   128

7 Completing the picture: from mix to screen   131
The 'contact'   132
Reprints and duplication   132
Opticals   134
Negative and original cutting   139
Grading and printing   140
Duplicating the master   144
Storage and retention of the master   144
The digital alternative   145
Conclusion   146

8 The elusive art: some editors and their work   148
Margaret Booth   149
William Hornbeck   149
Adrienne Fazan   150
Verna Fields   150
Dede Allen   151
Thelma Schoonmaker   152
Anne Coates   153
Carol Littleton   154
Roberto Perpignani   154
Lou Lombardo   156
Antony Gibbs   157
Richard Marks   157
Helen van Dongen   158
Stewart McAllister   158

Glossary   160
Suggested further reading   185
Index   189

Acknowledgements and thanks

Thanks to all those who have supplied stills. Those from *Fanny and Alexander* and *Tokyo Story* are from Artificial Eye, whose courtesy is particularly appreciated.

The stills and paperwork from the production of *Mary Reilly* are courtesy of Tristar Corporation, and I must express my gratitude to the producer Iain Smith and to the assistant editor Jeremy Hume.

Dede Allen, Thelma Schoonmaker and Roberto Perpignani kindly let me have the pictures of themselves. The photograph of Ms Schoonmaker is by Fred George.

The images of non-linear technology are from the manufacturers or distributors of Avid, Lightworks and Montage.

All other film stills were supplied by the British Film Institute Stills and Posters Department.

The picture of the director and editor at the Steenbeck was taken by my colleague Paddy Seale. This picture shows Michael Bentham and Felicity Moore, graduates of the National Film and Television School.

I would like to thank Barrie Vince for his advice on those sections which deal with the new technology, and Judith McDonnell for her stills research.

Lastly, thanks to my family for their tolerance and support of my latest venture into writing and to all those students at the National Film and Television School who have been a constant source of stimulus and fulfilment over the last twenty-four years.

Roger Crittenden, 1995

Introduction

Before the invention of cinema, popular entertainment was dominated by music hall, vaudeville, the circus and the various amusements and side shows available at the fair. Samuel McKechnie writes in his *Popular Entertainment through the Ages* that:

> The meanest show in the Bartholemew Fair of 1825 . . . was the peepshow. It consisted of rudely-painted scenes, which the proprietor successively let down by strings; and it was viewed through eye-glasses of magnifying power by several spectators at a time. They stood on the ground and a projecting rod was drawn round them while they were peeping at the scenes. These included the Visit of the Queen of Sheba to Solomon, Daniel in the Den of Lions, the Battle of Waterloo and the Coronation of George IV . . . it is only fair to say that more than any other exhibition (the) peepshow was the forerunner of a great new form of popular entertainment. It was a direct ancestor of the cinema.

Peepshows, Magic Lanterns or Phantasmagoria, all these devices for creating the illusion of an image, even sequences of images, were an established and popular part of mass entertainment in the nineteenth century. However they were extremely theatrical not only in content but in one very particular formal way: the point of view of the spectator was religiously consistent, i.e. as if you were sitting in the theatre in front of a performance.

If you have seen pictures of early cinematograph studios you will know that the theatrical approach was carried over into the point of view of the camera in primitive cinema; indeed we still refer to film studios as stages to this day. When the crucial breakthrough was made that took the camera close to and eventually inside the action of the drama, it was the craft of editing that had to be invented to bring coherence to the fragments of a scene.

In his book *The Parade's Gone By*, Kevin Brownlow described film editing as 'The Hidden Art'. The contribution that editing can make is still the least understood and most underestimated part of the whole process, and yet it is often the point at which the magic comes together or proves finally to be elusive.

I shall never forget the amazement that greeted Sylvia Ingemarson when she insisted, to an audience of fellow editors, that she had cut *Fanny and Alexander* in a few weeks. If you have seen Ingmar Bergman's masterpiece I think you will agree that it is a complex film that you would have expected to have given the editor and director many problems. Yet many films are the result of months of post-production work, none of which can turn poor material into a good film.

In the last few years there has been a revolution in the development of technology for the editing process. The combination of digital storage and random access to material has given the editor fingertip control in an instant. It is now possible to carry out editing decisions faster than the brain can envisage them. Never has it been more important for the prospective editor to master the craft to avoid being mastered by the machinery.

No editor can be guaranteed good material to work with, but he or she has no excuse if they are unable to use the craft to make the best use of that material. It is the aim of this book to encourage a better understanding of the craft of editing, so that the talented editor can create patterns and rhythms that give magical life to the art of storytelling. The computer game would have found a place alongside the peepshow at the Bartholemew Fair. The best of cinema and television can be more than a toy. Editing is part of the craft that can make it so.

Historical perspective: how editing has evolved

1

At the turn of the century in France two paths along which film would develop were being pioneered. The Lumière brothers were demonstrating how events could be the basis of film reality, and Georges Méliès was showing how manipulation of reality could become a film event.

Everything that has subsequently been recorded on film or video fits somewhere in the formal spectrum between these two extremes. In neither case however was the potential of editing even hinted at. The Lumières were content to show an event as it occurred before the lens, and Méliès enjoyed manipulating images through multiple exposure and creative legerdemain. The cut was not part of their language.

Yet the basic form of the cinema was established within ten years of the first public presentation of moving pictures. Although it is common practice to cite the films of D. W. Griffith as the first to contain the elements which allow us to juxtapose different types of shot when cutting, most of these elements had previously been used around the turn of the century by a group of British film-makers.

These pioneers (R. W. Paul, Cecil Hepworth, James Williamson, G. A. Smith and Alfred Collins) incorporated close-ups, sequencing of action, parallel action, variations of set-up and camera movement in their films. In *British Creators of Film Technique* (1948), Georges Sadoul suggested that these early film-makers were following the principles of sequence and change of view established before cinema in the telling of stories with lantern slides.

This sequencing with slides can be regarded as the direct antecedent of film editing, but in the early days film derived its impact from other traditions. Nineteenth-century popular theatre and literature were the sources of storytelling techniques which were allied to the crude methods of presentation perfected in the fairground. However one important factor made it imperative that film develop a language of its own: for thirty years it was a silent medium. Title cards were never going to be a sufficient substitute for verbal storytelling techniques developed over thousands of years of dramatic presentation.

Initially the title card provided a convenient bridge between two different shots, just as text was used to link a lantern slide performance, but mute tableaux seen from one point of view served to encourage a theatrical approach. Thus the early film-makers sensed that it was necessary to find ways of controlling rhythm and pace, establishing mood, providing emphasis and focusing attention in the scene.

D. W. GRIFFITH

The essential link between primitive film and the incorporation of most editing techniques in the films of D. W. Griffith was provided by Edwin S. Porter in his two famous films *The Life of an American Fireman* and *The Great Train Robbery*, both made in 1903. It was Porter who established that the intercutting of different shots not necessarily related to the same time and place could provide the basis for the structuring of narrative through editing.

Five years later D. W. Griffith began the process of refining his own methods of shooting which by 1914 included all the basic elements necessary for coherent visual narrative. It is of no little significance that his cameraman was Billy Bitzer who had earlier worked for Porter. Bitzer probably deserves more credit than he is given for applying the techniques in Griffith's films. Whatever the truth one thing is certain, with each succeeding film this pair of pioneers made, they were assuming an increasing degree of importance for the editing process. Some of their significant first uses of techniques were as follows:

Date	Film	Technique
1908	*Adventures of Dolly*	Flashback
1908	*For Love of Gold*	Full shot of two characters
1908	*After Many Years*	Close-up of one character and cutback to character being thought of in previous close-up
1909	*The Lonely Villa*	Parallel action
1910	*Ramona*	Extreme long shot
1911	*The Lonedale Operator*	Crosscut close-ups
1912	*The Massacre*	Moving camera, rapid cutting, crosscutting, and close-up detail
1914	*Home Sweet Home*	Tracking shot

Iris Barry delineated Griffith's achievements in her monograph published in 1940. Ernest Lindgren spelt them out even more clearly in *The Art of Film* (1948): 'Griffith instinctively saw the coherence he could achieve on the screen even though his material was fragmentary, filmed at different times in different places with a variety of shots, but all coming together to make one scene; (Griffith) succeeded in building up in the minds of his audience an association of ideas welded with such logic and charged with such emotional momentum that its truth was not questioned.'

Consider the alternatives available to the film-maker because of this establishment of the basic language. In 1908 Griffith started out as a director in the knowledge that the conventional film would show the whole scene, from beginning to end, from in front of the characters in a shot that included the whole area of the action (usually a three-walled set). When he and Bitzer decided to move into a closer shot of one character the convention was broken. Incidentally, when the studio bosses saw the result they complained that this was unacceptable since they had paid for the whole actor! As soon as this closer shot was seen it was no great step to show a closer shot of another character. Having done this you can intercut the two.

Perhaps the greatest step in this exploration of filmic space is the moment when the director realizes he is inside the area established in the wide shot. It is as if a member of the audience at a theatre performance has stepped on to the stage. The camera has to all intents and purposes become a

Figure 1.1   D. W. Griffith on the set with Lillian Gish.

character in the scene. So the dynamics of film language come to depend upon the sense that each member of the audience has of being present in the action through the agency of the camera.

Most cinema still proceeds as if Griffith were leaning over the shoulder of the director. Each director prepares the shooting script of a film with a very basic assumption in mind: that for each scene there exists an ideal point of view which establishes the position of the camera for the master shot. This ideal position is related to the best way of staging the action to allow the focus of the scene to be properly encompassed.

Once this position is established every subsequent shot that is incorporated must refer to the axis of this establishing shot. This is because we are working in a two-dimensional medium that represents three-dimensional space. The only ways of changing this axis are by character movement or camera movement.

As we have seen, Griffith was the first to make disparate elements cohere into convincing sequences. The culmination of his efforts came in two epic films: *Birth of a Nation* (1915) and *Intolerance* (1916). Iris Barry says: 'The film *Intolerance* is extremely important in the history of cinema. It is the end and justification of that whole school of American cinematography based on the terse cutting and disjunctive assembly of lengths of film.'

THE SOVIET CINEMA

Griffith had an enormous influence on the post-revolution generation of film-makers in the Soviet Union. Iris Barry states that it was: 'from his example that they derived their characteristic staccato shots, their measured and accurate rhythms and their skill in joining pictorial images together with a view to the emotional overtones of each so that two images in conjunction convey more than the sum of their visual content'.

In 1919, when the Moscow Film School was established, Griffith's films were being shown in Russia for the first time. Lenin himself, aware of the immense potential value of film to the new Bolshevik state, personally arranged the wide distribution of *Intolerance*. However, Lindgren points out that there was a deeper consciousness developing there:

It was the directors of the Soviet Union who were the first to understand the full significance of this fact (of film truth) and to exploit it; for editing, as the Russians saw, is nothing less than the deliberate guidance of the thoughts and convictions of the spectator.

Lindgren goes on:

They clearly perceived . . . that editing derived its power . . . from the fact that a succession of shots involved a complex set of relationships between them, relationships of idea, of duration, of physical movement and of form.

Among this generation of directors, all of whom came under the influence of Griffith, were V. I. Pudovkin, Lev Kuleshov, Dziga Vertov and Sergei Eisenstein. The writings and films of these four are worth careful study by all aspiring editors.

Kuleshov felt that editing was the heart of film-making. By cutting together the same shot of the face of a well-known Russian actor (Ivan Mosjoukine) with, for instance, a plate of soup on a table, a shot of a coffin containing a dead woman and a little girl playing with a toy, he was able to demonstrate that you could control the audience response by the nature of the juxtaposition, yielding in the above cases the feeling that the actor was expressing alternately hunger, sadness and joy.

Pudovkin worked with Kuleshov on the above experiment and it was he who carried the results forward into his filmic construction. He wrote at one point that he '. . . tried to affect the spectators, not by the psychological performance of the actor, but by plastic synthesis through editing'. He was scornful of Griffith's direct narrative techniques, preferring to create emotional effects through the careful montage of associative elements. His film *Mother* is the best demonstration of this approach.

EISENSTEIN

Sergei Eisenstein was just as interested as Pudovkin in the value of montage, but in his hands editing acquired intellectual force. His use of juxtaposition was meant to convey a synthesis of ideas much in the way that the Marxist theory of the dialectic proposed a dynamic progression in society. He was not content to tell stories even when they were related to the momentous events of the revolution. To Eisenstein it was of paramount importance that his montage gave the meaning behind the events.

The classic example is the Odessa Steps sequence in *Battleship Potemkin* (1925) where he uses more than 150 shots in less than seven minutes to portray an event through complex juxtapositions, whereas the surface drama could have been conveyed in no more than two dozen cuts. However, Eisenstein saw every cut as an opportunity to convey ideas about the events, rather than just as a means of pacing and focusing the scene. This point, incidentally, seems to be lost on Brian de Palma when he plagiarizes the Odessa Steps in the climactic scene of his film *The Untouchables*.

Although much of Eisenstein's approach seems contrived and obscure, it would be wrong to consign his work to the attic of film technique. The coming of sound put unbearable pressure on the effectiveness of pure visual metaphor, but he was as brilliant a thinker on the nature of the medium as we have so far seen, and his aesthetics regarding composition,

Figure 1.2 Sergei Eisenstein behind the camera.

colour and much else are still stimulating to contemporary minds if we can dust the cobwebs off our own resistance to earlier forms.

Indeed, when he was working with students at the Moscow Film School in the 1930s there was ample evidence that his approach to direction was anything but dry. We are indebted to a student, Vladimir Nizhny, for recording Eisenstein's pedagogical methods in his book *Lessons with Eisenstein* (1962). In it he describes intense work on the staging of a particular scene which Eisenstein used as a workshop example. It is the killing of the old moneylender by Raskolnikov in Dostoyevsky's *Crime and Punishment*. After exploring many ways of breaking down the scene, Eisenstein convinced his students of the feasibility of handling it in one long developing shot. By choreographing the two characters he was able to suggest a way of sustaining the drama through pacing and visual emphasis without resorting to editing.

Eisenstein summarized the work he had done with the class thus: 'It seems to me that the worry that was affecting many of you at the start, that for us to stage everything in one shot would be boring and uninteresting, has proved unjustified . . . In our work we have managed to fix all the striking and critical moments in a corresponding close view without changing the camera set-up . . . you have been convinced that mise-en-scène contains in itself all the elements concerned with editing break-up into shots.' He then coined the term 'mise-en-shot' to describe the way staging the action carefully can provide all the dramatic emphasis that would conventionally be conveyed by cutting.

His object was not to convince his students that shooting a scene in one shot is necessarily the best solution, but that proper staging will reveal the details of dramatic development that allow the director to decide how to photograph the scene. This analysis is still the essential task of each director and directly determines the nature of the editor's material.

In contrast and in opposition to Eisenstein's dramatic artifice, and inspired by Lenin's call to record the new Soviet reality, Dziga Vertov and his colleagues in 'Kino-eye' set out to use the medium in a way that was entirely reliant on what occurs in front of the camera, without being provoked by a script or performed by actors. The resulting energy and inventiveness is visible in *The Man with a Movie Camera*, where montage is only one element of the self-consciously manipulative style. Despite seeing himself as a significant recorder of post-revolutionary Russia, Vertov brought a refreshing playfulness to the form both in shooting and in the cutting room.

Not all early Soviet film-makers were concerned with either dramatic narrative or the representation of Soviet reality. Alexander Dovzhenko created the cinematic equivalent of poetic form by pioneering the montage of visual association not dependent on narrative progression. His film *Earth* (1930) presents a series of images which, whilst being thematically linked, do not add up to the coherent narrative which is inherent in conventional dramatic films. Dovzhenko has remained an inspiration for all film-makers who are attracted to the metaphorical use of visual language.

ROBERT FLAHERTY

Ironically it is the non-fiction film which has often provided more imaginative explorations of visual language. Pre-eminent amongst the progenitors was Robert Flaherty who has indeed been called 'The Father of Documentary'. As is often true of those who have a major influence on the development of a medium, Flaherty had few collaborators, especially in the early years, preferring to follow his own idiosyncratic path.

It might all have been so different if he had given up after the original material for his first film was burnt in a fire. Perhaps his determination to continue had something to do with the fact that the film had been shot under the punishing conditions of the arctic cold whilst observing a family of Eskimos. After a second period of shooting he eventually released *Nanook of the North* in 1922. No doubt the impact of this film at the time had something to do with its 'exotic' subject, but nothing can take away the fact

Figure 1.3 Robert Flaherty on location during the shooting of *Louisiana Story* with cameraman Richard Leacock, editor Helen van Dongen, the boy from the film and Mrs Flaherty.

that Flaherty's instinctive respect for his material conveyed a freshness which is still visible when the film is viewed today.

Flaherty's work from *Nanook* to *Louisiana Story* in 1948 demonstrates a continuity of development over three decades spanning silent and sound cinema. His techniques were refined from film to film without any radical change of approach. His work was admired by André Bazin, the French critic who inspired the New Wave. Bazin raised important questions regarding the validity of montage and used Flaherty's films as evidence to support his case.

Bazin felt strongly that the aesthetics of cinema demanded careful delineation. His essays, collected in *What is Cinema?*, present a particular and coherent view of the form and its relationship to content. Naturally editing comes in for stringent analysis, and part of his conclusion was enshrined in a law of aesthetics: 'When the essence of a scene demands the simultaneous presence of two or more factors in the action, montage is ruled out.'

He went on to say, '. . . it is inconceivable that the famous seal-hunt scene in *Nanook* should not show us hunter, hole and seal all in the same shot. It is simply a question of respect for the spatial unity of an event . . .' He was aware that his position was in direct opposition to the earlier theories and practices of the Russians: 'The editing of Kuleshov or Eisenstein and of Gance didn't show an event, they made an allusion to it', was his comment on the experiments of that previous era. However, Eisenstein was not the dogmatist many would have us believe.

If the object of a film is authenticity then Bazin believed that the audience must be presented with the proof within the frame, even if the reality we are asked to believe in is a fiction. This contract with the audience is at the root of all cutting decisions.

We do not have to agree with Bazin, but we must recognize that editing stands at the crossroads between film and audience. Flaherty often ignored the rule that Bazin proposed, for example in the scene between the boy and the alligator in *Louisiana Story*, but there is a clear line from Flaherty to contemporary documentary that continues to respect the relationships between subject, film-maker and audience.

BUÑUEL AND SURREALISM

Whilst Flaherty was working to strengthen the representation of reality, other artists were challenging the form of classic narrative. Luis Buñuel, in collaboration with Salvador Dali, produced those scandalous films of the surrealist movement *Un Chien Andalou* (1928) and *L'Age d'Or* (1931). Whilst it is true that these films contain some shocking imagery, their interest for us lies in the fact that they demonstrate that the conjunction of images can rely for coherence on symbolic meaning or even deliberate irrationality rather than the logical development of a narrative.

Indeed, we should be grateful to Buñuel for reminding us that the conventional narrative is a reactionary weapon, as much in film as it has always been in literature and theatre. The radical artist, he would say, must continuously subvert the form. Buñuel remained true to this approach throughout his career.

THE COMING OF SOUND

In many ways, by the end of the silent era, visual answers had been found to the challenge presented by the lack of sound. In any case the silent film had never been without sound. An orchestra, or at the very least a piano, invariably accompanied screenings, often using specially composed scores which were made available by the production company when the print was hired. There is no doubt however that cutting was a main support for narrative meaning, rhythm and emphasis in the absence of dialogue and other synchronous sound.

The irony was that for the first few years after sound arrived most cinema lost its energy and imagination. Since it was now possible to convey all essential narrative in words, all but the most disciplined and creative directors could depend upon the verbal as a substitute for the visual. This tended to inhibit the imaginative application of editing and to neutralize film style. The lazy habit of resorting to verbal exposition is still with us today: perhaps it is a function of the bias towards the verbal in our education, or simply a fear of the ambivalence which is inherent in the image.

For purely technical reasons, it is not surprising that the initial response to sound was unimaginative. In its early days sound recording technology was extremely primitive. To obtain a usable recording, microphones had to be placed very close to the actors and the camera had to be placed in a soundproof booth, and was therefore static. It was difficult to accommodate variations in voice level, and the artists could only move if the microphone position was adjustable. Also, early sound recording was virtually non-selective, so acoustics and the control of background sound were crucial.

THE SILENT COMEDIANS

Prior to the invention of cinema there was one particular art that worked its magic predominantly in silence: the art of the clown. Although Bazin considered that silent comedians such as Chaplin and Keaton depended on his principle of spatial unity, it is also true that much of their humour was made more effective by taking advantage of the cut. This was especially true once the concept of complicity with the audience was understood. This allowed visual gags to be signalled in advance and to be underlined

Figure 1.4 Buster Keaton and Kathryn McGuire in *The Navigator.*

afterwards, especially in relating the protagonist to the victim or to the object or situation which provoked the humour.

The classic example would be the banana skin joke, where we are with the person who has placed it for the victim and enjoy both the misfortune of the victim and the pleasure of the protagonist. Although the essence of this scene can be conveyed in one developing shot, the incorporation of cuts to show action and reaction as well as to control rhythm and emphasis gave the silent comics a very flexible form to play with. Although Chaplin and the rest did not write books about their craft, it did not stop Eisenstein and other theorists admiring the films they made.

Along with many other stars, the silent cinema comedians suffered rejection in the light of the coming of sound. The voice became the instrument of communication rather than the face and body. In the worst cases studios even substituted other actors' voices when they were dissatisfied with the original, a technique which was satirized in *Singin' in the Rain.* Often it was an excuse to end contracts with stars who had become too demanding or had lost their appeal at the box-office.

It is sad to reflect that much talent was lost due to short-sighted attitudes. None was more regrettable than the case of Louise Brooks, perhaps the most expressive of all silent stars, who was made to pay for abandoning

Hollywood to work in Germany with Pabst (*Pandora's Box* and *Diary of a Lost Girl*). On her return to Tinsel Town, at the start of the sound era, the offers were deliberately derisory and we were consequently denied the mature performances this artist would undoubtedly have given us. After all, she was only 25 at the time.

PERSISTENCE OF VISION

One crucial technical factor made it inevitable that sound would be given the serious consideration that it deserved. 'Moving pictures' were made possible because of the principle of persistence of vision: basically the human eye retains every image it sees for a split second. You can prove this by looking at a clearly defined object for a few seconds; close your eyes, turn your head to face a white wall and you will see the object 'projected' on the wall. So by recording a series of still images at a frequency that is fast enough to cheat the eye, they appear as continuous movement when projected at a similar speed.

The problem is that sound can only be recorded or reproduced satisfactorily as a continuous process. Therefore the picture and sound for any moment in time either have to be separated by sufficient distance on the same machine for one to be intermittent and the other to be continuous, or they have to be recorded and reproduced on separate machines which can be locked together in synchronous motion.

If it had been technically possible for sound and picture to be in parallel on the same strip of film, there would have been no need to consider the separate functions of the two elements. Everything could have been cut in parallel, and the consideration of other forms of sound such as music and effects would have required a much greater leap of the imagination. In the early days of video tape, when it had to be cut physically like film, the problem was repeated and it was common practice to make compromise cuts between the ideal 'frame' of picture and corresponding sound with the resultant lack of precision in the editing.

THE MOVIOLA

Fortunately the invention of the Moviola in 1929 allowed for the separate editing of picture and sound in parallel with each other. This meant that the brave and imaginative spirits of thirties cinema could feel free, both to express their ideas in exciting and effective imagery and to develop strong and evocative soundtracks. The approach to sound editing and its relationship to picture required a radical shift in the knowledge of film-makers who were used to constructing narratives based around captions and information that was inherent in the images.

Eisenstein and Pudovkin insisted that synchronous sound was the least interesting aspect of the new dimension. They were more interested in the contrapuntal potential of the constructed soundtrack, or the use of sound to complement a visual montage. In this they were at one with the most forward-looking directors in Hollywood and elsewhere.

SOUND PIONEERS

Kenneth MacGowan gives two examples in his book *Behind the Motion Picture Screen*; first:

> Alfred Hitchcock's first talkie, *Blackmail* (1929), showed us the power of off-screen speech to dramatize subjective fear . . . His heroine had stabbed a man who had attempted to seduce her. At breakfast she heard a neighbor (*sic*) discussing the murder and when she reached for a bread knife, the neighbor's conversation became indistinct except the word 'knife' which echoed on the soundtrack over her tortured face.

Secondly:

> In Fritz Lang's first talkie *M* (1931), the unseen mother of a missing child – whom the audience knew had been murdered – called her name again and again over the empty stairs, the girl's empty plate on the table, her ball in the grass, and the balloon that her murderer had given her, which was now entangled in some telephone wires . . . Lang used with equal skill and enormous effectiveness other off-screen but natural sounds.

In truth, we should be willing to acknowledge that the thirties saw a quiet revolution in film aesthetics in which editing of picture and sound played a practical and catalytic role. One of the best exercises for editors is playing chess. This is because the two activities are analogous in being games that play with space and time and where a decision made at any given point will have subsequent repercussions. The beauty of adding sound to the game is that it multiplies the options available to the editor.

LINEAR VERSUS REFLEXIVE

In a way we are constantly fighting to deny the purely linear nature of film and video, because if we can add a reflexive or circular aspect to the structure of a film there is a much greater possibility that it will mean more than the sum of its parts. The simplest example of these reflexive options is the repeated image or sound as exemplified in the examples described by MacGowan.

DEEP FOCUS

The next sea change in film language was made possible by the development of faster lenses that allowed a significant improvement in depth of field. By the late thirties directors were making demands of the camera which were to restore coherence to space and time on the screen, much in the way that Eisenstein was discussing with his students in Moscow.

JEAN RENOIR

Bazin describes how Jean Renoir was a pioneer in substituting composition in depth for conventional cutting. The subsequent achievements of William Wyler and Orson Welles were to confirm what Renoir had been hinting at for some time. Bazin, in his most eloquent essay *The Evolution of the Language of Cinema*, describes Renoir's achievement thus:

> He alone in his searchings as a director . . . forced himself to look back beyond the resources provided by montage and so uncovered the secret of a film form that would permit everything to be said without chopping the world up into little fragments, that would reveal the

Figure 1.5 Jean Renoir's *Partie de Campagne*, showing his appetite for staging in depth.

hidden meanings in people and things without disturbing the unity natural to them.

In the crudest terms, the conventional cut confirms a particular meaning by drawing attention to action and reaction in the chosen juxtaposition. The aim of staging in depth is to contain and emphasize meaning by choreographing camera and character action in such a way as to focus attention within the shot to allow the audience to see or perceive without the need to cut. In this aesthetic the editor uses the cut for rhythm and pacing rather than to create a meaning from fragments.

The conventionally cut film tends to lead the viewer by the hand, constructing a singular plot line and meaning, whereas staging in depth with long uninterrupted takes encourages the possibility of ambiguity and asks the audience to participate in the dilemmas facing the characters portrayed.

WILLIAM WYLER

As Bazin points out, two of the radical directors who espoused staging in depth worked in Hollywood: William Wyler and Orson Welles. Too little acknowledgement is accorded to Wyler, perhaps because much of his early work was adaptation from the stage, but to assume that his mastery of dramatizing in depth owes everything to the other medium is to grossly underestimate his command of the camera. A viewing of his film of Lillian Hellman's *The Childrens Hour* will prove the point, but his skill is visible years before in films like *The Little Foxes*. Indeed his later epics, like *Ben Hur* and *The Big Country*, prove his consummate skill in creating visual drama that owes very little to the theatre.

ORSON WELLES

Welles also had a background in the theatre, although before he made his first film, *Citizen Kane*, he was most notorious for his radio production of *The War of the Worlds*, which was so realistic that thousands of Americans believed the events were actually happening. Bazin is not the only writer who considers *Kane* to be of unique significance in the history of cinema.

On the face of it this film contains a rag-bag of styles, seemingly grabbed off the shelf by the precocious Welles: narration (by five different characters), one-shot scenes composed in depth, camera angles that defy gravity, montages of extreme temporal transition, the use of library footage of actual newsreels, model shots that expand the invented world, and against all this a soundtrack of corresponding complexity.

On careful analysis it is clear that none of this is careless or random. Whole books have been written attempting to give proper credit to Welles'

Figure 1.6 Orson Welles and Marlene Dietrich during the shooting of *Touch of Evil.*

major collaborators, especially his co-writer Herman J. Mankiewicz and his cameraman Gregg Toland, who had been instrumental in introducing William Wyler to deep focus. Both possessed the previous experience that Welles lacked, but their earlier work does not match the consummate skill that *Kane* demonstrates.

Bazin summarizes the achievement of Welles and his team thus: '. . . *Citizen Kane* is part of a general movement, of a vast stirring of the geological bed of cinema, confirming that everywhere up to a point there had been a revolution in the language of the screen . . . his (Welles) case is the most spectacular and by virtue of his very excesses, the most significant.'

In fact Welles represented both a culmination and a breakthrough. Even if Bazin was right in accusing him of baroque excesses, Welles at least demonstrated that the essential consistency was the matching of content to form, not a consistency which demands a neutrality of style. His was a belligerent challenge to the banality of mainstream cinema, perhaps more an echo of the sawdust and tinsel of the circus than the herald of a new poetics, but no less significant for all that.

DOCUMENTARY

There were other challenges to the conventions of mainstream cinema in the thirties and it is important that we look at some of them because of their impact on editing. First, documentary developed both through Flaherty and because of the work of others. Basil Wright's *Song of Ceylon* was a seminal work combining visual and aural montage in an innovative way, embracing with enthusiasm Eisenstein's rubric that asynchronous sound is the more expressive.

Pare Lorentz made similar use of unrealistic sounds in *The Plough that Broke the Plains*, but in the end contrapuntal effects between picture and sound were always going to be limited to the film of ideas rather than being easily applicable to narrative.

Whilst Wright and Lorentz were significant individual film-makers, the major impact of the documentary came from work done through public sponsorship in Britain. John Grierson masterminded the GPO Film Unit and nurtured a body of talent that culminated both in works of social significance and the poetic cinema of Humphrey Jennings. By encouraging the involvement of painters, composers and poets, he pushed the exploration of the medium beyond the normal parameters of propaganda. So much so that he and his cohorts were regularly at odds with the Ministry.

It was Basil Wright who directed the little gem of a film *Night Mail* for Grierson's unit. Today it would be unusual, if not unthinkable, certainly in England, for the leading poet and the leading composer to collaborate on the soundtrack of a short film for the Post Office, but W. H. Auden and Benjamin Britten did just that on this portrait of the London to Glasgow mail train.

The way the soundtrack combines natural sound with poetry and music, taking its rhythmic cue from the beat established by the train, is a unique construction in the history of the cinema. Indeed, the words of the poem were recorded **before** the images were cut, then the music was composed and recorded and finally the pictures and words were adjusted to the music. If we are nervous of adopting such a method today it may be through lack of both courage and a control of the form which demands talent and collaboration of the highest order.

HUMPHREY JENNINGS

The synthesis of individual talents that worked on *Night Mail* were all but combined in the one persona of Humphrey Jennings. Poet, painter, designer, social researcher, academic; he was all these things and he considered film-making to be a subsidiary activity.

During the short period when his films effectively enshrined the sombre but vital feelings of Britain confronted by the Nazi threat, Jennings produced a poetic cinema which few have emulated. He wished to 'tie knots in history' by using the image as metaphor. His work reminds me of Emily Dickinson's axiom 'Forever is composed of Nows', for his images encapsulated a particular era as if it were preserved in aspic.

Listen to Britain is Jennings' most thorough realization of the integration of evocative image and symbolic meaning. It is undoubtedly the joint achievement of Jennings and his editor Stewart McAllister. The magical quality of this film is related to the way the imagery is structured into a rhythm and line that seems inevitable and indeed derives its power from the inner dynamic. The way sound is used to complement the visuals without commentary (the introductory speech was not part of Jennings' conception) is an object lesson to all film-makers.

Every juxtaposition is both a natural progression and a comment. This film is structured like a poem: its style and content are inseparable. It is propaganda but it persuades through metaphor rather than polemic. It convinces because the images and sounds create their own resonances. It

Figure 1.7 Humphrey Jennings during the filming of *Family Portrait*.

uses the cut, the mix and the fade as positive elements in the overall style. It points to the fact that film can also work its magic when dealing with the action away from the centre of the stage. It is one thing to deal with the vortex of events, but quite another to focus on the heartbeat of those who 'only stand and wait'. It is to the soul of a nation what Leni Riefenstahl's *Triumph of the Will* was to the head.

Any sequence serves to illustrate the point: a quiet country village, a rumbling sound – tanks are seen disturbing the stillness – they rumble on to war – mix to sky – 'music while you work' – mix to road under railway bridge with train over – industrial landscape – factory girls – tannoy radio – girls singing at their work. The shot that gets the sequence moving and links from the sky to the factory is the travelling shot under the railway bridge, which coincides with the train passing over. This shot was taken at Denham, down the road from where the film was being cut. It seems that Jennings and McAllister could not decide how to get from the armoured column rumbling through the village to the factory girls and this shot was obtained during the editing. With the orchestrated sound it works like magic. The poet has found the right phrase.

As with other creative expression there is a difference between the work of a poet and the use of 'poetic' form in the cinema. Whilst Dovzhenko self-consciously employed poetic form, the true poets of the cinema, like Jennings, did not strive for such effects.

JEAN VIGO

The most influential poet of cinema was dead some years before Jennings appeared on the scene. Although he only made one full length film, Jean Vigo has influenced a great many subsequent film-makers. It must be remembered that Vigo's first film was a documentary, and that his cameraman was Boris Kaufman who had been part of Kino-eye.

This film, *A Propos de Nice*, exhibits a love-hate relationship with the city that Vigo knew intimately. It communicates an intense response entirely through choice of shot and juxtaposition. Kaufman was familiar with the 'montage of attraction' approach developed by Vertov, and although Vigo started out with the basis of a shot list the film was created by a process of interaction between the film-makers, the levels of 'reality' in Nice and the images that they recorded. Without the expositional potential of sound they were forced to construct a visual commentary through the editing.

Vigo's father was an anarchist whose death in prison was never fully explained. The son, in his short artistic life, managed to control any tendency to aggressive irrationality, and instead created bittersweet comments on the human condition in his two major films, *Zéro de Conduite* and *L'Atalante*. He only just survived the completion of the latter film, dying in 1934 at the age of 29.

I feel that he has inspired others, as much in his approach to editing as elsewhere in the craft. Whilst Lindsay Anderson was directly inspired by *Zéro de Conduite* in making his film *If*, Vigo's attitude to the form of cinema can be seen reflected directly in the work of Truffaut and others.

There is a wonderfully free-spirited approach to the editing of Vigo's films, which demonstrates the courage to depend on a continuity of emotion rather than the mechanics of action. In *L'Atalante* in particular there is often no surface logic to his juxtapositions, but his instinctive control of rhythm creates an aesthetic of feeling to replace the dependence on logical construction.

Figure 1.8   Jean Vigo and cast in production of *L'Atalante*.

Figure 1.9   A typical Ozu composition from *Tokyo Story*.

YASUJIRO OZU

The example of Jean Vigo should make us beware of rigid assumptions regarding film form and any one dominant aesthetic. Sometimes the cultural and artistic traditions of a particular part of the world have suggested alternative forms to that generally used in Europe and Hollywood. In the thirties in Japan, Ozu was developing a quite different approach to filmic syntax. Basil Wright, in his book on the history of cinema, *The Long View*, described Ozu's work thus:

> It is a world which is conveyed to us through a filmic technique which Ozu has stripped of all elaboration. The camera angle seldom varies, being centred on the action from a position a little above ground level. There are no fades, wipes, dissolves. Each sequence is introduced by a series of establishing shots – atmospheric and temporal as well as geographical – presented in a cool and completely unfussy manner. Nor is there any significant variation in editing tempo. Ozu's films tend to proceed at an ambling pace, and at moments of climax they slow down rather than speed up. Once one is accustomed to this unpretentious andante, a slight change of pace, one way or the other, is enough to quicken the nerves. . . . the films and the people in them

unfold before us like those paper flowers – also Japanese – which open gently to reveal their petals when we drop them into a bowl of water.

Ozu's rhythm and the apparent detachment of his mise-en-scène have invited comparison with Dreyer and Bresson. The similarities in the work of these three directors formed the basis of Paul Schrader's book *Transcendental Style in Film*, but we should not lose sight of Ozu's particular visual style. Not only is the camera static and invariably placed at the equivalent of eye level when seated on the floor, which in this case is as culturally specific as you could get, but also there is a respect for the space characters are inhabiting, in that the camera seldom penetrates between the actors.

Indeed, it is often the case that the audience has an unprivileged point of view, for instance in a two-shot from behind. Certainly, although the composition is invariably precise and elegant, it often feels as if the camera has been ignored. The dignity and respect accorded to the characters is partially conveyed by this lack of status accorded to the camera, and the editing is correspondingly discreet. Perhaps because Ozu does not resort to what we think of as conventional cover he also has no inhibitions about crossing the line; that is, he will move the camera 180 degrees even though by doing so the characters in a two-shot swap sides of the screen on the cut.

AFTER WELLES

It took a number of years for the artistry of the likes of Ozu and Vigo to seep into the creative consciousness of younger generations of film-makers. Meanwhile the influence of Welles after *Citizen Kane* was immediate, though not necessarily for the better. Aggressive montage, staccato rhythms and self-conscious camerawork coupled with vivid and arresting sound and music tracks are still the hallmark of many second-rate descendants of Welles. It is seldom that the subject material or treatment matches the energy and inventiveness of that epic original, and thus the vacuousness is not disguised by the sound and fury.

However it would be wrong to suggest that only the 'baroque excesses' have been imitated. Cinema since *Kane* has, at its best, learnt from the use of deep focus as much as from the structural and narrative techniques that Welles employed. Indeed, his next film, *The Magnificent Ambersons*, had the unity of style that the bric-a-brac (Welles' own phrase) of *Citizen Kane* lacked. In this film Welles relied to an even greater extent on long developing shots which conveyed the essence of each scene's meaning through the staging rather than cutting. He managed to control action in space so that montage became redundant.

In some ways the Second World War created a hiatus in the development of the cinema, partly because film making was often diverted to propaganda purposes and partly because there were considerable restrictions on distribution. At the end of the conflict in 1945, Marcel Carné's *Les Enfants du Paradis* reaffirmed the beauty of the best of cinema but did nothing for the development of film language.

NEO-REALISM

Ironically the mass suffering brought about by the war probably contributed to the development of the next influential movement: that of neo-realism. A paucity of resources and an awareness of the plight of ordinary people seemed to drive the likes of Roberto Rossellini, Vittorio de Sica and Luchino Visconti towards a simple cinema that dealt in stories of the human spirit remaining indomitable against the odds. Filming in the streets, sometimes with non-actors and employing the minimum of technology, these Italians created a rough cinema that had a direct appeal to the masses emerging from six terrible years of widespread suffering.

It is impossible to overestimate the subsequent influence of neo-realism on cinema all over the world. Whether or not the low budget film-makers in New York and elsewhere have seen *Rome, Open City* or *Bicycle Thieves* or *Paisa*, they have much in common with the neo-realists. Indeed the new Independents represent a revolt against Fascism too: the Fascism of the corporate control of big budget movie-making.

Figure 1.10 Vittorio de Sica's *Bicycle Thieves*.

We should remember that there is an inevitable connection between production conditions, chosen or imposed, and the style that is adopted. Worrying less about continuity than content, less about focus than feelings, less about exposure than emotion, gives encouragement to those who find the achievement of technical perfection too high a price to pay if meaning is sacrificed to mechanics. In editing everything becomes dependent on rhythm. It is as if the very pulse of the action must dictate the form rather than formulaic construction.

EDITORS TURNED DIRECTORS

Traditional cinema reasserted itself once the industry was back in shape after the war. Some of the most confident work in the late forties and fifties came from editors turned directors. David Lean was one such: Basil Wright admired his 'subtle camera movement and exquisitely timed editing' in *Brief Encounter*, qualities which were also evident in *Great Expectations*. The sweep of Lean's later large scale work, from *Lawrence of Arabia* to *A Passage to India*, continued to depend on his meticulous control of camera and his innate sense of pacing and rhythm in the cutting. This magisterial facility with the medium brought him many admirers, especially in Hollywood where Spielberg still quotes him as the master.

Kevin Brownlow has described editing as 'directing the film for the second time', and it is not surprising that the cutting room is the single most frequent source of directing talent from amongst the various crafts. Another example in the forties was Robert Wise, who had been Welles' editor on both *Citizen Kane* and *The Magnificent Ambersons*. Wise quickly established himself and worked in most genres including musicals: *West Side Story* and *The Sound of Music*. According to Geoff Andrew, 'Wise's finest work reveals that technical proficiency and sensitivity to performance, pace and setting may result in highly watchable even memorable cinema.'

THE NEW WAVE

In retrospect it is easy to see that the disillusionment with society that set in by the end of the forties would eventually lead to a widespread revolt both politically and artistically, and the cinema was to prove no exception. When the New Wave broke in France at the end of the fifties, one of the heroes most often referred to was Alfred Hitchcock. It was not that all of this group of French directors were keen to make thrillers, although François Truffaut, Jean-Luc Godard and especially Claude Chabrol did explore this genre. What they admired about Hitchcock was both his control of the medium and his ability to convey the disjuncture in society that lies only just beneath the surface. There is no doubt that Hitchcock's skill in economic exposition and his manipulation of the audience excited

Figure 1.11 François Truffaut shooting *Jules et Jim.*

these young talents who were eager to sweep away the tired formulae of the older generation.

In their writing for *Cahiers du Cinéma*, the magazine founded and edited by André Bazin, these young tyros showed particular admiration for the 'B' features, and their directors, which were an important part of the output of Hollywood in the thirties and forties.

'B' features were quickly and cheaply shot and edited. For these films to stand alongside main features in what used to be called 'double bills', they had to be superbly crafted. This demanded very careful planning down to the last shot, as they were made on ratios of two or three to one.

A number of directors graduated from this harsh training ground to become successful in the major league of Hollywood production. One such was Don Siegel, who later became the mentor of Clint Eastwood. Siegel learned his craft in the montage department at Warner Brothers. Montage in this context meant creating fast cut sequences to elide time and action, and thus achieve narrative economy; usually storyboarded and often taking advantage of optical techniques from fades and wipes to flips and whirls. Siegel created the montages for several hundred films, including *Yankee Doodle Dandy*, *The Roaring Twenties* and *Casablanca*; work for which he was seldom credited.

In addition, Siegel was second unit director on over forty features, another function where careful planning and fast and cheap work were essential. As a consequence of this training, Siegel's features are epitomes of the director's craft, and that includes editing, where his control of the shooting pays dividends. For ample evidence watch *Dirty Harry* or *The Shootist*.

Whether or not the New Wave understood the reasons for the skill of directors like Siegel or Samuel Fuller, they were certainly turned on by the energy and economy of these genre movie makers.

Although André Bazin was their mentor, it was François Truffaut, his 'adopted' son, who dared to go beyond the well-mannered questioning of past practices in a seminal article, *Une certaine tendance du cinema francais*, in which he named those guilty of binding cinema in a strait-jacket of literary pretension. He wanted to replace this cinema of 'litterateurs' with a 'cinema d'auteurs' in the line represented by Renoir, Bresson, Becker, Gance etc.

In 1959 the New Wave was launched with more than twenty first features by new directors in France. The result, in the work of Chabrol, Godard, Resnais, Truffaut and others, was a revitalization of the form of narrative film.

The New Wave achieved a great deal more by questioning the basic language of cinema. Until the 1960s dramatic film had been structured on the assumption that every scene had to contain narrative development. It seems simple now to ask why such weight should be applied to every scene. Once released from this prime function, editing can be used for so much more. We have at our disposal a medium which, while continuing to tell stories, can also concentrate on states of mind and the exploration of relationships.

In 1959, Michelangelo Antonioni's *L'Aventura* had been based on no more story than the dilatory search for a missing woman, but within that framework it managed to explore the empty lives of a group of upper-class Italians. Truffaut used a triangle of relationships in *Jules et Jim* (1961) where the events are dependent on the whims of the heroine, Catherine. Godard used some elements of the thriller genre in *Pierrot le Fou* (1965) to explore attitudes to surface reality and some of the influences on life in capitalist society.

Godard it was who challenged the value of all continuity editing. He was determined to avoid the smooth cutting which seduced the audience into that suspension of disbelief that 'fiction' film normally depends on. To create a truly radical cinema he believed that the audience must remain conscious of the artifice on the screen. Discontinuity in editing was a major weapon in his attempt to achieve this.

Some critics have labelled his technique as 'jump cutting', which is regrettable since the true jump cut only applies to the use of two sections of the same shot with a section removed in the middle. Godard's technique was far wider in that he deliberately used mismatched shots to jolt the audience from their conventional screen hypnosis.

Whether or not individual film-makers decided to jump on the

Figure 1.12 Jean-Luc Godard with Anna Karina.

Godardian bandwagon, there was much food for thought provoked by his work. For editors the questioning of invisible continuity cutting as a worthwhile objective is particularly unsettling. The trouble is that many less talented directors have used his abrogation of the conventional craft to excuse sloppy technique in the service of second-rate ideas.

Alain Resnais' exploration of time, memory and the imagination represents another extreme of this new-found freedom. Resnais is linked with the literary movement that included Marguerite Duras and Alain Robbe-Grillet. Their desire to invest the novel with the ability to imitate the complexity of mental states had a natural corollary in cinematic experimentation.

Resnais first explored the relationship between past and present and our reactions to imagery in his moving documentary on Auschwitz, *Nuit et Brouillard*. Black-and-white archive material of the concentration camp

Figure 1.13 Alain Resnais in the cutting room.

juxtaposed with colour images of the grass-covered remains were complemented by a narration by the novelist Jean Cayrol. This produced an
eloquently simple but affecting message about remembrance or rather not
forgetting. The features that followed, especially *Hiroshima mon Amour*,
L'Année Dernière à Marienbad and *Muriel*, were attempts to use the
essentially linear medium of film to describe the complexities of our
psychological existence.

We should not be put off by the density and seeming obscurity of
Resnais' work. All editing which requires more than the efficient presentation of strictly linear narrative deals in the coexistence of different times,
places, events and the thoughts that connect them. The structuring of
images in Resnais' work and the way this is supported by the soundtrack
will reward close examination. He has himself influenced a number of
subsequent directors concerned with the ambiguity of human existence.

In contrast to the detachment which marks the work of Resnais, the
films of Federico Fellini are full of convoluted self-analysis, often to the
neglect of narrative coherence. In works like *Eight-and-a-Half* and *Roma*,
the imagery and structure are dependent on, or victims of, Fellini's
self-doubt as he mercilessly examines his own life. Yet we do not have to

be aficionados of this particular director to admire the daring and disturbing imagery. His films are another strong reminder that structure can as easily depend on a personal, even obscure train of thought, as on the demands of a linear and straightforward plot.

THE EFFECT OF TELEVISION

By the 1960s the omnipotence of cinema as the medium of popular entertainment was coming under threat from television. The result was twofold: firstly the cinema attempted to reinforce those aspects which television could not imitate. Projects were given more scope by the application of wide-screen and stereo sound. Secondly television began to provide both new talent and new techniques which were gradually assimilated by the cinema.

WIDE SCREEN

The possibility of the use of the wide screen had existed since the silent era. Abel Gance's *Napoleon* (1925) employed a technique that appeared on the screen as a triptych. Commercially it was the advent of Cinemascope in 1953 with *The Robe* that made alternative aspect ratios a reality. This involved the use of anamorphic lenses which squeezed the image on to a normal negative in the shooting and required that projectors reverse the process to restore the image to its correct shape on the screen.

Subsequent developments have mostly compromised between Cinemascope's 2.35:1 and the old Academy ratio of 1.33:1 and avoided the expense and complication of anamorphic lenses by masking the print. The effect of wide screen on framing and cutting is well analysed by my old friend Gavin Millar in *The Technique of Film Editing*, the classic book of Karel Reisz which Gavin updated in 1968.

Many directors find Cinemascope intimidating because the single close-up in particular leaves a large proportion of the frame unfilled. Many films have been compromised because television, until very recently, would not show 'scope in its original shape. Framing for the central third of the screen is a negation of its value. However in the hands of a master the wide screen is a revelation. Elia Kazan, in such films as *East of Eden* (1955), *Wild River* (1960) and *The Arrangement* (1969), made marvellous use of visual composition to reinforce the drama. For instance when James Dean, as Cal in *East of Eden*, finds his mother, played by Jo van Fleet, and follows her, the camera tracks back along the deserted main street framing the two characters walking on either side: he cagily watching, she nervous of this young stranger. The space between them is visually eloquent in a way that would have been impossible in the academy frame and would have been spoilt by cutting.

Some aspects of editing are rendered more difficult by the wide screen. One of the assumptions of continuity cutting, where the action is continued over the cut, is that the eyes will follow movement and thus accept the cut almost subliminally. To a degree this is dependent on the frame being perceived as a whole so that the continued movement is effective even if its position in the frame alters on the cut.

In 'scope, assuming we are watching on a big screen, a continuity cut, say on fast linear movement when the action jumps from extreme left to extreme right of frame, means that the eyes will need a split second to adjust. Thus the cut loses its immediacy, a fact that has been confirmed by research carried out in Japan using a device that registers the frame by frame focus of attention of the pupils.

For some directors this seems to be a release from the tyranny of continuity. Luchino Visconti's *Death in Venice* is a succession of beautifully composed shots which make no concessions to continuity, even when movement continues over a cut. At one point the protagonist, played by Dirk Bogarde, is shown walking in a medium shot which then cuts to an extremely wide high angle where he is an insignificant detail in the top right-hand corner of the frame. By the time that the audience finds the focus of interest, the value of movement as a bridging device is lost.

If we believe that following movement is the least viable motivation for cutting, because it conveys no meaning not already contained in the original shot, then wide screen allows for the possibility of continuing the action within the frame. This is consistent both with Eisenstein's mise-en-shot principle and with Bazin's preference for containing all significant elements within the shot.

To study the use of cutting in wide screen, do not use video copies unless the title is available in the original shape. Remember also that the effect was meant to be appreciated on a big screen.

STEREOPHONIC SOUND

As with wide screen, the idea and even the practical possibility of stereophonic sound existed much earlier than its general application in the 1950s, when it was the natural complement to Cinemascope. Adding width to the aural perspective gave another dimension, especially to the more epic productions of the time.

THE SMALL SCREEN

Neither wide screen nor stereo sound were enough to hold back the growing influence of television in the 1960s. In truth the small screen has yet to be treated with enough seriousness for its real significance to be appreciated. Yet it has bred both ideas and people that continue to influence the form, including the craft of editing.

The size of the image is the most obvious influence on the nature of television, and the predominance of the close-up is the direct result. The word has dominated television from the outset, so that faces talking to each other represent a very high percentage of the images to be seen in most living rooms each day. The art of acting for the small screen is concentrated into speech and facial expression, whereas the cinema, at its best, demands much more from the whole actor. As Louise Brooks once told me, 'The best actors are dancers.'

When I was learning to cut, an important piece of advice that I received was to save the close-ups until their value was crucial to a scene. Once you have cut in close there is no further emphasis available to you, unless you cut wide again first, and this may not be a valid option. The best of television, both in drama and documentary, makes effective use of the whole range of shots, but the tendency to shoot close is very tempting, especially under the pressure of ever tightening schedules.

Although television makes use of and adapts the different genres which already existed in the cinema, it also generates new or modified forms. Editing situation comedy, soap opera or current affairs programmes makes particular demands on the craft, although the emphasis on verbal exposition is the main difference from cinema. Borrowing from other forms, especially theatre for drama and journalism for documentary, makes the small screen less cinematic, and it takes courage and talent to buck the trend.

Television also encouraged the growth of the commercial as a major form and the art of telling stories in one minute or less has since had a major influence on the aesthetics of the medium, whether for the large or small screen. This is both exciting and alarming because the economy of visual exposition allows for ever increasing shorthand in presentation, but at the same time we seem to be in danger of losing the audience's capacity to enjoy a more discursive style.

Both television and commercials have provided a training ground for major talents who have enriched the form. The vitality of the documentary has depended on the small screen for some time now, since that is both where the commissions come from and where the work is shown. In general television has encouraged a generation of realists whilst the world of advertising seems to spawn fantasists, as far as fiction is concerned. Of the former, Penn, Lumet and Frankenheimer are examples in America and Ridley Scott is the epitome of a graduate from commercials in Britain.

SONS OF POETS

As always, it is the genius of the special individual which brings new vitality to the form. Two who have given the cinema a much needed transfusion are Bernardo Bertolucci and the late Andrei Tarkovsky, both sons of poets who had considerable reputations in their respective home countries of Italy and Russia. In both cases the parental influence has been transmuted into a strong visual sense which marries pictorial expression to the metaphorical strength derived from literature. At the same time both Bertolucci and Tarkovsky exhibit a cadence and scansion which can be felt in the rhythm of their editing, as much as in the mise-en-scène itself.

Of the two, Bertolucci possesses the more energetic style, and his editors Perpignani, Arcalli and now Gabriella Cristiani have had to match this in their cutting. Often this is a nervous energy, as in the sequence in *The Conformist* when the protagonist and his new wife are travelling by train on their honeymoon. The sexual tension is heightened by the woman, played by Stefania Sandrelli, confessing to her husband, played by Jean Louis Trintignant, how she lost her virginity. His indifference slowly turns to passion and they make love. The cutting, in the confines of a closed railway compartment, is surprisingly edgy, but this superbly complements the atmosphere of the scene.

The proof that this has nothing to do with editing to get round the problems of shooting in a confined space is evidenced by a similar edginess in the editing when John Malkovitz and Debra Winger make love on a ridge in the desert in *The Sheltering Sky*. All kinds of ambivalences are reflected in the personalities of characters in Bertolucci's films and both his camera and his editing support this, never more so than in *Last Tango in Paris*.

Tarkovsky's cinema was both more intellectual and more elemental. Earth, Air, Fire, and Water merged in a mystical transcendance in films like *Mirror* and *Stalker*. Even in his two films made in exile, *Nostalghia* and *The Sacrifice*, there was no compromise either in form or substance.

In a godless age his images seemed to prophesy the coming of a new spirituality. Coming close to reflecting the iconic notion that form and meaning are one continuum, his synthesis demanded that we accept that each juxtaposition had the potential of the ineffable rather than causal or narrative connections. His book *Sculpting in Time* is a testament to his artistic journey and his diaries a record of the Via Dolorosa which the Soviet State made of that life. We may not wish to make films in his manner, but we should not be intimidated by their nature into rejecting the lessons they can teach: as much about life as the potential of cinema. 'He that has eyes to see, let him see.'

There is a belief that the dominant convention of filmic expression, certainly in the West, is partly a result of 'male' attitudes to visualization. It is therefore exciting that in the last twenty years a number of female

Figure 1.14   Andrei Tarkovsky.

directors have emerged who are not interested in imitating their male peers.

Of these one of the most interesting is Chantal Ackerman. In early films like *Jeanne Dielman* and *Les Rendez-vous d'Anna* she deliberately chose an alternative aesthetic. Although it owes something to Robert Bresson, there is an added dimension which affects every aspect of her work from choice of subject through scripting, mise-en-scène to editing. It is signalled most dramatically at the very beginning of *Les Rendez-vous d'Anna*. The camera is facing down the platform of a large railway station much as it does in that image from the birth of cinema taken by Lumière almost a hundred years before. However the train arrives from **behind** the camera and the woman who turns out to be the central character gets off and walks **away** from us. Thus the form is inverted.

In *Jeanne Dielman* the static camera watches Delphine Seyrig throughout, but is powerless to follow her in and out of frame as she goes about the drudgery of her everyday life. This owes much to Ozu, but is somehow transmuted into another kind of pathos. In this form cutting can be a deliberate fracturing when you are least expecting it, or sometimes comes only after a painful wait, when the conventional film would satisfy our need for punctuation more frequently.

RECENT TRENDS

Since the sixties, there have been 'New Waves' of various shapes and sizes in Europe and elsewhere in the world. All have challenged the practice of the previous generation, usually to liberating effect; none more so than in the former Eastern Europe, especially in Czechoslovakia, but also in Hungary and Poland.

The present trend is towards an internationalism which risks burying the particular qualities of an individual or regional cinema under a deluge of sanitized banality. This is encouraged by the ravenous appetite of television, without which very little production can be financed. Editing can become cutting by numbers in this climate, and the craft is bound to suffer.

A major issue is the question of language. Style and form are partially a cultural response and that is embedded in linguistics. If we wish to preserve diversity we must protect the indigenous language. If Kieslowski continues to make films they should be in Polish and the Taviani brothers should stick to Italian.

Yet the best directors can understand and absorb influences from outside their own culture and still make personal cinema rooted in their own specific background. Bertrand Tavernier, a Frenchman from Lyons, is one such. In films such as *Coup de Torchon, Sunday in the Country* and *La Vie et Rien d'Autre* he uses the diverse inspirations of an American pulp novel, a homage to Renoir and a statistic from the First World War to create cinema that is always intelligent and thought-provoking.

Throughout his work, Tavernier uses camera, editing and sound with courage and conviction. In transposing the plot of *Coup de Torchon* (Clean Slate) from the American context of Jim Thompson's novel to French colonial Africa, Tavernier still retains the sharp disturbing contours of the narrative. This is reflected in the abrasive and unsettling editing, despite the lassitude exhibited by the characters whose lives have neither purpose nor direction. Tavernier is in a line from the New Wave, but at the same time rejects the excessive antipathies of Truffaut and Godard. This allows him to appreciate the work of Michael Powell, for instance, and even to acknowledge the value in the films of some of his countrymen who were defiled by *Cahiers du Cinèma* at its most acerbic and brutal.

It is individuals like Tavernier who always have the ability to remind us of the true potential of the medium and we should be prepared to examine and understand their work so that it can inform our own practice. In a later chapter we shall consider some more recent work that continues to use the medium in the best traditions but at the same time with a new voice.

Shooting with cutting in mind

2

It is essential to be aware from the start of the effect of different styles on the same material. There are many examples from the history of cinema of different directors tackling the same or similar stories. A classic example is how Renoir (in 1945) and Buñuel (in 1964) treated *Le Journal d'une Femme de Chambre*. Had the two films been given different titles, it would be some time before one became aware that they both had their origin in the same story by Octave Mirabeau. The translation of Akira Kurosawa's *Rashomon* (1950) into *The Outrage* (1964) by Martin Ritt, and his *Seven Samurai* (1954) into *The Magnificent Seven* (1961) by John Sturges, though inspired by the originals, have little in common with Kurosawa's style. The various adaptations of Raymond Chandler's detective thrillers from Edward Dymytryk's *Farewell My Lovely* to Robert Altman's *The Long Goodbye* show the breadth of interpretation available to directors ostensibly working in the same convention.

We should also acknowledge the distinct and crucial contribution made by Directors of Photography (DOPs). Henri Decae and Raoul Coutard created as much of the style of the New Wave as the directors, whose approach spawned the auteur concept. Indeed, you will remember how much this has been true from the beginning of cinema: Billy Bitzer and Greg Toland are two examples. The person behind the camera is the final proof of the importance of style. The Hollywood veteran James Wong Howe worked with many directors, some brilliant, some competent, and some downright mediocre, but no matter for whom he was working he managed to put his stamp on the imagery that ended up on the screen. It must have been a real pleasure to put his rushes together. Other examples of close collaboration between directors and DOPs have been Walter Lassally with Michael Cacoyannis, Sven Nykvist for Ingmar Bergman, and Vittorio Stararo for Bernardo Bertolucci. It is impossible to separate the contributions made by these partnerships in the finished films. There are also many examples of very good camera people working with talented directors producing work which is disappointing to both. The 'chemistry' is very important: if partnerships are unsuccessful the results will be irredeemable in the cutting room.

So style is not something to be applied in the cutting room. The true function of editing is to respect and support the aesthetic choices made during the shooting. If there is nothing to respect there is nothing to contribute and all the wizardry available to the editor will be to no avail.

THE SHOOTING PROCESS

The shooting script or, in the case of documentary, the shotlist, is meant to provide us with a template for the film or video before it exists. However, each director is dealing, at the moment of shooting, with the fundamental question: how do I shoot to provide the most effective material for editing? If we understand the dramaturgy of the script we can analyse how the details of the mise-en-scène can be captured on the film or tape to provide the raw material that the editor needs. So what questions should be kept in mind during the shooting? Each scene should be examined to identify the following:

1. Where is the focus of interest?
2. When and to what does that focus shift?
3. What is the mood and consequent pace of the scene?
4. Does that mood/pace change?
5. Are there natural pauses which should be reflected in silence and stillness?
6. What significant detail **must** be seen?
7. Conversely, when is it important to see the whole area in which the action takes place?
8. When is a reaction more important than an action?
9. How should movement be encompassed?
10. Does any off-screen or non-synchronous sound contribute to the scene?
11. How do the beginning and end of the scene relate to those immediately before and after?
12. Does the setting occur more than once in the script, and therefore need to be established in a particular way?
13. Can the turning point of the scene be pinpointed?
14. What is the function of the scene in the overall script?

Finding the answers to these questions allows us to refine the way the scene is shot. In practice the lazy or insecure director will play safe and adopt a neutral style, going for 'conventional cover'. This comprises: a master shot, wide enough to encompass the whole action; medium shots, usually isolating significant interaction; and close-ups for emphasis and reaction.

If however the above questions are confronted rigorously, two significant benefits can be obtained. First the ratio of shot material to edited footage is likely to be reduced considerably, and secondly and more importantly the director will have chosen a positive style; one which the editor can respect and which provides a clear sense of the form that is preferred. The camera is not the only contributor to this point of view. Casting, performance, art direction, choice of locations and many other elements need the same careful appraisal. The best scenarios will already contain implicit answers to these questions, although the best directors bend the script to their desires and predilections. When Roman Polanski was hired to direct *Chinatown* he spent several months refining Robert Towne's script. Essentially his rewriting established that the story would be told from the point of view of the protagonist, Jake Gittes, played by Jack Nicholson. There is virtually no shot in the film that isn't either showing what Jake is seeing or showing his reaction. If you apply the questions listed earlier to such a clear visual approach you can see that the answers are easily translated into images, and this explains why most audiences find this particular film so easy to identify with. If there is sufficient potential in a script the perceptive director will be able to extract the essence and match the original conception with an appropriate style.

It is important to understand the basic and fundamental interdependence of image and sound. The best of cinema and television gives the impression that everything seen and heard is part of the deliberate intention of the film-maker, except in those films which set out to allow chance and improvisation to play a significant role. Joseph Losey was once asked during a television interview why he continued to struggle to make films against the odds. He replied that he was 'fascinated by the rhythm of silence'. The interviewer obviously thought that Losey was being clever and ignored his reply, but if I were asked to write a book on the language of film I would plagiarize Losey and call it *The Rhythms of Silence*. Anyone who has seen Losey's best films, for example *The Servant* or *Accident*, will appreciate that he was a master of eloquent silences, but the fact is that his statement is relevant to all film-making.

Robert Bresson said, 'Build your film on white, on silence and on stillness', and this is ideal advice to encourage the film-maker to ensure that everything seen and heard is intentional. In a scene in Francis Ford Coppola's *The Conversation* (1974), Gene Hackman visits his old girlfriend played by Teri Garr. There is a tension between them born of his too infrequent visits, and his secretiveness about his work as a private investigator. At the point at which one feels that he wants to convey to her that he may not be calling again he wanders into the kitchenette, and the silence, stillness and distance are broken by the line, 'Your rent is due this week'.

As Bresson also said, 'Don't run after poetry. It penetrates unaided through the joins.'

There are a number of mechanical procedures which have to be followed during shooting to ease the task of editing. These are explained in the sections which follow.

IDENTIFICATION AND SYNCHRONIZATION

The clapperboard or slate is the aid to identification and synchronization and it is filmed or recorded at the beginning or end of each take. The 'clapping' of the hinged section provides an exact aural and visual reference point; it also provides essential and precise information. It presumably originated circa 1929–30 when everything, including the inclination of actors' heads, became slave to the new sound film, if we are to believe the evidence of *Singin' in the Rain* (1952). It is a remarkably crude device which does nothing to improve the neurotic atmosphere that often pervades the shooting of a film. There are now substitute devices for providing a sync reference, including the filmic equivalent of 'time-coding', but nothing fulfils the task of identification quite as well as the clapper. The procedure should be as follows:

Person	Verbal Instruction	Mechanical Operation
1 Director or Asst. dir.	Quiet	Clapper in shot
2 Asst. dir.	Run sound	Switch on recorder
3 Sound recordist	Running/Speed	
4 Asst. dir.	Run camera	Switch on camera
5 Camera operator	Running/Speed	
6 Asst. dir.	Mark it	
7 Camera asst.	Slate 5 Take 3	Clap and exit frame
8 Director	Action	

In the shooting of fiction films by American crews, the slate number corresponds to the shot as numbered in the script. This means that there is an instant reference when cutting without having to correlate two sets of numbers. If you allow flexibility during shooting and begin to add shots not scripted, the numbering system can become complicated.

Directors should encourage their cast not to treat the word 'Action' as if they are greyhounds being let out of their traps. It is entirely the wrong word as a cue to begin acting. In a theatrical situation the director says 'In your own time' or 'When you're ready'. The best performers will, in any case, set off at the pace and rhythm that suits the scene, but those less experienced or nervous will hit the end of 'Action' with their first line, as if they have just received the blast from a twelve-bore shot-gun.

This can have an effect on the edited film for two reasons. Firstly the pace and rhythm of speech and movement of sections that are meant to cut together must be consistent, so it is essential that the mechanics of shooting do not dictate that pace and rhythm. Secondly the existence of a pause after 'Action' allows the editor a useful second or two of extra sound overlap and static visual. The best way of achieving these objectives is by taking two or three deep breaths before beginning the action. The same criterion applies to the end of each shot. The cast should complete the action and then pause before the director calls 'Cut'. In any case, at the beginning and end of every shot both action and dialogue should extend beyond that part of the script for which the shot is intended. For instance, if someone has just sat down on a chair in the previous shot and you have moved the camera in for a closer shot, always repeat the sit down action. A cut at the point where an action has just been completed is the most uncomfortable of all.

Sometimes it proves impossible to put a clap on the beginning of a shot, maybe because the director has carefully established the mood for a shot and wants as little as possible to disturb the performers' concentration. This also happens in documentaries when the film-maker has no control of the situation and switches on in time for the start of interesting dialogue or action. In these cases an end-board or slate may have to be used, so before saying 'Cut' the director calls 'End-board' and the clapper is inserted upside down to distinguish it from the front slate.

For the clapperboard to be used efficiently the following points should be remembered; the whole process should not take more than a few seconds:

1. The board must be marked up clearly and accurately.
2. The verbal identification should precede the clap, and not be simultaneous with it, to ensure a clear recording.
3. If there is a false start to the take, and the clap has to be repeated, 'second clap' should be added to the announcement.
4. The camera operator should confirm that the board is in focus.
5. The board must be big enough in frame to be readable.
6. If lighting or exposure for the shot are low, you may need to open up the lens or spotlight the board.
7. If the shot is too close to include the whole board, show the area of identification for the verbal cue and then move down for the clap.
8. Start with the hinged section raised and clap crisply.
9. Hold the board closed and steady for a moment after the clap.
10. Leave the shot quietly and quickly, and have your escape route planned.

When a clapperboard is unavailable or inconvenient, possible alternatives include clapping the hands together horizontally or tapping the head of a microphone with a finger. In documentary shooting, you can avoid interrupting the flow with an 'alien' voice by using one of these two methods and showing an increasing number of fingers to the camera for every shot. If a crew is well co-ordinated this can be an efficient identification system. A visual indication of the slate number is a useful bonus, so carry a notebook and felt-tip pen with you in case it can substitute for the board. Even so-called 'blip-sync', where the film is fogged and a high pitched bleep is recorded on to the tape, works better with the addition of an audible and visible indication of sequential numbering. All systems, including video, where there is no need to incorporate a synchronizing method, can benefit from a number reference at the start of each shot.

CONTINUITY

All aspects of aural and visual continuity or matching are crucial for the editor. It is not surprising that the job of checking continuity is a responsible and specialized role in all fiction shooting. Not only is the consistency of appearance, clothing, props, make-up and so on the direct concern of the continuity person, but many other aspects too. Lighting, details of design and setting, matching shots and action, provision of cover, consistency of dialogue, indeed everything that will ensure that footage is usable by the editor should be monitored by the continuity person. Inconsistencies that find their way on to film must be noted on continuity sheets, as must the reasons why takes are preferred.

THE LINE

This is the mother of all cinematic conventions. Every camera position establishes a flat plane which, when projected as a two-dimensional image, presents a left-to-right orientation of all objects in the frame. To avoid the risk of disorientating the audience, convention dictates that all subsequent camera positions should be restricted to the 180 degree arc established by the first shot (Figure 2.1). Avoiding crossing the line seems to give inexperienced film-makers their biggest problems, and it is extremely frustrating in the cutting room to be presented with shots which, although valid in themselves, cannot be intercut with the rest of the shots for that sequence.

It is possible to establish a new line during a scene, but this can only be done by moving the camera across the line during a shot, or by a character moving to establish a new orientation. An analysis of most good dramatic films will reveal the positive use of moving to a new line for dramatic emphasis – an effect akin to that experienced in reality when someone moves their position in relation to us sufficiently to require us to decide whether to accept the need to turn round in order to face them again. Antonioni is particularly fond of using realignment of this sort to mark psychological shifts in a scene.

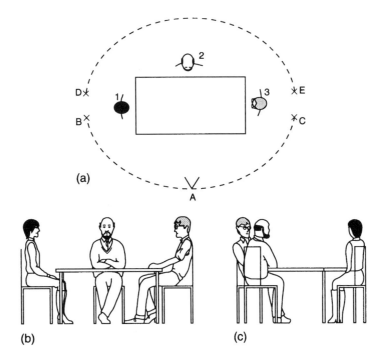

Figure 2.1 The line: if the master shot (b) is taken from camera position A all other shots should be taken from within the arc B to C, unless a new 'line' is established. Cutting directly from b to c for example is disorientating because the characters appear to have changed their positions relative to left and right of the screen.

EYELINES

This is closely related to the question of the line. A shot of two characters establishes the 'eyelines' or direction of look between them. If the characters remain static, this eyeline must be maintained in every shot. Even if we take a close-up of one of the characters from exactly in front, the angle of the head and the look of the eyes must match that established in the wider shot. As with the principle of the line, movement of the camera or the subject can vary the eyeline, and again dramatic emphasis can be gained. A particular value of establishing the eyeline is the use of the 'look away' to signal rejection, embarrassment, disinterest, guilt or any other emotion which can cause one person to avoid another's eyes.

DIRECTION OF MOVEMENT

Consistency is needed both within the frame and in and out of it. Most simply, if a person or object exits right of frame they should enter the next shot on the left, and vice versa. This remains the case whether they are going across the screen, towards camera or away. If we ignore this rule it will appear that the person has changed direction on the cut. However, there are many distinguished examples of breaking this rule – John Ford, for one, is inclined to ignore this convention, especially when dealing with sweeping movement of indians, cavalry or cowboys. Usually it is the strength of the movement which carries across the cut that allows him to get away with it.

PACE OF MOVEMENT

Compared with the task of matching direction of movement, the problems with matching pace are less obvious and therefore more often not addressed properly. We have all seen the Western where the posse is riding hell-for-leather in a wide panning shot, when on the cut to a medium head-on tracking shot it seems to have slowed to a sedate trot. All movement needs matching to be convincing and to allow the greatest flexibility in cutting. Walking shots seem to be the hardest to match and it is easy to delude ourselves into believing that if the legs are not visible the pace does not matter. With any action that is meant to be assembled with other material of the same action, even the turn of a head or the flick of a finger, the pace must be matched. One of the most frequent mis-matches is the cut from the exterior to the interior of a moving vehicle, which may well be shot on separate days. Speed can be dictated by the ability of the camera operator to follow action. If possible it is always best to shoot the more difficult shot first and match the speed subsequently.

There is a similar problem with dialogue: performers often raise the volume and increase their speaking speed when being shot in close-up. I can only surmise that this phenomenon is a reaction to a feeling of intimidation at the proximity of the camera, when the logic is to talk more quietly in a closer situation. It can have an alarming effect on the usefulness of cover in a sequence. Acting for the camera demands a consistency of pace both in speech and movement. Some performers, often with a background in the theatre, have a tendency to modify each next rendition of a line, and this can be the editor's ultimate nightmare.

ANGLE AND DISTANCE

Unless the intention is to shock or to give strong emphasis to a character or object, it is important to vary angle as well as distance in alternative shots. Kurosawa is fond of cutting closer on the same angle for effect, for instance at the dramatic climax of *Sanjuro* or as the villagers approach the water-mill to consult the Sage in *The Seven Samurai*. However, in normal circumstances the demands of continuity make it safer to move the camera at least 30 degrees from the line of other shots, especially if you are shooting a single person. The zoom lens makes directors lazy as it enables the size of the subject in the frame to be changed without moving the camera. A slow zoom-in on the focus of attention in the frame can be very effective, but the temptation to use the beginning and end of the zoom as separate shots should normally be avoided unless intercut with other angles.

SET DISCIPLINE

One of the most frequently voiced reasons for building a set is the advantage to be gained by 'floating' a wall and giving a wider perspective of the space than would be possible in the real room. The problem is that the audience can lose faith in the artifice we present if there is no logic to the space the camera shows. I have been given rushes where a character was seated on a sofa right up against a wall and found that the reverse angle was a shot taken from at least six feet behind the sofa. Sometimes extreme wide angle lenses are used to contain all the action in a confined space, and this can be very ugly. The challenge of shooting relatively small interiors provokes a variety of ingenious responses in directors. Ozu and Chantal Ackerman are happy to let the action move in and out of a static frame, implying the space beyond but not showing it. Bertolucci and the more baroque directors will use a fluid approach, including the implication that the camera can ignore walls; moving from room to room, and even through windows. Steadicam and similar devices encourage this fluidity at the risk of losing believability, but if realism is not the aim then the space in front of the camera is what you make it.

THE OVERLAP

It is a common error to assume that if you closely storyboard a film you can avoid shooting overlap action for the front and end of adjacent shots. Even the most experienced director will allow for the possibility of adjusting the cutting point in editing. Although action may be the easiest point to match, the cut may be better used to emphasize the moment of decision before the action, or the subsequent effect of the action. We must remember that editing is not about the mechanics of physical movement. It is much more an opportunity to support the dramatic ebb and flow. In any case the performers should not be expected to pitch their performances by going cold into the next move or line; their craft is not mechanical either.

The mediocre film demonstrates a foolhardy belief that efficient application of the mechanics of conventional screen language is all you need to be successful. In truth this is no substitute for having a clear conception of what you want to show and how you want to show it. Even so the unconventional film must also confront the problems described above. For instance the film that is shot in long takes must deal with questions of rhythm and pace, focus of interest and the other factors affecting the use of the camera; and some substitute will have to be found for the language of individual close-ups, medium shots and long shots. Miklos Jancso choreographs the camera and the action with a precision far exceeding that demanded by the convention; for example *The Round-up* and *The Confrontation*. Conversely Rainer Werner Fassbinder often left the camera as a passive spectator, albeit in a carefully chosen position, whilst the action or inaction unfolded before it; for example, *The Bitter Tears of Petra von Kant*.

DOCUMENTARY SHOOTING

So far in this chapter we have been dealing with questions that arise mainly during the shooting of fiction, where everything is ostensibly under the control of the director and crew. The same strictures will apply in non-fiction if it is appropriate to dictate what happens in front of the camera; for instance in the filming of a mechanical process or for educational programmes where the script, including both words and images, is predetermined. In these cases the equivalent of a script or at least a detailed shot list will often provide a cutting guide too.

However, most documentary shooting occurs without the film-makers being in control of what happens in front of the camera. There is still considerable variation in the precision with which a crew approaches shooting. A news crew are well aware of the 'story' they are following and in many cases the images suggest themselves. The best news and current affairs camera operators will supply material that has a natural structure, often the result of collaboration over many years with a particular reporter. The fact is that dramatic events can substitute for a script and an intelligent crew will follow the natural arc of the story.

On the other hand, most of what we broadly label documentary is unpredictable and in a way formless. The natural history film-maker will use his or her knowledge and observation to decide the best vantage point from which to shoot an activity, but the footage will still contain surprises. Once we get away from mechanical processes the documentary film-maker has to learn particular skills in order to provide the best material for editing.

The following points about documentary shooting will help to ensure fewer problems in editing:

Identification and sync reference

There are situations in documentary where neither of these is possible, but it is better to get into the habit rather than to be casual about it. This ensures better co-ordination between camera and sound, since most forms of sync reference require a conscious effort from both. It can be very frustrating in the cutting room to find that the camera pans off a subject too soon, or that the recordist switches on too late to register the sync point. End slates are often less intrusive.

Static at front and end of shots

Where possible allow a static hold at the beginning and end of movement, either of the camera or the subject of the shot. Pans, tilts, tracking, zooms and hand-held movement are always much easier to cut if there is static at the front and end of significant action. A pause of this kind is a stylized intervention in the action and may be considered inappropriate, but the right psychological moment can be punctuated in this way.

Speech and silence

It is valuable to allow pauses at the front and end of dialogue, be it conversation or interview. Apart from allowing more flexibility in the editing, sometimes the silent look is more eloquent than the words.

Shooting for usability

There is a school of thought amongst documentary camerapersons that moments of awkward shooting should be deliberately sabotaged to avoid the possibility of being used by the errant editor. As the more experienced professional knows, unless the camera is actually switched off the editor is likely to use the bit in question anyway. The need to refocus is the classic example, but if achieved effectively the change of focus can be a useful detail that is worth incorporating. Panning from one person to another should be achieved carefully for similar reasons. In highly charged circumstances a whip-pan may be exactly complementary to the scene.

Continuity in documentary

The demands of continuity still obtain even when filming reality. The line and eyelines do not cease to exist because events are real. It is just as disconcerting in an interview as in a drama if screen continuity is disturbed. Continuity of time and action must also be considered. Smoking, eating and drinking can be particularly awkward for the editor. In the end, however, the film is more important than any problem of continuity and the editor has to live with such irritations.

The value of an establishing shot

The 'frame' in which any film exists is never the ideal that a painter creates. There is a sense in which Magritte's attempts to prevent the convention of the frame dominating our perception is relevant to film. We present a partial reality which is only justified by the particular relevance of its content to each moment in the film. Often it is sound which implies the space beyond the frame. Western pictorial art has refined a theory of compositional balance which is a trap for film-makers. The audience knows in documentary that we are determining their view of a partial reality, and this is different from inventing a reality in fiction. It is often true that the space inhabited by a person or persons is part of their character or situation. We should try to show it therefore, if only to allow the audience to feel they know where they are. The editor may well choose to establish the space early on, and then not feel the need to cut to it again.

The problem of shooting too close

I have never understood why some documentarists want us to be able to count the nostril hairs on the subject they are filming. If being so close is meant to concentrate attention, the obverse is true. Unless we are in an antagonistic situation, we are most at ease listening at a comfortable distance. It is said that this tendency to shoot very close is a product of television and the small screen. Certainly documentaries shot in the days when they were regularly shown in the cinema used the close-up very sparingly. The guideline should be to attempt to contain all relevant visual information within the frame, otherwise the editor may complain that he or she is forced to cut away to show a relevant detail. A good example is where a spokesperson for a group is holding forth and we can see his sentiments confirmed (or not!) on the faces of his comrades. This is far superior to the cutaway of one of them nodding, which is now given no more credibility than it deserves.

Looking and listening

To judge how much of the available information should be contained within the frame, skilled documentarists use their other eye (and both their ears) just as much, if not more than, the one that is pressed against the viewfinder. Unless you are looking and listening beyond the frame, every reaction to a change in the focus of interest in a scene will result in a badly executed movement that happens too late. The frame you are holding may be indeterminate if you are using the viewfinder as the equivalent of a periscope.

A simple experiment will prove the point. Choose a moment when you can observe a group of people. Put some cotton wool in your ears, close one eye, and use your hands as a substitute for looking through a viewfinder. Ask yourself what criteria are available to you for judging the frame you should hold. The one eye, restricted to the normal angle of view through a lens, has no perspective except its own narrow silent arbitrary frame. You have no way of knowing why people are doing things, who is talking to whom, or what is likely to happen next, and you will use the camera as a visual vacuum cleaner.

The significant detail

Both during and after a particular shoot it is useful to consider if there are any objects that are relevant to the content of the scene which have been poorly covered in the main body of the shoot. If you feel the need to take supplementary shots you should be careful that they match the dominant perspective or that they can be used as point-of-view shots. The lack of such detail can prevent the construction of a satisfactory sequence.

Filming with a purpose

The cardinal sin in documentary making is to be filming without really knowing why. This indicates a lack of clarity over what the film is really about, and the foolhardy assumption that the cutting room is the place where miracles are performed to bring coherence to unrelated material. This produces the kind of documentary which is sewn together by the ubiquitous narrator whose words are supposed to justify a rag-bag of ideas. The trouble is that ideas are ten-a-penny. Any subject could be the basis of a documentary, but if you have not thought through your approach there will be no focus to the shooting and superimposing an attitude in the cutting room is too late.

Know your style

Above all in documentary you must be clear in your choice of style. If you are structuring reality into a predetermined form each shot will have a function. If on the other hand you wish to let reality take its own form, the shooting and therefore the editing must not interfere with that life in front of the lens and mike any more than is absolutely unavoidable. Whatever choice we make there is an unwritten contract with the audience that makes it important to be clear about the approach we are taking. If we cheat we risk losing their trust. This is tantamount to professional suicide because switching off is only a remote control away.

THE PROPER USE OF SOUND

It has always seemed strange to me that whereas only one person is responsible for the look of a film, the quality of its sound is the divided responsibility of at least three people: the recordist, the sound editor and the mixer. When you add the fact that sound editing on major features is usually subdivided between dialogue, effects and music editors, it is something of a miracle that the final results have any coherence at all. This is an indication of the lack of priority given to sound and the results are often disappointing. The tone must be set from the beginning in the attitude to sound during the shoot.

SYNC(HRONOUS) SOUND

There are two traditions in world cinema: one says that shooting synchronously is preferable, represented by Britain and America; the other favours post-synchronization, represented by Italy, Spain and the Orient. The advantages of a sync recording include:

- Sound adds to the perspective when evaluating the shot.
- Performance is an integration of speech and action.
- If post-sync is necessary a guide track is invaluable.
- Sync effects can only be approximated in dubbing.
- Atmospheres are location specific.

Obtaining a usable sync recording may be impossible because of:

- Anachronistic background sound on a period subject.
- Uncontrollable noise, e.g. planes, trains etc.
- Natural phenomena, e.g. high winds.
- Camera noise enhanced by reflective surfaces.
- Wide shots that prevent effective microphone placement.

When sync shooting is impossible the camera is not hampered by sound considerations. This can shorten shooting time and can lead to a more imaginative visual style. The films of Bertolucci and the Tavianni brothers, for instance, benefit from this opportunity.

WILD SOUND

Even if sync recording is impossible, there are distinct advantages to obtaining wild tracks, including dialogue, since the actors can match the rhythm, pace and feel of the performance they have just given for the camera. If circumstances prevent a good dialogue recording it is useful to have a wild track of the background to place against the eventual post-sync voices.

The quality of wild tracks is the best yardstick with which to measure the commitment of a sound recordist. The one who is prepared to get up early and stay late in order to obtain imaginative additional sound will earn the eternal gratitude of the editor. One such trojan was a certain John Murphy, whose experience as a relief mixer made him acutely aware of the needs of the editor both in documentary and drama.

Two examples will show what I mean. First a documentary. The subject was the city of Florence. The camera operator supplied a selection of mute shots which were moulded into a decent sequence by the editor Dave King. However, what made it special were the wild tracks. A tracking shot past narrow streets was made magical by a recording of distant traffic over which could be heard the sound of arpeggios being practised on a piano in an upstairs room, heard through an open window. The panorama of the city from the Piazzale Michelangelo, which panned from the release of balloons in the square to the skyline, was eloquently complemented by the sounds of laughing and squealing children which were mixed through to the distant bells of the churches across the Arno.

The drama was Ken Russell's film about Delius, *Song of Summer*. Murphy was faced with difficult conditions for dialogue recording. In one case, a hand-held walking shot, it was impossible to get a clean track, so he grabbed the actors immediately after the shot and obtained two or three takes of the dialogue. With only minor adjustment these fitted perfectly and no post-sync was necessary. In another case aircraft noise prevented any recording. Knowing that in this case post-synchronization was unavoidable, Murphy went to the location at dawn the following morning and obtained an atmosphere track and several footstep recordings, using his assistant who walked over the same ground that the performers had the day before.

Unfortunately, in my experience, these examples are exceptional. More often than not wild tracks are inadequate or unusable, and library effects are a poor substitute.

PAPERWORK

The editor's primary materials are the picture and sound rushes. However, written information can be an important aid to work in the cutting room. This takes several forms:

Camera sheet (negative report)

Along with the sound report, this provides the guide to the process of synchronizing the rushes. It also shows the cameraperson's preferences, which do not always accord with those of the director.

Sound report

This is where you will first see evidence of the recordist's performance. Helpful notes on sync and wild recordings alongside the technical information are very welcome in the cutting room.

Continuity notes

The best continuity persons are a boon to the editor. Through their understanding of the value of each shot and the reactions of the director to each take, they allow the editor to view the material with open eyes.

Shot lists

These are the equivalent of continuity notes for documentaries, but also contain much more information. At best they are a diary of the shoot that includes details that would have been forgotten had they not been committed to paper at the time of shooting.

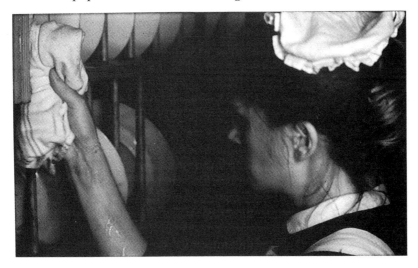

Figure 2.2 Shot from *Mary Reilly* referred to in the continuity report (Figure 2.3).

DAILY CONTINUITY REPORT

Production:	"MARY REILLY"	Date:	Monday, June 6, 1994
Cameras & Set Ups:		Set:	INT KITCHEN – NIGHT
A CAM: 75 mm 5′6–7′ T3.8 1SFX		Screentime:	.03″
Cam on dolly on rails – facing sink profile & tr r/l		Time Shot:	12.55–13.15
from steps		Weather:	

SLATE NO:	39
SCENE NO:	43

ACTION & DIALOGUE

> CLOSE SHOT MARY – STANDING AT
> SINK IN R/L PROFILE – CAMERA
> TRACKS R/L (FOR ANNIE'S O.S.
> MOVE) – MARY WIPES PLATE RACK,
> REVEALING HER SCARS

CLOSE SHOT MARY standing in L/R PROFILE at the sink, washing up – she looks up – eyeline L/R for ANNIE (in the scullery) – CAMERA TILTING UP with her head move. CAMERA TRACKS R/L holding MARY, (for ANNIE's o.s. move down the steps). MARY leans to C.R. to take the cloth from ANNIE. MARY lifts her left hand up, holding the cloth, she wipes the bottom rim of the top plate rack, her hand starting at arms length away from her, and moving twds herself (L–R), revealing the SCARS on her wrist.

TAKE 6 ONWARDS: MARY turns over right shoulder, twds CAM, and looks up as if to the floors of the house above.

DIALOGUE:

ANNIE: (os) Bradshaw says he goes tohouses.

conts down to

ANNIE: (os) Thanks.

Noise of tap dripping throughout scene.

Take 1	NG	.31	Scars not visible – wrists too wet
Take 2	NG	.20	Not good for speed of track
Take 3	NG	.33	Not pref
Take 4	NG	.42	Don't see both Mary's eyes
Take 5	PRINT	.38	
Take 6	PRINT	.40	
Take 7	NG	.40	Not pref for Mary's last look up
Take 8	PRINT	.44	
Take 9	PRINT	.41	

W/T 39X – ANNIE'S LINE: BRADSHAW SAYS HE GOES TO HOUSE.

Figure 2.3 Continuity report page from Tristar Production's *Mary Reilly*.

Marked-up script

This gives the editor a graphic guide to the way each scene is covered and a reference to the alternatives available at each moment.

The guideline when completing these forms should be: what information should the editor have which is not obvious from the material itself. After all is said and done, weeks or maybe months of effort are finally reduced to a few cans of celluloid and magnetic film. It makes sense to ensure that the person who is supposed to breathe life into that footage is given all the support possible.

From cutting room to edit suite: the development of the technology

3

In *The Parade's Gone By*, Kevin Brownlow chronicled the early days of editing thus: 'Editing, in common with other aspects of techniques, settled down to a solid professionalism around 1918. Astonishingly most editors worked without the animated viewers considered essential today. They cut in the hand. Modern editors are baffled by this; how could they possibly judge the pace or the rhythm?' He goes on to describe how 'cutting in the hand' only died out when sound brought synchronization problems, and quotes Bebe Daniels' comment on Moviolas, the new editing machines: 'The old cutters would not use them – they were like old cooks who refused to use pressure cookers.'

It is only now, in the 1990s, that we are faced with a similar technological revolution. Non-linear or more strictly random access editing from digitized rushes is making cutting on film the redoubt of those who must have a physical relationship with their material. As Michael Rubin puts it in his book *Non-linear*: 'There is no replacement for the simplicity and physicality of working on film. If the life style and tactile nature of film are the appeal, as is the case with many film-makers, the process and labor IS the joy of film making, and editing electronically may offer little benefit.' A new generation is growing up that may never know the difference: in ten years cutting on film may be a thing of the past.

The process has always been a simple one: all you really need is a pair of scissors, a razor blade, some glue, a light box, a pair of rewinds and a projector. It must be remembered that for many years editors always cut on 35mm and each frame was visible to the naked eye. Matching action on 35mm is easily done by aligning frames in the hand over a light box. The beauty of a projector as the only viewing device is that you are forced to

Figure 3.1 Not the best advertisement for the well organized cutting room in Lescarboura's *Behind the Motion Picture Screen* (1920).

watch the film, rather than having the facility to stop and start and constantly to analyse each frame. The establishment of good pace, rhythm and indeed structure depends upon building up the sense of a whole sequence, and avoiding concern for what happens at the static moment that exists at each cut.

There is no doubt, however, that the right devices and good organization are as beneficial to the cutting room and editing as they are to the kitchen and cooking; if only to avoid the chaos pictured in Austin C. Lescarboura's *Behind the Motion Picture Screen* (1920), where editing merits half a page in a 420-page book!

Until recently editing technology was the poor relation, the least considered of the tools of the trade. It would have been even worse had it not been for Iwan Serurier, the inventor of the Moviola. This machine has changed very little since it was adapted for sound in 1929. It is a little recognized fact that no technology is neutral in its effect on the process for which it is designed. The Moviola is an outstanding example of a machine dictating attitudes to the craft it is used for.

The development of flat-bed or table editing machines using a continuous prism movement showed that there are no innate reasons why the characteristics of the Moviola are essential to editing. The intermittent motion of the picture head, the vertical movement, the small screen and the standing position for operating were all part of a mode that was abandoned in the alternative design.

The characteristics of the Moviola may not have been a conscious decision. Since the camera and projector pre-dated editing machinery, it was their design detail that provided the reference point for the Moviola; indeed the earliest machines were simply crude adaptations of camera and projector mechanisms. We should also bear in mind that the designer was conscious of the habitual cutting method – in the hand, over a light box – and assumed that he was producing an occasional aid to the editing process, and not a replacement for the well established routine for silent movies. The Moviola was conceived as a way of checking a few feet of film which also, unintentionally, gave editors a chance to match action and reaction in a way not possible in the hand. It is one thing to make a cut that allows a movement to continue over it; it is quite another to determine, by running the two shots several times through a mechanism at correct film speed, when is the best moment to match that movement. It has been claimed that rhythm and pacing were mastered by editors of silent movies to such an extent that they could see the moving image at the correct speed in the hand. However I am sure the advent of the Moviola gave editors a distinct advantage in gauging the rhythm of cutting.

Once established in the 1930s, the Moviola dictated much more than the mechanics of cutting: the cutting room was designed around it, indeed the original bench with synchronizer and rewinds only works as an adjunct to the Moviola, but its most significant effect is the way it encourages editors to relate to their material. Editing at the Moviola, as is obvious from a few moments observation, is a positive, even aggressive operation. You can sense that the editor feels an almost physical challenge as the film rattles back and forth through the gate. The editor stands in dominating fashion slapping and slamming pieces in and out of the mechanism, like a lion tamer determined to prove who is king of the editing jungle. You can imagine Howard Hawks or Quentin Tarantino exercising on a Moviola on getting out of bed in the morning, rather than indulging in callisthenics. Indeed it's a man's world at the Moviola, though in my opinion the best Moviola editor is a woman: Dede Allen.

Contrast this with a visit to a well established cutting room in Germany, where a Steenbeck or other flat-bed machine is holding court. You enter a world of soft lights and attentive service with coffee on tap and a vase of flowers decorating a carpeted room. The film runs silently back and forth with only the occasional click signifying a change of direction. You hear the odd comment, hardly above a whisper, between director and editor. You wonder why your teeth are beginning to ache, until you realize that the ambience reminds you of nothing so much as your dentist's surgery, with everything calculated to prevent the director's ulcers from flaring up.

This contrast is of greater significance than most people realize. Neither machine dictates such an extreme and different attitude to cutting, but each encourages a particular mode of working. It can be argued that the Moviola

Figure 3.2 Director and editor discuss a cut at the Steenbeck.

is best suited to dramatic films shot for continuity cutting and that the flat-bed is appropriate for the more discursive kind of documentary. In the end the quality of the editing, whichever machine is used, will depend on the skill and experience of the person using it.

In some circles the flat-bed is only considered useful for viewing, and this may well have been its prime function when first introduced. The best are very kind to film and can be used to run show copies and reversal masters, though this must be done with extreme care. With the advent of 16mm a gentler machine than the Moviola was desirable and table machines came into their own. In a sense the Moviola had relied on the toughness of 35mm for its effective operation. Since then the two types have become real alternatives, a fact recognized by the Moviola Company when they developed their own flat-bed in the 1970s. To this day film editors strongly prefer either the upright or flat-bed type of machine, just as camera people are wedded to one or other camera.

For many years the synchronizer has been an essential aid to editing. Combined with the Moviola it completed the cutting room technology in Hollywood and elsewhere until the advent of the flat-bed machine. The most obvious use for the original synchronizer was to match the negative or reversal master to the cutting copy before printing the final film, but once sound heads had been added much more elaborate use became feasible.

When 16mm became the dominant gauge in television, all equipment had to be adapted to cope with a frame size that was too small to view with the naked eye. For the synchronizer to remain a valuable device it was necessary to incorporate a way of viewing the picture. Once this was achieved it was a small step to add a motor to allow picture and sound to be run at normal speed. Refinements created a very flexible machine; good enough for some editors to choose to work exclusively at the 'picture-synchronizer' except when wishing to view cut sequences properly. In various guises the pic-sync or Compeditor has remained an effective cheaper cutting device to this day.

In the heyday of the Moviola, editors worked with optical sound and cement joiners. These were replaced by magnetic sound and tape splicers in the sixties. Optical sound had the advantage of being visible. Experienced editors learnt to read simple and common words and could cut close to a modulation by sight. Cement joiners had the disadvantage of losing frames every time a cut was made, thus preventing experimenting with a cut since the shots could not be restored without reprinting. On the other hand editors had to learn to judge the best cut before committing themselves; a discipline which had its advantages.

Tape joiners allow for the possibility of trying alternative cuts, but being able to restore shots is a mixed blessing. Too many joins can make it impossible to judge the cutting, especially when projected, as each join shudders through the gate. Both magnetic track and tape joins are subject to deterioration. It is essential to avoid running your track over sound heads at speed and under tension any more than is absolutely necessary, especially if you intend to use the cutting track as an element in the mixing.

In Moviola style editing, and when using a Compeditor, an essential piece of equipment is the sync-bench. This can be used to facilitate synchronizing the rushes, assembly editing, track laying and negative or master cutting. The essential characteristics incorporate rewinds, bins and a centrally placed pic-sync which can be replaced by a simple synchronizer for negative cutting. It is unusual to find a sync bench in a flat-bed cutting room.

Perhaps the most ubiquitous gadget is the trim bin. This primitive apparatus is the lazy editor's filing system, and should be treated with a degree of scepticism. A trim bin has a limited capacity: trims hung in it should be returned to their original cans when the sequence they belong to has been edited, otherwise the amount of material will get out of hand and you will have far less chance of finding those few essential frames that you are bound to need in a hurry.

Spacer and leaders are also essential in the cutting room. Spacer can, of course, be any waste film, though ideally single perforation white spacer is the best (single perforation to ensure it is inserted into picture and soundtrack rolls the right way round for machines and projectors, and white to allow the clearest possible marking). Standard leaders (or, according to the specific function, projection leaders, academy leaders, dubbing leaders and printer leaders) are all used to cue the start of a roll of film. It is possible to use marked-up spacer as a substitute leader but eventually a proper leader will have to be used.

Production companies, television stations and laboratories all produce different species of leader but they universally exhibit the basic markings which were established by the American Academy of Motion Picture Arts and Sciences in the 1930s. Working from the head inwards, a plain section for identification is followed by some kind of start-mark for synchronous lacing in the projector or editing machine – this mark is usually twelve 35mm feet from the first frame of picture, although television often works with a fifteen-foot equivalent. After this there is a count-down leader with windows showing the number of feet decreasing progressively to three (3). At this point the numbers stop to ensure that projectionists can allow the image to reach the screen without revealing further numbers, ensuring a neat change-over between reels.

If such a leader is attached to your cutting-copy picture all the sound track needs is a sync mark opposite the start, identification on the front and a sync bleep at the '3'. This device allows for positive synchronization where there may be variable run-up speeds between projector and sound reproducers, and gives the laboratory a reference point when marrying picture and sound into a combined print. The bleep consists of one frame of thousand-cycle tone and can be obtained from any dubbing theatre or transfer suite.

The cutting room does not require an abundance of paper beyond the various information sheets that we talked about in the last chapter. The log book will be dealt with in chapter 4. It is useful to have a film footage/time conversion chart but remember they exist for 24 *and* 25 frames per second running speeds and you must refer to the right one. It is also worth having a laboratory price list (as long as it is current!). A constant reminder of the cost of reprints should make you more careful when handling the material. Also any information on laboratory processes, especially an optical chart, can be helpful. Laboratories also supply a specially designed optical order pad – it is as well to follow this since you will then be giving that department the information they require in the form they are used to.

It is also necessary to have the following consumables: joining tape, camera tape, cleaning fluid, spare bulbs (and fuses) for equipment, dusters, anti-static cloths for dry-cleaning film, rubber bands and/or paper clips for securing pieces of film.

Ideally the room should have good ventilation, a subdued light source for viewing, venetian or roller blinds for the windows, a rewind bench to avoid having to rewind on the editing machine, and chairs of adjustable height. The floors, walls and working surfaces should be easy to clean, although some people prefer carpeted floors to reduce ambient noise. Above all the best use should be made of space with sufficient shelving to store all material.

These general requirements allow for considerable variation in layout and design. Whatever you end up with will have been considerably influenced by the machinery in your particular cutting room. Experience will demonstrate that the position of the machine is the most important variable to get right. Its relation to the sync bench is also very important if your method of working includes considerable moving to and fro between the synchronizer and the machine. There is no point in having a very neat room if the relationship between the various items in it is at variance to the way they are used.

In 1960, when I first entered the cutting rooms, video did not function as an editing medium. Engineers took up to ten minutes to make a physical cut in 2 inch video masters. The result was not something an editor would be proud of. Even recognizing the video equivalent of a frame was difficult, and in any case picture and sound were not parallel on the tape. For some time, certainly in the BBC, if serious editing was required a 'film recording' would be made and the sound transferred to 35mm magnetic film. To be fair, video recording was originally developed to allow the transmission of 'live' performances to be time shifted for different areas or, as in the case of the USA, to accommodate different time zones in the same country. It is only now being realized that this purely functional reason for taping meant that for some years nothing was archived, and masters do not exist for much of the quality television from that time. Even if it did you would have to rebuild the machines it was played on at the time, which is exactly what the University of California in Los Angeles did a few years ago in order to copy, amongst other treasures, Fred Astaire TV specials. Even so this was only possible because they traced the man who designed the original Ampex, who had the blueprints in his loft!

Through the 70s and early 80s video editing gradually became more sophisticated. The potential of timecode was understood as early as 1962 but standards were only adopted ten years later. Narrow video tape began to come into general use in the 70s, and linear off-line video editing became an industry standard, with EDL (Edit Decision List) systems allowing conforming of masters (as an equivalent to negative cutting and printing in film) in the on-line situation.

The limitations of video editing are analogous to the process of assembly editing on film. If film editors favour the assembly method it is usually a job that is delegated to the assistant. Basically, chosen takes are put together in script order before the editor starts the real job of cutting. In linear video editing this assembly method is dictated by the system: the original tape(s) are replayed from one or more decks and the sections are re-recorded onto blank tape through another deck. Thus the cut accumulates, with each editing decision relating only to the **next** cut. Any subsequent desire to make alterations in the order or balance of a cut sequence will usually involve starting again, and is thus a major task. The only alternative is to use the first cut as a new master and to go down a generation, with inevitable loss of quality, which will eventually make it difficult to judge the editing itself.

Talented and experienced video editors can think through the cutting of material in such a way that their first attempts are as good as some film editors would arrive at only after much reworking. They are probably good chess players too. When I worked in current affairs television, in the early 60s, film editors cut the work print for transmission and the joins were made with cement: there was no second chance. Some of those pieces were exquisite little documentaries. Is a wood engraver less of an artist than a painter?

The best people in any craft will overcome the limitations of the tools at their disposal; however, the development of new technology will always encourage the idea that its application can improve the situation. In the mid-80s the confluence of computers and digital storage systems created the breakthrough in post-production that some people had been yearning for, and the implications are more far-reaching than could have been imagined even ten years ago.

Let us be absolutely clear about this. Non-linear electronic editing systems replace not only the Moviola or off-line machine, they substitute for the cutting room or edit suite and even the assistant, once the material has been digitized and logged. The cans of film or video, the sync bench, rewinds, trim bin: the whole environment in which the editor has traditionally worked is reduced to a computer screen display, a keyboard and some form of controller.

There are two other distinct advantages of non-linear editing environments. First, each attempt at a cut can be preserved and several alternatives tried before any particular one is committed to. This is possible because you are working at a simulator which can begin from scratch each time, rather than actually cutting. Secondly, the material can be 'random accessed' almost instantly, compared with the delay that is normal even in the most well organized cutting room.

If this seems like Eldorado for the editor there are some drawbacks with current technology. It does take time to digitize and log the material, but this may not faze the film editor who is used to going through similar processes before cutting. Although digital storage is extraordinarily compact there is a limit to capacity. The alternative is to reduce the quality of the image, but a balance has to be struck between retrieval potential and the need for adequate visualization. However, it has to be said that there are no in-built technical limits which prevent gradual improvement in both storage capacity and image quality.

Perhaps the most revolutionary changes are only now coming on stream. It is now possible to achieve a high percentage of normal editing work in the non-linear mode based on an ordinary PC or personal computer. This brings the new technology within the capacity of everyone's pocket. Advances in digital sound are making non-linear a viable system for creating mixed sound tracks. All effects which were previously only possible through expensive laboratory work can be achieved with the added advantage of being able to preview them. Editing from multiple sources can be achieved with simultaneous display of sync-locked material. The keyboard is becoming less and less necessary, so even the manipulation of the material is as simple as the handle on a Steenbeck.

Technology has its own effect on the way we work and the results we achieve. In the near future sophisticated editing systems could be available in schools, colleges and all institutions that have access to a video camera. Indeed every home could have one. Perhaps the craze for games that simulate reality on a video screen might be replaced by an obsession with manipulating 'real' images. In the profession it is clear that there is nothing to stop directors cutting their own films at home, making the editor redundant. What worries the traditionalist is that because the technology can offer infinite alternatives at the flick of a switch, the need to understand the material before you make a cutting decision no longer exists.

In any case there is a desire, driven by accountants and corporate executives, to speed up the post-production process and, in theory, non-linear should make faster editing possible as long as the infinite opportunities to play with the material are avoided. If formulaic techniques are applied to the way material is shot everything can be turned into a production line. If you combine this with clever but meaningless effects the whole quality base of the best of film and video will be eroded. It is a nightmare scenario comparable to that let loose by the sorcerer's apprentice.

On the other hand, making the technology available to all could result in a wider understanding of the potential of good editing, and thereby foster a better knowledge of the language. Talented people could come from a wider base in society and challenge the more gross aspects of 'pure' commercialism with a new artistry. The independent movement, especially in the United States, has shown in recent years that quality does not depend on large budgets. Perhaps the technology now exists to give society at large the chance to express itself and the dangerous hegemony of media moguls could soon be over.

One other aspect of technological development should be mentioned. High Definition Television (HDTV) will become the norm in the next decade. Our homes will become mini-cinemas in the sense that large wide screen television with digital stereo sound will replace the present sets. This may encourage a more visual attitude even amongst the makers of broadcast programmes. There is nothing inherently better about a bias towards the visual dimension but it does place a different emphasis on the skill of editing. HDTV is also a challenge to film itself. Although 35mm has a greater resolution and the projected photographic image has a very particular quality, there is no technical inhibition to the use of video in all parts of the production and exhibition process. The compensation is that non-linear editing has the potential to re-invent the craft that has always been part of the special nature of the film cutting room.

Editing procedure 4

It should never be forgotten that film editing is a craft in which those involved have a tactile relationship with their 'material'. Although the 'material' is not shaped by the editor as clay is shaped by the potter, the way in which the editor relates physically to the footage will affect his sympathy and harmony with the process of shaping the cut film. I cannot stress this too strongly for those aiming to become editors or to edit their own material; watch any first-rate editor and it will not be long before you sense his relationship with film as a substance.

This basic tactile nature explains the logic of much about the way editors tend to work. Like good cooks, they prefer to have all their ingredients to hand – consequently the material must be organized and accessible. For some reason many people find the need for systems in a cutting room hard to accept. Actually, there is nothing obsessive or curious about it at all. Putting together a film is a complex process, and anyone successfully engaged in it will tell you that the greatest enemy, assuming good material, is anything that inhibits a positive work rhythm or stifles the development of momentum. I have known people so anxious to see a first cut of their material that they have ignored all advice to do the preparatory work, dived straight in, produced a cut in record time, and subsequently only avoided becoming suicidal when trying to re-cut by reprinting large amounts of material.

So the bulk of this chapter is about organizing the material to make it most accessible during the cutting process – a day spent preparing at this stage will save a week at a later stage of frustrating searches, resynchronization, re-transfers, reprinting and all such admissions of defeat which the editor cannot afford. One further point to bear in mind while reading this chapter: different kinds of film require different approaches in cutting. For instance, no one in their right mind would treat the footage for an observational documentary in the same way as the slates for a scripted drama.

By its very nature, film requires a number of careful procedures that are unnecessary with video. However this does not mean that less care should be taken when preparing to edit from video material. It is especially important to protect your master recordings which, like the negative of a film, are irreplaceable. I shall come back to video later in this chapter.

CHECKING YOUR MATERIAL FOR FAULTS

No film should be looked at (after the mute viewing to check for camera, stock and laboratory faults) until the paperwork has been organized. If the film is fiction this written material may include camera sheets, sound reports, continuity notes, shot lists and marked-up script, all of which affect the way the footage is viewed and contain information about possible faults and sources of conflict which make choice of take and section of shot always a matter for compromise. For example, the best take for camera will not always be the best for sound and neither may be the one the director prefers for performance.

The laboratory rushes report is the other main source of information which will tell you if there are faults to be dealt with. However, as it does not always tell you everything about the state of the material, a proper viewing of mute rushes, on a projector, should be held **immediately** after processing, preferably attended by director, cameraperson and editor to ensure nothing escapes unnoticed. This assumes that the editor is on the production during shooting, a luxury seldom possible except with feature films and the most elaborate of television programmes. (On most features the rushes are synchronized and viewed by lunchtime on the day after being shot, so the mute viewing is rendered redundant.) There are obvious advantages in having the editor on the pay-roll from the start of shooting, especially if they can achieve a rough cut of sequences very soon after they are processed. This gives the director and crew the chance to be sure they have obtained all the necessary material satisfactorily. The editor may well make useful suggestions for additional shots or re-shoots, and directors who have confidence in their editors will ring from location to ask specific questions about the effectiveness of material.

The following checklist should assist in the interpretation of remarks in the laboratory report and other paperwork and in dealing with faults discerned by yourself:

1. *Scratches* Check if on print or in negative.
   (a) *Positive* Ensure that the projector and editing equipment are clean and properly aligned to avoid further damage (badly scratched cutting copy is a hindrance to good judgment in cutting).

(b) *Negative* Check if they are emulsion or base scratches. Base scratches will usually polish out but emulsion scratches are a bigger problem and can be a reason to reject material. Also check if they are caused by camera or in processing and take remedial action.

2. *Dirt or 'sparkle'* In general, positive dirt is black and negative white.

(a) *Positive* Dirt on the print usually implies that equipment needs cleaning. A dirty cutting copy is as much a hindrance as a scratched one.

(b) *Negative* If negative 'sparkle' is sufficiently worrying it is advisable to ask the laboratory to clean the negative and supply another rush print for checking. (N.B. It is unfortunately all too common to receive rushes which are dirty at the front and end of camera rolls on 16mm. With luck this will not spoil your irreplaceable shot that was snatched just before the film ran out.)

(c) *Hairs etc. in camera gate* These usually appear at the top, bottom or side of frame. Check whether they are in the camera or projector by asking the projectionist to rack the picture to reveal the frame line.

3. *Fogging* Head-, tail- and edge-fogging can all result from inefficient loading or from a badly fitting magazine. If the rush print is black-and-white the full extent of fogging will only be appreciated if a colour print is obtained.

4. *Static* If your stock becomes electrically charged during exposure, patterns (known as 'Christmas trees' which they sometimes resemble) will appear on the processed material. There is no treatment for this, but it is sometimes caused by friction or rubbing in the camera, so the camera operator should be notified.

5. *Over- or under-exposure* Since rush prints are almost invariably not corrected for variations in exposure, there will normally be a degree of variation in density. However, if there is unacceptable heaviness or lightness in the print a check should be made of the negative and, if the laboratory thinks it is correctable, a graded print should be obtained. If there is a general trend away from the norm of exposure, checks should be made of the film stock and lens ratings (speeds) and efficiency of exposure meters.

6. *Soft focus* Remember that differential focus and shots in which the focus is altered will probably be related to changes in the point of interest. The effectiveness of change of focus can consequently only be judged when material is synchronized. General out-of-focus rushes imply bad columnation of lenses, 'finger trouble' or just plain carelessness.

7. *Camera mechanism* Your laboratory report may mention a number of faults which are due to irregularities in the camera:

(a) Intermittent exposure variations: 'flicker'.

(b) Irregularity of focus: 'breathing'.

(c) Unsteadiness of image: 'weaving' or 'floating'.

8. *Lens aberrations* Various forms of image distortion can be caused by faults in the lenses. With careful and regular testing these problems are very rare.

9. *Stock faults* There are several ways in which faulty stock can affect your material and you should always consider this a possible cause. The manufacturers admit the minimal liability of stock replacement if they accept responsibility.

10. *Processing* Mistakes are also made in the laboratory and, prevention always being better than cure, you should ensure (a) that camera sheets are clearly written and special instructions always included where necessary, and (b) that you establish an immediate rapport with your 'contact' at the laboratory to whom any problems can then be referred personally.

11. *Extraneous objects* Last but not least, boom shadows, microphones and cables in shot can easily be overlooked when viewing rushes for the first time.

SYNCHRONIZING THE RUSHES

Let us assume that all the rushes have been viewed and any necessary steps taken to rectify faults. The next task of the editing department is to see that the ¼-in. tapes are sent for transfer to magnetic film – they are almost always dealt with by a specialist sound facility, either in plant or elsewhere. If, however, you are able to do the transfer yourself then it is just a matter of gaining access to the facilities.

Assuming there is no bad news from the transfer you now proceed to synchronize your rushes. The most common form of sync marking is still the clapperboard but the basic method holds true for 'bleep' or 'blip' sync and even for the mike tap or hand clap (p. 40). Nothing is either more important or more boring than this process – unless each and every take of every slate is synchronized to the exact frame, you are storing up trouble for yourself when you embark on cutting. A synchronizer should always be used because it locks together picture and sound without any system of linkage that allows differential movement. Machines that are belt driven or can be decoupled between the picture and sound transport encourage error in synchronization. Since 16mm sync is already relatively imprecise (35mm, having 4 perforations to each frame, is much more accurate), anything which encourages this imprecision is to be avoided at all cost.

The advantage of a viewing machine with a larger screen than that available on a picture synchronizer is obvious. Even the most efficient crew is sometimes unable to provide in-focus, well-lit, large, steady clapperboards and so it may be necessary to run picture rushes for marking up on a Steenbeck or Moviola – essential if there is no sync reference. Some editors prefer always to mark up picture rushes by this method – it certainly has advantages and, with all due deference to camera assistants, provides an immediate and thorough check against the camera sheets. Also, laboratories often join camera rolls together out of order and, by running all picture rushes on the machine, rolls can be broken down and marked up in chronological slate order.

The following points take you step by step through the process of synchronization:

1. Place the roll of picture on the horse and insert in the synchronizer.
2. Find the first clapperboard and isolate the first frame which shows the board closed.
3. Mark up with white or yellow chinagraph, using the standard mark for picture sync, thus:

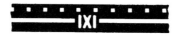

The horizontal lead-in line (extended over several frames) allows for quick identification when searching for sync at speed.

4. Remove picture from synchronizer, place the relevant sound roll on the horse and insert this in the synchronizer.
5. Locate the corresponding sound announcement and mark up the frame which contains the FRONT EDGE of the noise of the clapperboard closing, with the standard mark for sound sync, thus:

6. Reinsert the picture 'in synchronization' and write the slate and take numbers next to the lead-in line on both picture and track, e.g. - - - - ×
    - - - - 13 – 2. (N.B. It is best not to use a diagonal line, e.g. 13/2, between slate and take since this can easily be mistaken for a 1; some editors even prefer 13T2 for total clarity.)
7. Always retain 2–3 feet in front of the sync frame to allow for lacing of each slate on an editing machine when you have broken down the film. This is more essential on a Steenbeck since a Moviola requires only a few frames to engage.
8. This being the front of the sync roll, join 20–30 feet of single perforation spacing to the front of this slate and add sync marks half way along both for ease of lacing when projected and for the coding machine.
9. Mark the front of each roll thus: 'TITLE', SYNC RUSHES, SLATES: X–Y, HEAD, ACTION OR SOUND. If white spacer is used it is possible to use colour coding to allow quick identification of picture and sound, e.g. black felt-tip pen for picture and red for sound.

10. The front of these rolls can now be attached to spools on the take-up arm and reeled down to the end of the marked-up slate.
11. Level sync should now be marked across the frame line. However, where either sound or picture continues beyond the other and is considered important enough to retain (if in doubt **always** retain material), then spacing must be inserted in the roll that has stopped first, until the other one finishes.
12. Either in level sync or after spacing has been added, both rolls can be guillotined and the next take put into sync and joined on to the tail of the previous one.
13. This process should be continued until you have about 1000 feet. Then add spacing to the tail with a level sync mark for checking.
14. Now remove this roll from the take-up arm and rewind it in sync, using the tail sync mark, for an immediate check of the complete roll.
15. These rolls of picture and sound should now be put into cans, clearly labelled with the same information as the front of the roll (see 9 above). The material is now ready for the coding machine.

Additional points to note in synchronizing rushes:

- Wild tracks are best removed from the sound material, rewound and identified before being put into a can for later use. It is a good idea to list the wild tracks in terms of purpose, approximate length and quality to avoid lengthy and often disappointing searches at the end of the cutting. Never assume because a wild track has been recorded to cover a scene or specific effect, that it is any more than a token effort on the part of the recordist to supply what he or she divines as necessary. The very fact that sync sound has not been recorded is often a good enough reason to suspect that wild tracks will not be usable. Therefore the list is only worthwhile if it is an accurate representation of what is usable. (Otherwise at midnight when you are laying tracks for mixing the following day you will realize too late that library sound should have been obtained to cover the scene in question.)
- Mute picture should also be removed and identified, unless it is very short and directly related to the sync slates immediately adjacent, when it is best left in the sync roll and spacing added to the sound roll.
- Both wild tracks and mute picture should be identified in chinagraph. Normally reference is made to the scene or slate to which they are relevant, thus: W/T after 13–2 and M after 13–2. Some mute of course is identified with the clapperboard. There are exceptions to this, e.g. wild track is sometimes recorded as general background and is then identified as W/T to cover scene X or slates X to Y. Occasionally a shot intended as sync lacks sound and will have to be post-recorded. In this

case it can be labelled 13–2 No Sound, to differentiate it from a strictly mute shot.

- If a take has been end-boarded, then a simple sync mark and identification should be added near the front for lacing up when it is separated from the roll.
- When using spacing in the sound roll, always ensure that the emulsion side of the spacing is joined so that it faces the opposite way to the oxide of the magnetic track. Otherwise the emulsion will clog the sound heads and cause wear to the track itself.
- There is no need to use the diagonal cutter for sound when synchronizing rushes as the cuts made at this stage will not be used in the final film. This helps to speed the process and makes for easier handling when the film is broken down.
- Never assume that because the clapperboard is in sync, the whole take remains in sync. A faulty lead or a low battery can cause loss of sync in recording and mistakes can be made in transfer. Therefore always make spot-checks, taking advantage of any natural substitute for a clapperboard, such as door slams or – the best alternative – words beginning with a B or P. If a take is found to be out of sync it is best to confirm **all** the slates on that tape roll since the checks necessary when reloading the tape recorder may not have been done properly. You can then explore the possibility of whether a transfer can be made to adjust the sync. If this is out of the question you should determine whether sound or picture is longer and by how much. If sound is slightly longer (say by a frame per foot), it is possible to remove the excess frames at regular intervals. If either is a great deal longer it is probably best to consider post-synchronization or, in the last resort, to reject the material. If picture is slightly longer you have a trickier situation. Obviously, removing frames from the picture will not work as, when the negative is cut to match, the ensuing print will jump; and adding frames to the sound is awkward, especially with distinctive background on the track. It is possible to stretch or concertina the sound whilst retaining the pitch of the original, but this is an expensive process and only to be recommended if the track is irreplaceable and essential.
- Never treat sound (at this or any other stage) as the element you are adding to the picture. The best marriage of the two is a total synthesis, so you must apply the same sort of quality checks to your sound that I outlined for picture during the mute viewing. One factor that reduces the respect accorded to sound is that, except in feature films, the sound you synchronize to the picture cutting copy is the same that is used to re-record from when mixing, whereas the cutting copy is a mere work print. (In feature films no one would normally dare to take the mutilated, worn-out, working track to the dubbing theatre; indeed the higher

status accorded the sound track in feature films is recognized by there being a separate sound editor.)

CODING THE RUSHES

Once all material has been synchronized, or as each roll is rewound and checked, it is ready for coding or numbering. Except in large studios it is unusual for cutting rooms to have access to their own coding machine, so it is normal to use a firm that provides a numbering service.

The coding machine indelibly marks your picture and sound material at 1-foot intervals along the edge, with numbers which progress automatically by one digit at a time. On 16mm the numbering block usually has 6 digits which consist of 2 letters and 4 numbers, or 6 numbers. So your first roll of picture and sound can be numbered AA0000–AA1000 or 01 0000–01 1000, the second AB or 02 and so on. It is worth noting that with an 8-digit block it becomes possible to code using the appropriate slate and take, e.g. slate 243 take 7 becomes 24370000 onwards.

All professional editors prefer to work with coded material. It has the following advantages:

- The alternative for logging purposes is to use key numbers. Coding is preferable because:
  (a) Key numbers are often indistinct in the rush print.
  (b) Coding supplies you with the same reference for picture and sound.
- It provides a level sync mark every foot.
- Trims can be easily located.

I am convinced that the slight delay involved before cutting can commence is a small price to pay for the value of coding your material.

LOGGING

The nature of the log that you must now make of your material will be determined by several factors, the most important of which are (a) the kind of film you are working on and (b) what other paperwork already exists as reference for the editor. On a scripted drama, where shot lists, camera and sound reports, continuity notes and a marked-up script are also available, the log may only need to consist of slate and take numbers, and the corresponding head and tail code numbers. However, on documentary much more information is usually added, including descriptions and quality of each shot. Illustrated here is a simple form of log sheet. Remember that the prime purpose of your log is to enable you to find material from a simple number reference.

THE NATIONAL FILM SCHOOL BEACONSFIELD			RUSHES LOG			
DATE 6 · 3 · 81		TITLE ' HIATUS '				

ROLL No	SLATE No - Tk	SCENE No	RUBBER NUMBERS FROM	TO	MUTE OR SYNC	DESCRIPTION	OK NG
1	1 − 1	5	AA0000	0012	S	C·U· JOHN - (LINES WRONG)	N/G
	1 - 2	5	0013	0025	S	" "	OK
	2 − 1	5	0026	0031	M	C·U· DAVID REACTION	
	3 · 1	5	0032	0040	S	TWO-SHOT JOHN / DAVID (mike inshot)	N/G
	3 - 2	5	0041	0049	S	" " —	OK
	3 · 3	5	0050	0057	S	·· " ··	OK
	4 - 1	17	0058	0066	M	C·U· PHONE	OK
	5 - 1	17	0067	0093	M	C·U· PHONE (ALTERNATIVE ANGLE)	OK
	6 - 1	17	0094	0134	S	WIDE-SHOT FIGHT (CAMERA FAULT)	N/G
	6 · 2	17	0135	0176	S	·· ~ · (CAMP KNOCKED OVER)	N/G
	6 · 3	17	0177	0238	S	·· " ··	OK
	6 - 4	17	0239	0280	S	·· " "	OK
	6 · 5	17	0281	0324	S	·· " ·	OK
	7 - 1	17	0325	0337	S	B·C·U HANDS ON THROAT	OK
	7 - 2	17	0338	0349	S	·· " " "	OK
	8 · 1	17	0350	0371	M	C·U REVERSE ANGLE	OK
	9 - 1	17	0372	0385	M	WIDE SHOT DAVID RELEASES JOHN & STANDS UP	OK

Figure 4.1 A sample log of rushes incorporating short shot descriptions for easy identification.

TRANSCRIBING OR MARKING UP THE SCRIPT

The next step depends entirely on whether your film is documentary or fiction. With documentary, it is best now carefully to transcribe all interview or conversational material, with slate reference, as a shorthand guide to cutting. However, never treat the transcription as a substitute for cutting the film itself, because the words on paper cannot convey voice inflexion or the rhythm. So it is best to use the transcription in conjunction with viewing the material. With fiction, it is the practice of some editors at this stage to mark up the script. If continuity notes have been provided, this is a simple process of representing the coverage for each scene on the relevant page of the script. However, there are refinements to this system. One is to wait until the synchronized rushes have been seen with the director, and only to mark up the script with those takes that are chosen to be used rather than all that have been printed. Another is to obtain polythene sleeves for the script pages, so that the marking up can be done in chinagraph on the sleeve and altered when decisions are made, thus representing the cut film in a graphic form. This will be a very useful cross-reference (and will protect the script from the otherwise inevitable deterioration).

VIEWING THE SYNC RUSHES

Everything described so far should have happened before the viewing of sync rushes, unless they are being viewed daily as shooting progresses. This

Figure 4.2 Shots from *Mary Reilly*: part of the coverage referred to in the script example (Figure 4.3).

viewing is important not least for the relationship and understanding between director and editor. You should not, however, expect too many concrete decisions to be reached at this stage: it is much more important to get a feel of the material and to begin to relate the script as written to the film as realized. There are many editors who find it impossible to imagine the 'look' of a film even from the most lucid scenario, but this is not necessarily a disadvantage since the particular vision a director brings to a film will invariably not mesh with the perceptions of others. Indeed, if the editor has too clear an idea of how the film should look he stands the chance of being very disappointed at rushes. If director and editor are one and the

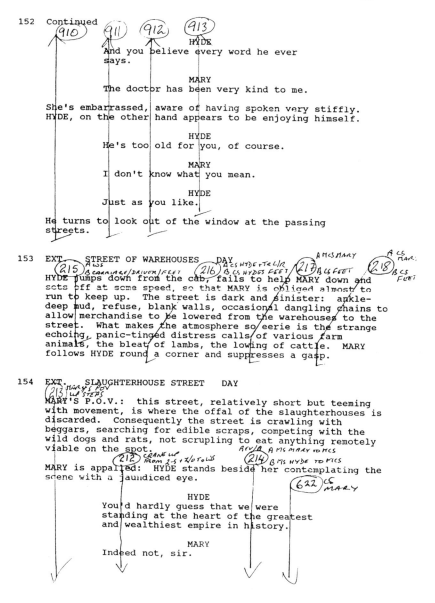

152 Continued

⑨⑩ ⑨⑪ ⑨⑫ ⑨⑬

                    HYDE
        And you believe every word he ever
        says.

                    MARY
        The doctor has been very kind to me.

    She's embarrassed, aware of having spoken very stiffly.
    HYDE, on the other hand appears to be enjoying himself.

                    HYDE
        He's too old for you, of course.

                    MARY
        I don't know what you mean.

                    HYDE
        Just as you like.

    He turns to look out of the window at the passing
    streets.

153 EXT. STREET OF WAREHOUSES DAY   A MCS MARY   A CS MAR.
    ②⑮ B CARRIAGE/DRIVEN/FEET ②⑯ B CS HYDES FEET ②⑰ B CS FEET ②⑱ B CS FEET
    A WS   A CS HYDE rTR L/R
    HYDE jumps down from the cab, fails to help MARY down and
    sets off at some speed, so that MARY is obliged almost to
    run to keep up. The street is dark and sinister: ankle-
    deep mud, refuse, blank walls, occasional dangling chains to
    allow merchandise to be lowered from the warehouses to the
    street. What makes the atmosphere so eerie is the strange
    echoing, panic-tinged distress calls of various farm
    animals, the bleat of lambs, the lowing of cattle. MARY
    follows HYDE round a corner and suppresses a gasp.

154 EXT. SLAUGHTERHOUSE STREET DAY
    ②⑬ MARY'S POV UP STEPS
    MARY'S P.O.V.: this street, relatively short but teeming
    with movement, is where the offal of the slaughterhouses is
    discarded. Consequently the street is crawling with
    beggars, searching for edible scraps, competing with the
    wild dogs and rats, not scrupling to eat anything remotely
    viable on the spot.   ArY/B A MS MARY TO MCS
    ②⑫ CRANE UP   ②⑭ B MS HYDE TO MCS
    FROM 2-5 r X/OTO WS
    MARY is appalled: HYDE stands beside her contemplating the
    scene with a jaundiced eye.   ⑥②② CS MARY

                    HYDE
        You'd hardly guess that we were
        standing at the heart of the greatest
        and wealthiest empire in history.

                    MARY
        Indeed not, sir.

Figure 4.3 Marked-up script page from *Mary Reilly*, showing clearly the editor's options for this scene.

same person, this is the time when you come face to face with the reality of your material. There is no way that the experience of shooting the film can be wiped from your memory, but the more you can treat what you see on the screen in the viewing theatre as the reality, and forget any imagined ideal realization of the script, the easier it will be to make the most of editing's contribution to the final result.

If possible the material should be assembled in scene order for this screening, to give an immediate sense of the whole material for each scene and of the way scenes may or may not be constructed to flow together. New and exciting juxtapositions may emerge later but the ideas that can transform a cut that is slave to the script are always more likely to emerge if the editor has digested the expected form first.

At this viewing it is very useful to make notes of particular reactions you have to the material aside from the indications given you in the paperwork supplied from various members of the crew. You should now begin to feel the possible shape of sequences. Remember that one element in a few seconds of an otherwise poor take may make it the best alternative for that moment in the film. It is too easy to fall into the trap of looking for the perfect combination of these elements, when there is advantage to be had from choosing a nuance of performance in a take that is less good than others for lighting, operation, sound and overall rhythm. Judging which elements are more important than the rest is also part of this effort to familiarize yourself with the footage. It will not all happen at once, and first impressions, right or wrong, are often superficial: the relevance of a shot may only be revealed as the overall structure takes shape during cutting.

Even if little seems to sink in as a result of projecting your synchronized rushes, it is always a better approach than plunging straight into cutting without a clear map of the outline of the material in your mind. Of course, if you are cutting fiction, you have a map in the shape of a shooting script, but even attempting to cut to that script may lead you up blind alleys which you can avoid if the viewing is held first.

BREAKING DOWN THE FILM

After screening, the footage is broken down for ease of working. Several factors may affect the system employed. Let us take the example of a scripted fiction film first. Assuming that a reasonably clear idea has emerged of which takes are to be employed in the cut, each of these chosen takes is broken out of its sync roll and rewound, on 16mm usually with both picture and sound on the same core, and clearly labelled. If possible all the slates for a particular scene should be put in the same can. The takes remaining on the roll are canned separately and labelled as 'spares' for the appropriate scene or scenes. This system is ideal for editing with a synchronizer and Moviola or with a motorized picture-synchronizer. It can also be employed when using a table editing-machine, but in that case the first cut working from broken-down rushes is inevitably more laborious and less fluid (see comments on use of different machinery, pp. 56–7). The machine you are using may affect how you decide to file the material.

Documentary footage is seldom broken down into single shots unless those shots are inordinately long. The guideline here is to leave the subject material in rolls that make sense of it but that are not too long to prevent relatively swift reference to any particular shot. In any case 16mm rolls of more than 400 feet (10 minutes) are very cumbersome when you are searching for a few frames – which invariably turn out to be at the far end of the roll!

Sometimes the dialogue will be post-synchronized before cutting. This is usually because there is a greater chance of the artist being available at this early stage. Post-synchronization is discussed in detail in chapter 6.

CUTTING

Once all the material has been broken down and filed you can proceed with the cutting of the first sequence. Unless there are specific reasons to do otherwise, such as the need to cut a sequence early for post-synchronization, always start at the beginning. This may seem obvious, but it is sometimes very tempting to begin with a particularly vivid scene or one that has struck you as attractive when reading the script. In documentary there is some- times no way of knowing what is the beginning, in which case devise some guideline to give you a sense of overall structure to allow the first cut to emerge: chronology is the most obvious yardstick but there may be others.

The next chapter deals in detail with attitudes to and reasons for cutting. Remember that in all cases where you as editor are expected to make a substantial contribution to the form of the final film the way you approach each stage of the cut will inevitably affect your perception of the structure. It is always better if you end up revealing an essentially innate form rather than seeking to impose an artificial shape.

To begin cutting arrange all the material for the sequence on the bench in front of you, in the order you expect to use the shots, using the marked-up script as reference. At this point I am unable to avoid what to many editors is a heresy. The widely accepted procedure is to construct an assembly from which a rough cut and eventually a fine cut are produced. It has always seemed to me to be counter-productive to insert extra stages in the process, when the only way that you can tell whether each sequence is working is to cut it properly. The assembly seems to me to be a way of reducing editing to the level of 'painting by numbers'. It makes the framework pre- determined and allows less flexibility later. Whereas, even if it does not work first time, an attempt at a real cut gives you information that can be applied to a re-cut. More than that: as the cut comes together the cumulative effect of each cut and each scene on the rest will emerge dynamically. Editing has to be a process of cause and effect, of the synthesis created from juxtapositions. The first few cuts when jumping in the deep end are always hard, not to say traumatic, but there is nothing worse than the limp structure that results from nibbling away rather than tackling the task head-on.

Of course, there are sequences that can only be constructed little by little but, even if you are presented with two or three rolls of material than are supposed to be magically transformed into a dazzling montage, always look for the core idea. If the sequence is worth having it must have a point in the film. Finding that purpose and applying it to the evaluation of each shot will always give you more of a basis for constructing a sequence than the principle of 'stick it together and see how it goes'. Sometimes the criterion is as simple as direction of movement within the shots, or some form of progression that allows the film to flow from one scene to the next.

Whatever approach to cutting you come to favour, a positive attitude is essential. No procedure should be applied for its own sake, but only because you believe that by the method you employ you stand the best chance of making the most of the material.

The actual process of cutting with a tape joiner has been described (p. 58). Some of the cuts you make will not remain the same, so the most important part of organizing the way you edit is to ensure that the material remains as accessible as possible. Remember that the trim bin is no substitute for a proper filing system (p. 59). It is also best to rejoin head and tail trims of each shot so that they can be easily re-run when considering alterations. If this is not done you will begin to experience the worst aspect of disorganization in the cutting room. As each cut is made the trims become a separate collection of pieces so that towards the end of the process you find that every time a few frames are required there are three or four places to look: the original can, the trim bins and various cans marked 'assembly trims' or 'fourth fine cut trims'! The exasperation this produces can be soul-destroying, and the refinement that is invariably necessary to arrive at a fine cut worth the name may be seriously jeopardized.

For consistency it is as well to apply the following marks during cutting:

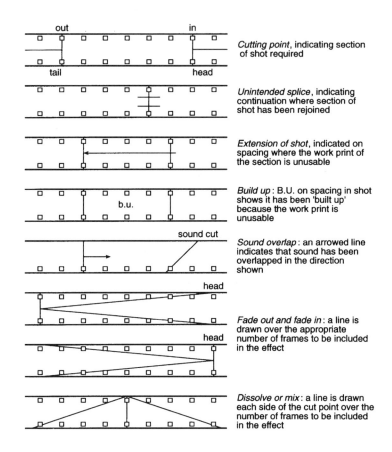

Figure 4.4 Standard markings used during cutting.

VIDEO EDITING

The procedure for video editing is remarkably simple. With the use of the 'Smart Slate' or 'Digi-slate' in shooting, time-code is incorporated to allow easy synchronization. Once the copy tape has been made for editing the time-code can be used to log the material for efficient retrieval. The editor then proceeds to build up the cut in a linear fashion, adding each next shot after previewing the options. An EDL or Edit Decision List is created and modified as the process continues. Any alteration to an existing cut will require copying to a further generation unless you simply want to alter a cut position or insert another shot without changing the overall length of the sequence.

Video editing is often done using another soundtrack, the most common being the use of music as in pop videos. The electronic medium also allows the editor to experiment with simple effects such as fades, wipes and dissolves, though the more complex effects will be incorporated on-line.

RANDOM ACCESS

The development of non-linear or random access editing has gradually moved towards a system which potentially replicates the traditional craft of film editing whilst at the same time taking advantage of computer and digital technology. Although there are now a considerable number of systems vying for the approval of the industry, there are indications that a degree of standardization is developing. Before long it seems likely that the choice will be a matter of taste rather than between radically different machines.

The procedure to be followed will initially depend on the medium of origination, i.e. film or video. Once you have the material in a format that the system will accept it can be input up to the limit of the particular disk or machine capacity. Next the material is logged. This can be as simple as the shot number, but the more sophisticated systems allow you to incorporate descriptions, script pages, or any useful information that may assist the editing. The point is that the on-screen display substitutes for everything that is available in a cutting room. As with film, careful and detailed logging will help make editing go much more smoothly.

Once the rushes are logged editing can begin. Working can be through a keyboard, mouse or controller, or a combination of these methods depending on the particular system. The shots for a sequence are accessed by typing in the appropriate code. Key frames from each shot can be displayed and cued for review. Part of the monitor shows the evolving cut whilst another area can be used to run the shot(s) currently being considered. Each attempt at a cut can be considered and filed away while alternatives are tried. Graphic displays represent the cut as it evolves and indicate where you are in the process.

Picture and sound can be given composite or separate treatment. The picture can be electronically altered or visual effects added. Sound mixing from multiple sources can be achieved, in some cases up to broadcast standard. Although cost and the particular editing needs are important, your choice of non-linear editing system may be just as much a matter of taste as it has been between Moviola and Steenbeck.

There are now a large number of non-linear editing systems. It should be borne in mind that new versions of existing models are appearing frequently, often offering a considerable modification. The basic format will be similar however and once you have mastered one system each subsequent type you encounter will be relatively easy to use.

Figure 4.5 The Avid Technology Europe Ltd 'Media Composer' provides sophisticated picture and sound random access editing.

Figure 4.6 The Lightworks Editing Systems Ltd 'Heavyworks One' which is capable of handling multi-camera productions and which has considerable soundtrack capacity.

Figure 4.7 The 'Montage' non-linear editing set-up which brings random access within the financial capacity of a wider range of production.

THE RELATIONSHIP BETWEEN DIRECTOR AND EDITOR

One indication of the importance of the relationship between directors and their editors is that frequently the same editor will work with a director on a number of films. It has even been known for directors to alter their schedule to fit in with the availability of their favourite editor. There are many cases of consistent and continuing collaboration between directors and editors: Truffaut worked frequently with Martine Barraqué; Thelma Schoonmaker has been Scorsese's editor for many years; and Tony Lawson is Nicolas Roeg's regular collaborator.

The relationship will vary enormously in each case. Some directors merely require a good and reliable technician, others expect and depend upon a much more creative contribution. There is also considerable variation in working methods. Most editors do not like to have the directors breathing down their necks all the time; by far the most effective way is to meet regularly, say for an hour each day, and to discuss what has been cut since the last meeting and to review the material for the next sequence or sequences due to be cut. Of course, the nature of the material will affect how often and for how long consultations need to take place, but only where director and editor are completely relaxed and in tune with each other will it be possible to work together constantly without considerable tension developing.

It is not enough just to be sympathetic in attitude to your director. To make the most positive contribution an editor should take the following steps:

1. Read the script in advance of cutting.
2. Become familiar with the director's previous work.
3. Read any background material relevant to the film.
4. Meet the cameraperson, sound recordist and other major contributors to the film who might affect your own job.
5. Liaise with the continuity or production assistant for documentation.
6. Make yourself known to the laboratory contact.
7. Choose your assistant carefully for both efficiency and tact.
8. Find out your director's preferred working hours and eating habits!
9. Ensure that the cutting room is properly set up before cutting starts.
10. Make sure that reliable maintenance can be obtained for your equipment.

If you think any of the above is unnecessary then you should not be an editor. It is easy enough to be a good technician, but the satisfaction to be gained from editing is in direct proportion to the effort you make to demonstrate a real commitment.

The language of editing: giving your material form and refining its meaning

5

In *The Parade's Gone By* Brownlow wrote: 'Editing is directing the film for the second time. To gauge the psychological moment – to know exactly where to cut – requires the same intuitive skill as that needed by a director.' Every film presents the editor with an imprecise agenda. Without experience it is natural to conclude that a well-cut film only requires the editor to put the pieces together in the right order. In fact, no editor believes that his task is simply to find the one perfect conjunction that is just waiting to be discovered. If this were so cutting would be analogous to jigsaw solving.

The difference between editing a film and assembling a jigsaw is that with a film nothing is completely predetermined. The film-maker may claim that the film already exists in his head, and that it is also on paper in the script, but the film that emerges from the cutting room has never existed before, neither in someone's head nor on paper. It is only through the editing process that the material is translated into the form that can communicate its narrative and meaning to the audience.

To understand the language of editing requires us to define in what ways it involves 'directing the film for the second time'. In that way we can unearth what Brownlow calls 'the hidden power' of the editor.

SELECTION

The way films are conceived and shot assumes the function of editing. This is especially true in the selection of what is to be shot, a process that leaves levels of decision-making to be refined in the cutting. In dramatic films this provides the editor with different kinds of choices. The first is the choice between several attempts at the same shot. Every time two or more takes are shot on the same slate selection in the editing is being allowed for. This implies both the desire to obtain the most effective version of the action for a particular shot and the realization that the choice of take may depend on which one dovetails best into other shots which cover the same segment of the script. Secondly, it is normal to shoot the same action in more than one set-up: the resulting changes of angle and sizes of shot allow a further level of selection in the cutting. Thirdly, this kind of shooting leaves open the question of when to cut and what to cut to.

STRUCTURING

To be able to understand the way in which editing selects, you must first understand the structuring of a scene and also the placing of each scene in the overall film. To be able to structure a scene effectively you must understand its function. It is the misunderstanding of function that leads to the most superficial use of editing technique. If the writing and/or shooting of a film is meant to convey more than just the words and actions of its characters then the cutting must be used to serve those aspects of the drama that lie beneath the surface. If you edit merely to ensure that the dialogue is heard and the actions seen then your structuring will be only something mechanical.

Helen van Dongen arrived at her own list of factors affecting the structuring of material through her experience as Flaherty's editor: the subject matter of the scene; spatial movement in each image; the tonal value of each shot (atmosphere); the emotional content. This can be taken to represent the specific agenda for documentaries, although in general terms it overlaps in its application to dramatic material.

BALANCE AND EMPHASIS

The real contribution of editing is to provide support to the inherent drama through balance and emphasis. The balance in a scene is a delicate matter which must be retained with every cut, and if we use emphasis correctly it will help this balance. For instance, each time you cut to a closer shot it is imperative that the shift in visual emphasis supports the dramatic balance at that point.

THE DYNAMIC AXIS

Already in the way a scene is staged – in the way character and camera movement are controlled – the director is seeking to use physical space to support the emotional content of the scene by balance and emphasis. Editing should respect and reinforce these intentions. As each scene evolves the editor must be aware of changes in the dominant line of dramatic tension, or what I like to call the dynamic axis. This is not simply a matter of analysing the flow of a scene and deciding who is 'centre stage' at any point; any such obvious dominance must be taken in conjunction with the point of the scene and its purpose in the overall drama. To take a simple example, if a fight occurs between two characters it may be that the effect on a third party not directly involved in the fight is more important in the film than the actual conflict. The reactions of this third party could be the element that the cutting needs to emphasize. Even here, you have to be careful not to over-emphasize by cutting: for instance, the director may have carefully staged the action to focus on reactions of the third party while still including the other two characters in the shot. Understanding this dynamic axis in a scene will always give the editor the right clues in deciding what to cut to and when.

MOTIVATION

All cuts should be motivated. Again it must be emphasized that this is not something mechanical. Just because there is movement that could be followed or emphasized by a cut is not necessarily enough reason for the cut. The dramatic focus of a scene and the point of view that has been established are often far more important than the details of the action. Staying wide can sometimes serve the tension far better than cutting in close, and the cut to a close-up may provide undue emphasis on the insignificant.

POINT OF FOCUS

The editor must be aware that at each moment in a shot the audience's attention is focused on a particular area of the frame. Often a cut that is sufficiently motivated is prevented from working properly by the switch of attention on the cut. If the eye has to adjust its focus in an unexpected way the moment of the cut will be a dead spot and will dislocate the flow of the scene.

SEQUENCING

We must also be aware of the way in which cuts work at the junctions between scenes. Much will depend upon the way the director has ensured that the shots that are meant to open and close each adjacent scene can be matched in the cutting. The success of sequencing will be affected by the composition and, of course, by the control of pace and rhythm.

PARALLEL ACTION

Scenes that are meant to be cut in parallel are often conceived without due attention being given to the pacing and balance. Such intercutting will seldom work unless the material has been preconceived for that purpose, especially since the normal function of parallel action is to lead to a denouement which brings together the separate dramatic threads.

RHYTHM AND PACING

As we construct a scene the aim must be to provide the right pacing and to establish or emphasize the inherent rhythm. In both dramatic and documentary films the events being shown have a natural rhythm. It is important to be able to use this rhythm to motivatehe cutting. Of all the elements which must be considered for effective use of the editing process, the use of and control of rhythm and pace are finally what will determine the contribution that cutting makes to your film.

Kurosawa had in mind a particular piece of music when conceiving oneequence of *Red Beard* (1964). According to Donald Ritchie in *The Films of Akira Kurosawa* (1965), when Kurosawa had cut the sequence together, he 'put on a recording of the Haydn, the second movement, and played it along with the film to see what the effect was. Well, the effect was just fine, but what really surprised me was that I had cut the sequence so that it came to an end precisely at the end of the Haydn . . . Somewhere in the back of my head some kind of clock kept count.' Of course, the material had the potential to work effectively but it was the editing that confirmed the inherent rhythm and pace.

In his article *Montage mon beau souci* (1956), Godard stated: 'If direction is a look, montage is a heartbeat. To foresee is the characteristic of both, but what one seeks to foresee in space the other seeks in time.' When he wrote this Godard had only made two short films, but foreseeing in time is indeed the prime function of editing. Everything we do in cutting is in some sense a manipulation of time. We speed it up, slow it down, repeat it, truncate it, stop it, go forwards and backwards in it, and remove the need for it to get us from one place to another or indeed from one camera set-up to another. We even combine the same time in more than one place by parallel cutting. We use our perceptions of time to cheat time.

Ultimately it is our ability to control the rhythm and pace in cutting that makes it possible to play with time in this way, but because we have this power as editors it is also possible to lose control. For no shot is neutral, both its content and its form already contain the elements which contribute to the innate rhythm that reacts upon any juxtaposition we create. If you make one significant change in a sequence, even if it seems to be well cut, the result will always have a rippling effect on the feeling of the rest of the sequence, and it is unlikely that you will get away with making just that one adjustment.

REASONS FOR CUTTING

Cutting is always a matter of balance and emphasis, a delicate structuring of elements, and while a cut is never right or wrong in an absolute sense, we can say it works or does not work in relation to the rest of a sequence. Unfortunately it is a common error in cutting to rationalize the logic of particular cuts without due reference to their place in a sequence. If you watch a good editor at work you will notice the way he or she backs up a considerable number of feet before running the film to check a change. This procedure springs from an awareness that the cut is not simply a matter of what happens at the junction of two shots. That junction may be a perfect match of an action that continues across the cut, but the effect can still be wrong. This structural balance is not like strict tempo music. In fact, every cut involves a series of decisions which, with experience, become a subconscious checklist.

POSITIVE REASONS: ANALYSING THE ELEMENTS OF DRAMATIC DEVELOPMENT

The most important thing is that your decision to cut should be based on positive reasons. An awareness of the general factors just discussed – structuring, balance and emphasis, the dynamic axis, rhythm and pacing, etc. – is the essential starting point. But it is only by then analysing the elements of dramatic development in the scene under consideration that you will be able to arrive at the correct **particular** solutions.

In attempting to respect dramatic development in cutting you should be aware of the following elements:

1. Is the audience to identify with a particular character or are we merely observers?
2. Does a particular character dominate; does that dominance shift during the scene?
3. Does the dialogue function as narrative or is it mere embroidery, i.e. aside from the real drama of the scene?
4. Is there a necessary eloquence in the silences?
5. How does the movement of camera and/or characters contribute to the scene?
6. Should the scene be carried wide or are close shots essential?
7. If we cut in close will it preclude cutting wide again?
8. Are there significant details that must be seen?
9. Does a reaction need to be explained?

10. Does a moment in the scene demand a shock cut to point up the drama?
11. Does the scene have a natural climax?
12. What elements apart from the characters are important to the scene?
13. Do other sounds have significance apart from the dialogue?
    and of course:
14. What is the function of the scene?
15. How does the scene fit into the overall film?

If you can answer these questions at each point that a cut seems appropriate, it will help to determine what to cut to and when. I am not claiming that during the process of editing these questions are consciously confronted, but they should be part of the unspoken agenda behind the way each sequence is structured.

OVERCOMING PROBLEMS BY CUTTING

Although the hundred and one bad reasons for cutting do not teach us positive lessons about editing, the remedies for such shortcomings can produce positive results:

Uneven performance

The best delivery and characterization is sometimes spread in sections over more than one take. This can be improved by inserting reaction shots or by cutting to a different angle so that the best parts can each be used.

Fluffs

If a word or short phrase contains a 'fluff' or wrong emphasis in an otherwise reasonable take it is often possible to replace the offending sound with the same words from another take or shot covering the same dialogue.

Lack of reaction

Where a facial expression is 'dead' or the reaction shot does not even exist, look elsewhere in the scene for similar reactions which may not be needed in their proper place. It may even be possible to snatch the required few seconds from before the clapperboard or after the director shouts 'Cut'. This is one good reason for retaining all properly framed and exposed picture when syncing up.

Mismatched action

Sometimes an action cut that is essential will not work either because the change of angle is strange or because of considerable discrepancy in pace. In this case try cutting before the action or, if the sequence depends on rhythm for its effectiveness, you can sometimes use the movement of another character to match that in the outgoing shot. Indeed, it is always too easy to fall into the trap of trying to make a direct cut work when the best answer is to insert an alternative that does not depend on matching action or pace.

Discrepancies in pacing

You must remain aware of whether the overall pace suits the mood of a scene. Where it seems too slow it may be necessary to overlap the dialogue or intercut more. Where the pace is too fast make use of the silences by inserting pauses contained in complementary shots.

Unconvincing action

If action is unconvincing when cut together, the reactions of a third party with sound laid over often compensates (e.g. with a badly staged or performed fight scene). This does assume, of course, that the director has had the foresight to shoot such reactions.

Lack of static before or after movement

Tracks and pans occasionally lack a satisfactory hold on the beginning or the end. Mixing from or to a relevant static shot can be an effective substitute or even improve the structure of the scene. Given even pace it is also effective to mix one movement into another, although this is hard when the movement continues in the same direction. A track or pan mixing to a zoom can often provide dramatic concentration.

Problems of matching sound and picture

In dialogue scenes the best cutting point is often not available without offsetting the junction on the soundtrack. Firstly, what seems to be the best place in the dialogue may not provide a convincing picture cut. In this case there are two solutions. You can either overlap the dialogue if this is appropriate to the mood of the scene, so that a good visual cut is created, or it may be possible to remove a phrase from the dialogue to achieve a similar result.

Secondly, where the dialogue already overlaps it may be necessary to continue the track from one of the two shots over the cut to retain the sense of the dialogue and still achieve an effective picture cut.

Other unsatisfactory juxtapositions can be improved by making use of hard sounds, such as door slams or gun shots, to bridge or signal the cut.

Unconvincing dialogue

The scripted words are never sacrosanct and it is important to remain aware that dramatic flow can often be helped by removing phrases or even whole sentences. Again this is facilitated by inserting a reaction or just ending a scene sooner.

Junctions between scenes

These are perhaps the most vital cutting points: always be prepared to acknowledge that a scene is overstaying its welcome or that it can start later. Once a scene has served its purpose it is criminal to hold on to it. However, the very essence of a particular sequence can be contained in the pause at the end, and in any case remember that the initial impact of each subsequent scene is dynamically affected by the last moments of the scene that precedes it.

CUTTING AND REACTION: DRAMATIC EMPHASIS

The psychology of film language is constantly being modified by the interactions between film-makers and the audience. Consider, for instance, the reaction shot. Reaction is perhaps the most basic tool of dramatic construction, without which all narrative lacks its essential driving force. Once movies had confirmed the validity of showing someone reacting to the words or actions of others, it seemed only natural to cut to that reaction. But once this possibility had been established film-makers soon became aware that cutting to the reaction was not necessarily the only way of dealing with the expectation provoked in the audience. In film the cut is now only one way of using this device. Staging can incorporate the reaction in several ways:

- The camera can pan to the reaction.
- The camera can track or zoom in or out to include the reaction.
- Focus can be changed to emphasize the reaction.
- The protagonist can turn or move in shot to include or reveal the reaction.
- The person reacting can turn or move into shot for the reaction.
- The reaction can be given in dialogue out of the shot, while the camera remains on the protagonist.

- Conversely the build-up to the reaction can all be taken on the character from whom that reaction is expected.
- The provocation and reaction can be represented by the way a 'neutral' observer responds to the whole interaction.

Most of these alternatives apply equally to both fiction and documentary filming, the only difference being that whereas in scripted films the **director** can choose in advance, in documentary the decision has to be made by the director and/or cameraperson at the moment of shooting. The important point is that the cut is not the only way to deal with a shift in dramatic emphasis. However, more often than not the cover for a scene will still leave some choices available to the editor. For instance, a pan that reveals a reaction in wide shot can still lead to the feeling that a subsequent cut to close-up is justified. Indeed, the pan may alternatively give you the opportunity to cut back to the person who has provoked the reaction.

DIRECTORS AND EDITING – SOME EXAMPLES

There is great variance in the degree to which selection, structuring, pacing and rhythm are left to the cutting stage. Even in the same film a director may decide that some scenes are best structured in the way they are staged and that others are best handled in the cutting room.

The following examples are meant as a stimulus to the study of particular films. The choice is personal and obviously cannot be comprehensive.

KUROSAWA *RASHOMON* (1950)

This film confronts the audience with four different versions of the story of a violent attack on a nobleman and his wife in a forest in medieval Japan. In many ways Kurosawa's use of the form is daring and unconventional.

When we first meet the woodman the most important shot is one where the camera tracks alongside him as he runs through the forest. To begin with the camera is at some distance; but eventually it crosses his path in front of him in close-up and continues tracking, having reversed our point of view. Thus one shot has contained the man and his natural habitat from different perspectives and also conveyed a sense of movement. It is difficult to imagine a cut sequence that would have been as effective.

Later the bandit is sitting under a tree, beside a path through the forest. Eventually we see the woman being led past the spot on a horse by her husband. To increase the tension, Kurosawa intercuts several times between the bandit and his point of view and each time cheats the movement so that the progression is elongated (i.e. if you were to cut together the shots of the travellers the action would overlap at each cut). In this case if Kurosawa had contained the action in a wide shot the tension would have

Figure 5.1 Akira Kurosawa (centre) directing *Rashomon*.

depended on real time and the spatial relationship between the characters. Also in *Rashomon*, as in many of his films, Kurosawa makes use of the American Cut: a cut in on the same angle for dramatic emphasis. In less sure hands this would merely appear clumsy but by controlling the *rhythm* he is able to defy the convention of change of angle.

One further aspect of *Rashomon* should be noted. The proceedings of the court are **always** seen from the point of view of the magistrate, who is **never** seen, only heard. This gives the court scenes an unremitting intensity and forces the audience to act as judge. The director sacrifices the possibility of controlling pace in the cutting because he is concerned with other aspects of dramatic emphasis. The camera is the magistrate, therefore the axis of the scene is the line between each member of the audience and the prisoner or witness being interrogated. Any change of angle or cut would have destroyed this line. The value of Kurosawa in examples like these is that he prevents us from considering that the conventional answer is necessarily the only one.

It is also very valuable to analyse Kurosawa's shooting and editing of action, especially in his Samurai trilogy: *Seven Samurai, Yojimbo* and *Sanjuro*. The roots of his rhythms are embedded in the style of kabuki theatre where the drama can simmer for an inordinate amount of time then suddenly erupt. Action, including death, happens in an instant, and yet with extraordinary grace. Both the quiet simmering and the eruptions of action are elegantly handled by Kurosawa who brings both camera and cutting to bear on his mastery of the genre. Sergio Leone is not the only director to plagiarize him without shame.

BERGMAN *PERSONA* (1966)

In an interview with Peter Cowie in 1969 Bergman stated: 'Film is concerned above all with rhythm. . . . The primary factor is the image, the secondary factor is the sound, the dialogue; and the tension between these two creates the third dimension.'

In *Persona* Bergman is at times as audacious as Kurosawa in denying the conventional approach to editing. Through a narrative that has as a central dramatic element the wilful silence of one of the two main characters, he is able to construct sequences that emphasize the inaction and silence of this character through the restlessness and verbosity of the other. The watershed of the film and of the relationship between the two characters comes when Alma (the nurse) recounts her interpretation of Elisabet's (the silent patient) attitude to having a child. First the statement is made while we watch Elisabet's face and then it is repeated whilst the camera is on Alma. At the end of this repetition the two faces merge in one image as if one or other of the two women has taken on the 'persona' of both.

Conventionally we would have expected an intercut sequence, building to a climax through the editing, but the impact that Bergman achieves makes us consider the implications behind the statement rather than the superficial effect on the characters. This is not a technique that can be easily applied to other situations in films, but it does point to a more general problem. The close-up is the most telling weapon in the armoury of cinema, but it has one particular disadvantage. In scenes between two characters there are invariably moments in the cutting when you feel torn between the alternatives of seeing either one or the other. Seeing both is a compromise that may not have the advantage of either. Constant intercutting can call attention to the technique. Bergman's answer is really only an extension of the way all editing plays with time, and it is paid off by the masterly merging of the faces.

Apart from *Persona* there are many of Bergman's films which reward careful examination, from *Summer with Monika* (1952) through *The Seventh Seal* (1957) and *Wild Strawberries* (1957) to *Cries and Whispers* (1973) and *Fanny and Alexander* (1982). The clarity of his narratives are always complemented by precise and unfussy construction, making the editing a model of its kind.

BUÑUEL *THE DISCREET CHARM OF THE BOURGEOISIE* (1972) AND
PHANTOM OF THE LIBERTY (1974)

In a conversation with Marianne Kärré, Bergman remarked: 'Have I borrowed anything in *Persona*? But of course, why wouldn't I borrow? Buñuel was my first cinematic revelation. He remained the most important for me ... I entirely share his theory of initial shock to attract the public's attention.'

Buñuel's influence is most keenly felt in the opening montage of *Persona* which is climaxed by the jamming of the film in the projector and the image burning out. But his relevance to the contemporary film-maker is not limited to the anarchic, surreal elements that persist from his early attempts at cinema; for Buñuel, perhaps more than any other director, turned the use of the basic grammar of film into magic and mystery.

In relatively late work such as *The Discreet Charm of the Bourgeoisie* and *Phantom of the Liberty* he effectively took the linear nature of cinematic expression and resisted the audience's desire for a continuously coherent narrative. By providing coincidental, accidental and providential connections between people and situations he used conventional techniques to carry us along so that, instead of expecting and looking for a story, we become concerned with what Buñuel had to say about situations and attitudes.

Figure 5.2 Luis Buñuel (left) discussing a scene during shooting of *Phantom of the Liberty.*

In *Discreet Charm* dreams become reality, or do they? And the film is punctuated by the main characters walking along a flat uninteresting road as if Buñuel is saying: if you want narrative progression, this is all you are going to get. In *Phantom of the Liberty*, after the nurse has spent a bizarre and surreal night at the inn on her journey to Argenton, the film cuts to an older man having breakfast in the foreground as she comes down to pay the bill and leave. The man asks for a lift in her car and, without an elaborate cut sequence, they leave together and we find that when she drops him off, it is his story that we next follow. Our curiosity is aroused without any indulgence in fancy devices and the world within the film has its own irrefutable coherence. Each cut or substitute for it within the shot has superficial logic but the drama and Buñuel's comment on it are working continuously on other levels. This 'thrower of bombs', as Henry Miller called him in the 1930s, was a magician with a difference: he was more likely to produce hats out of rabbits than vice versa and to do it in such a way that the audience accepts it in terms other than those of logic. We all now can recognize and reject the library shot of the ferocious lion when it is intercut with the intrepid hero standing his ground, but when in *Phantom of the Liberty* the husband wakes up and sees animals and birds stalking about at the end of the bed we accept it because Buñuel has established his own *un*logic.

Since the hypocrisy of bourgeois, social, political and religious morality was his main target, the nonsensical becomes frighteningly rational. A study of Buñuel's editing, especially in these films, will confirm the way he used conventional expectation in cutting, as well as in staging, to serve his own purposes.

BRESSON *UNE FEMME DOUCE* (1969)

Buñuel's characters are vivid and his situations extraordinary, a stark contrast to the cool, detached, ascetic approach of Bresson. He, like Bergman, is convinced that rhythm is the omnipotent aspect of cinematic language: 'Nothing is durable but what is caught up in rhythms. Bend context to form and sense to rhythms.' His object is 'to translate the invisible wind by the water it sculpts in passing'.

In his best films Bresson practises what he preaches with compelling success. Take the opening of *Une Femme Douce*. We start on a door handle, which seems to be held almost too long – an elderly woman opens the door – stands in the doorway – moves. The subjective camera sees a french window open on to a balcony – a rocking chair – a table – a plant pot falls – the table falls – the woman moves into frame – outside a towel floats down (it starts too high). We cut to the road, cars – feet – pan to girl's body. The tragedy around which the film revolves is established without melodrama but the effect is devastating. There is an intense parallel between this film and Bergman's *Persona* in that silence plays a large part in the drama. The past remains the subject of the film. It is about one hour into the film before the future is referred to and then it is by the old maid Anna: 'After the funeral I would like to go away for a week.'

There are many one-shot scenes, often faces are not shown at all and very seldom in close-up. Bresson's desire for stillness, silence and emptiness

Figure 5.3 Robert Bresson on the set of *Le Passion de Jeanne d'Arc*.

(whiteness) conveys the intensity of the situation. At one point he has the man and the girl at the theatre hearing Hamlet's advice to the players: 'Speak the speech I pray you.' It is Shakespeare's equivalent of Bresson's aesthetic. Later he emphasizes the point by showing the girl's disgust at how Shakespeare's text has been mangled.

Very seldom does Bresson structure a scene by intercutting. (An exception is the soup-drinking scene when silence and stillness emphasize the emptiness between the characters.) More typical is the scene where the man is watching the girl listening to a record. We see her from over his shoulder, which is very much on the edge of frame. This shot is held for a considerable time, then the man moves his head and the newspaper he is holding very slightly, and we are reminded of his presence without a cut to the reverse angle of him watching.

Bresson's unique style is best seen in early work such as *Au hasard Balthasar* and *Mouchette* (both 1966) and also in his most recent film *L'Argent* (1983) which many consider to be his masterpiece. Although it may not be immediately obvious from their work he has had a strong influence on a number of directors, including Martin Scorsese and Paul Schrader. This is clear evidence that admiration does not necessarily create imitation when the talented film-maker absorbs aspects of a master that go deeper than surface mechanics.

GODARD *PIERROT LE FOU* (1966)

Godard, as we have already noted, is another director who has articulated the central contribution of cutting to the film process. In *Montage mon beau souci* he wrote: 'Montage is above all an integral part of mise-en-scène. Only at peril can one be separated from the other. One might as well try to separate the rhythm from the melody. . . . Editing can restore to actuality that ephemeral grace, neglected by both snob and film-lover, or can transform chance into destiny.'

For Godard, however, there has always been a degree of tension between his awareness of the power of editing and the way it functions in the conventional commercial film: 'The most that efficient editing will give a film otherwise without interest is precisely the initial impression of having been directed.' Consequently he has always been at pains to resist the seductive elements of editing technique.

Perhaps the watershed in his work was *Pierrot Le Fou*. He prefaced the film with Elie Faure's description of the work of the painter Velasquez in old age, taken from Faure's *Histoire de l'art* (1921–7), and read largely in voice-over by Ferdinand, played by Jean-Paul Belmondo:

'His only experience of the world was those mysterious copulations which united the forms and tones with a secret but inevitable movement . . . space reigned supreme. It was as if some tenuous radiation gliding over the surfaces imbued itself of their visible emanations modelling them and endowing them with forms carrying elsewhere a perfume like an echo, which would thus be dispersed like an imponderable dusk, over all the surrounding frames.'

At the end of the quotation we see Belmondo in his bath reading from the book to his young daughter. Godard explained the purpose of the quotation: 'This is the theme. Its definition . . . one should not describe people but what lies between them.' (*Cahiers du Cinéma*, 171, 1965.) In another scene Belmondo says to Samuel Fuller, the American film director: 'I've always wanted to know what the cinema is.' Fuller's reply is underlined by being translated into French by a girl. He says: 'The film is like a battleground – love – hate – action – violence – death – in one word "Emotion" '; to which the Belmondo character exclaims 'Ah!'. This exchange is handled in one shot of Belmondo flanked by Fuller and the girl, and happens at a party where all the imagery and dialogue are concerned with the clichés of the medium of advertising. Godard provides ample evidence of the attitude we should take to the surface narrative. He periodically interrupts the flow to reawaken our awareness of his lack of concern with the story as such. As Belmondo and Anna Karina career in a car towards the Riviera, the former turns at one point and addresses a remark to the camera. She asks whom he is talking to and he replies: 'The audience.'

Nevertheless, Godard is not cavalier with his use of editing technique. In this and other films, such as *Weekend* (1967), his awareness of when the audience will expect a cut allows him to stimulate our consciousness of the medium simply by not cutting, or shooting in such a way that the camera movement or the movement of characters in and out of frame substitutes for the cut. It is his confidence, when shooting, in the way editing works, that allows him to control the way he uses the process.

ROHMER *LOVE IN THE AFTERNOON* (1972)

For another French director, Eric Rohmer, the space between people and between words is even more central to his style. In the six *Contes Moraux*, and especially in *Love in the Afternoon*, words hang in the air between characters as if nothing that can be said is significant enough to prevent the inevitable process of people being trapped by their own fate. Superficially his films are empty of drama, but he allows the existence of such a vacuum to resonate, by not cutting until we are painfully aware that a confrontation can have no resolution. He will hold a character's uneasy reaction to the words of another, usually in a wide shot, until we know there is nowhere to go. More often than most directors he uses the fade-out as an articulate comment on the inconclusiveness of situations. His films are preoccupied with human relationships that remain locked in a sterile non-communication as if socialization has guaranteed the impossibility of his characters coming to terms with the dichotomy between their desires and the 'rules of the game'.

In *Love in the Afternoon* the protagonist is confronted with the nakedness of three women in his life and on each occasion he is unable to integrate his reaction with the relationship that his social attitudes demand. The sight of his wife in the shower is unnerving to him because he realizes he takes her body for granted; the au-pair rushes past him to deal with the baby and we feel his embarrassment; and the woman he wants to make love to is too much of a threat when she finally invites attention. The beauty of each scene is that Rohmer makes them seem accidental. It is as if they provoke a counter-rhythm to the mental life of the protagonist and thus become barriers to his attempts to come to terms with his own psychology. There is a richness in Rohmer's work which is almost in spite of his economic unfussy style. The camera only moves when it is unavoidable, and cutting functions as periodic punctuation rather than fracturing each moment artificially. The cut or the fade thus become important punctuation and are not used as mechanical devices.

PENN *NIGHT MOVES* (1975)

In this film the character played by Gene Hackman responds to an invitation from his wife, played by Susan Clark, to see a Rohmer movie by saying: 'No thanks, I saw a Rohmer movie once – it was like watching paint dry.' Penn, or rather Alan Sharp, the writer, would probably argue that Rohmer intimidates an audience that expects a more conventional narrative style. Rohmer and the rest of the French New Wave had articulated their awareness of the values in mainstream American cinema through the magazine *Cahiers du Cinéma*. Penn and others of his generation have, to a degree, absorbed this analysis and countered it with an intelligent reworking of the 'straight' narrative film. *Night Moves* is a case in point. Sharp believes that movies continue to feed off their own antecedents, implying that they cull from the imagery and style of other films a resonant continuum that acknowledges the tradition that has evolved – at least since the coming of sound.

Night Moves has scenes that illustrate the way a craftsman such as Penn can complement the feeling that exists in the script with a shooting style that seems to come out of the writing rather than being imposed upon it. A vital contribution to this is Dede Allen's cutting. When Hackman confronts his wife's boyfriend and asks, 'How is it between you and Ellen?', there are five cuts before the reply. They are paced so well that we are not conscious of them as cuts but only of the build-up in tension that they provide. Earlier, when Hackman sees his wife and her boyfriend come out of the cinema and go off together, his emotional response is built over twelve cuts all on medium or long shots, only coming to a close shot of Hackman as he decides finally not to confront the couple. Each shot of Hackman can be said to represent a changing emotion from pleasure at seeing his wife, through curiosity, amazement, apprehension, indecision and finally action.

The counterpoint of the progression of the couple from the front of the cinema to the boyfriend's car acts as the 'moves' provoking Hackman's changing response. What Allen has actually done is to construct a very telling parallel action sequence from what are basically only two shots. The end sequence of *Night Moves* contains a dramatic section with 22 shots in the space of 10 seconds. Detailed analysis reveals no 'cheating' in the sense that no shot, even of a few frames, is other than a relevant part of the action as the sea-plane first kills Jennifer Warren and then plunges into the sea within inches of the motor boat on which Hackman is helplessly stranded. It is a model of economic action-cutting, with none of the fussy flamboyance of earlier Penn movies, e.g. *Bonnie and Clyde* (1967), where slow motion and other devices artificially extend the moment of high drama.

Penn subsequently made *The Missouri Breaks* (1976), an unconventional Western whose discursiveness is well supported by the editing which was supervised by Dede Allen.

These aspects of *Night Moves* indicate the availability of 'commercial' cinema for detailed dissection. Previous examples in this chapter resist such analysis. Cutting functions as a more conscious device in the conventional movie, but because this makes it more accessible we should neither be discouraged by its limitations nor use such evidence to make value judgments about style. Editing, as Eisenstein was emphasizing in the 1930s, is not about what happens at the cut but what is placed between the cuts. It is not the juxtaposition that is important but the elements that we choose to juxtapose.

POLANSKI *CHINATOWN* (1974)

Occasionally Hollywood and Europe meet without the tension between their stylistic traditions causing a negative result. Roman Polanski achieved a remarkable synthesis of these traditions in *Chinatown*. He had already demonstrated a sure hand in earlier films, especially in the opening sequences of *Rosemary's Baby* (1968), where the economy of exposition, while developing an atmosphere of foreboding, is founded on shooting and cutting that exhibit an admirable conviction about the right shot, its angle and size, how long it is held, and an inevitable progression from scene to scene. These values are further enhanced in the superbly scripted (by Robert Towne) and performed *Chinatown*. What Polanski has absorbed, consciously or unconsciously, can be traced back to Eisenstein's mise-en-shot principle, which allows the director to confront the way each scene works without treating the cut as the only punctuating device available to him. In a number of crucial scenes cutting is virtually absent, but the positioning and movement of characters, and the pacing of action and dialogue, provide a rhythm that works better than editing construction could.

When Jack Nicholson, as Gittes, confronts John Huston as Noah Cross, no elaborate cover of the scene is allowed to interrupt the flow. Cuts are made only for emphasis and not as mere mechanistic devices. The same is true in Nicholson's visits to Mulwray's office – the uneasiness of the latter's secretary is conveyed by the private-eye prowling in front of her in wide shot. Again when Nicholson and Faye Dunnaway are talking in bed, a static high-angle shot concentrates our attention on their exchange in a way cutting would not.

However, Polanski is not averse to cutting. The proceedings of the city council early in the film, when the new dam is being discussed, contains a number of cuts which allow us to digest information about characters and situation, while the debate is carried on in words as often as not against images of people other than the speaker. The climax of the scene, when sheep are driven into the council chamber, works well partly because the editing avoids planting such an event as the likely dénouement of the scene. *Chinatown* is the kind of film which demonstrates a real control over the kind of questions we have asked ourselves with regard to the function of editing in the total process. If the function of each scene and the focus of attention are analysed, almost no examples of loose or lazy construction are

Figure 5.4 Roman Polanski directs Jack Nicholson in *Chinatown*.

revealed. Polanski has said that he considers himself a bad writer but a good scenarist. His films, especially *Chinatown*, are cogent evidence of this.

ALTMAN *THE LONG GOODBYE* (1972)

One American director who in recent years has consistently conducted his own exploration of the contribution of editing to his films is Robert Altman. His attitudes to camera, sound and performance as well as to editing have demonstrated his search for a more effective and interesting language. Although he is unable to make the dramatic leaps that Griffith incorporated, his work has a similar awareness of the need to expand and extend the craft. In *The Long Goodbye* he adopts radical technique. The camera is hardly, if ever, still. Sometimes the movement is marginal but it is always used to good purpose. The camera, like Elliot Gould's cat, prowls about as if restlessly seeking the only sustenance that will satisfy it. The character played by Gould deals with surface reality with as little effort as necessary, always conscious that there is something beyond the apparent that will give a clue to the mystery. Often the 'rule' that maintains that cutting on camera movement is difficult and dangerous is ignored, and because Altman has control over rhythm and pacing it seldom falters. The scene which culminates in the awareness of Nina von Pallandt and Gould of Sterling Hayden's drowning is handled through reflection and background action of the suicide, played against the conversation in foreground. A dog provides a restless counterpoint to the action and as it drops the dead man's walking stick we cut to the search for the body with telling conclusiveness. The tension throughout the sequence is sustained without the conventional reliance on intercutting.

In Altman's best work both picture and sound editing play a crucial role. This is especially true in his mosaic-like work, especially the splendid *Nashville* (1975) and *Short-cuts* (1993). He has a refreshingly unpedantic yet never superficial vitality that uses the craft available in the cutting room to telling effect, in that he complements a fluid camera style with an unconventional approach to editing and sound design that is always making you aware of the space beyond the frame.

CUTTING AND THE PRIVATE-EYE GENRE

It is no accident that the last three films discussed – *Night Moves, Chinatown* and *The Long Goodbye* – are from the same genre. There is a natural affinity between the private-eye thriller and certain aspects of the particular contribution that editing can provide. In this genre there is invariably close identification with the detective who seems caught up in events beyond his control, and the dynamic of the film depends upon the way twists in the story are complemented by juxtapositions in the editing. The emphasis is on the visual detail and not merely on the occasional moment of high drama. Every image is potentially a clue, either to the understanding of the mystery or to feed our desire to get inside the character and motivation of the protagonist. There is a vital difference between Raymond Chandler and, say, Agatha Christie whose *Death on the Nile* (1978) remains literary and theatrical because it depends on direct verbal exposition and the melodrama of obvious and overtly threatening situations. The danger in private-eye movies is always beneath the surface of the narrative, and this allows for a uniquely cinematic structure where the cut, along with composition, camera movement and sound can carry the development of a scene while the superficial narrative is working in dialogue and action. Used in this way the cut becomes a weapon, and constructing a sequence becomes analogous to fencing where each thrust and parry gives rhythmic counterpoint to the narrative progression. The distillation of this style is the action film. In such films cutting contributes a great deal to, for instance, car chases, fights and gun battles, but in such instances the cut is usually serving the action directly rather than providing a deeper perspective.

EDITING AND GENRE

Editing within a particular genre has its own specifics and conventions which directors choose to adhere to, ignore or alter to their own desires. The trouble with strict genre film-making is that the form can become tired and predictable, which has encouraged mavericks to mix genres or simply to ignore the conventions. However, there are particular types of sequence which present similar agendas for the editor whether they are part of a standard genre movie or not.

Comedy was probably the original genre, unless we count Méliès' *Voyage to the Moon* as the first sci-fi film. Cutting for laughs, both verbal and visual, can suffer more than any other genre from being removed from the live audience situation. If the humour is working well you may find you have cut too fast and some jokes are buried. If it is working badly the material becomes dead meat on the screen. Comedy is the form which is most affected by the differences between particular audiences, and pacing cannot allow for the reactions in different countries or even in the same cinema on different days of the week.

What saves the editor with comedy is the quality of the script and the performances. Often the biggest decision in cutting is the transition between sequences: whether to let a gag subside or carry its momentum over to the next scene. It is hardly ever possible for the editor to use cutting to create humour that does not already exist in the material. On the other hand the editor can very easily kill funny material by clumsy cutting.

Comedy, especially situation comedy, has become the staple of television. In modern times the cinema has few great comedians, perhaps because television encourages both parochial humour and the verbal over the visual. Apart from Woody Allen, it is Chaplin and Keaton and the other silent comedians who are the touchstones of the best in comedy, and Allen hardly ever achieves his humour through cutting.

An exception amongst directors of comedy was Billy Wilder, often with the support of his arch collaborator, the writer I. A. L. Diamond. The classic product of their work together was *Some Like it Hot* (1959). In this wonderful film, musicians Jack Lemmon and Tony Curtis escape from the mob in Chicago by joining an all-female band on a jaunt to Miami, having been unwitting observers of the infamous Saint Valentine's Day Massacre. Curtis falls for the band's singer, played by Marilyn Monroe, and Lemmon (in

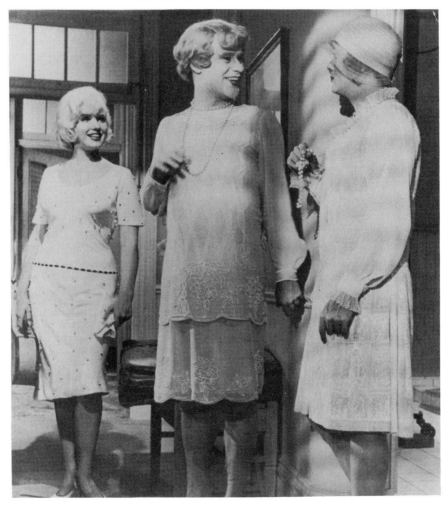

Figure 5.5 The stars of Billy Wilder's hilarious *Some Like it Hot*: Marilyn Monroe, Jack Lemmon and Tony Curtis vying for best dressed 'woman'.

drag) is courted by an old lecher played by Joe E. Brown. The many humorous situations that naturally ensue are made particularly effective by the elan of the editing, without which the numerous switches from male to 'female' would lack pace and conviction.

Occasionally contemporary comedy has the wit to exploit the contribution of editing. There is a natural affinity in the collusion between comedian and audience and the similar connivance that the editor exploits. *Groundhog Day* (1993), directed by Harold Ramis, chronicles the purgatory suffered by the protagonist played by Bill Murray, who must literally relive a particular day again and again, locked in his own cynical conceit. We enjoy the repetition at his expense in a film that bravely denies the linear nature of conventional narrative. It is a piece of cinema whose very conception depended on an understanding of the craft of editing from the inside.

Perhaps the most testing of genres for the editor is the musical. Superficially the opportunity to depend on a rhythm and structure that already exists may seem to make editing easier. The truth is that you should never cut **to** music, only **with** music. For many years dance sequences have been shot to playback and often covered by several cameras simultaneously. Where the choreography has been camera conscious, editing choices are theoretically predetermined. However, in practice this is often not the case, and the editor must attempt to adjust the structure whilst being locked in the rhythm of the music.

The more adventurous directors of musicals prefer to shoot a number of alternative shots and to structure their material in the editing. *All that Jazz* (1979), for which Alan Heim won the editing academy award, is a strong example of the exploitation of the combined energy of music performance and cutting, for which Bob Fosse, the director, must have been mainly responsible.

In recent years the musical has become an infrequent form, but the habit of including a song or strong theme tune to help the commercial exploitation of straight dramatic films often provides the editor with the opportunity to indulge in something like good old montage. This is hardly comparable with the real thing, and anyone wanting to understand the possibilities of musical construction would be better advised to watch the films of Fred Astaire or Gene Kelly.

The western is perhaps the archetypal genre, depending as it does on characters who unambivalently represent good and evil and predictable situations and events. Even here in recent years the mould has been broken, as America comes to terms with its past. Now Indians are allowed to be heroes and to have true wisdom, as our social and ecological crimes catch up with us. Yet the editing in Westerns, especially of battles and gunfights, usually follows well-established patterns. *Dances with Wolves* (1990) and *The Last of the Mohicans* (1993) are recent examples which are cut well and return the form to its roots from the operatic alternative represented by the 'spaghetti' variety, which usually avoided the inconvenience of having to establish motivation before characters drilled each other full of bullets.

As with westerns, horror films, thrillers and war films often rely heavily on action cutting. The secret is often in the rhythm and pacing and not in the slavish adherence to continuity. All vigorous movement can be convincing on the screen if you control the rhythm in the frame, as long as the cutting provides the right overall impression, preferably using elements that are specific to the action, as in the example in *Night Moves* described earlier.

The proliferation of television channels and the development of satellite and cable systems creates an ever increasing pressure on the need to produce material quickly and cheaply. The danger is that the craft, including that of editing, is reduced to cliché and banality. Genre films at their best retained an individuality but the formulaic product now dominating our screens is mostly second rate.

Figure 5.6 Bob Hoskins and Cheryl Campbell in Dennis Potter's ground-breaking *Pennies from Heaven.*

Two beacons stand out against this tide inside television. First, the work that is inspired by quality writing. One of the best examples in British television was Dennis Potter. *Pennies from Heaven* (1978) and *The Singing Detective* (1986) stand out in particular as prime examples of the writer understanding his medium so intimately that he can inspire a courage in the use of the form to support radical drama for the screen. In both of these series Potter chose to structure his narrative to include the miming of the characters to thirties and forties popular songs, thus avoiding the dread hand of naturalism.

On the other hand, the writers of soaps have debased the structure of drama by their arbitrary use of intercutting between scenes, ostensibly to create a continuum in several parallel situations at once. The result is ugly at the cut and illogical in the narrative since the audience is frequently taken back to a scene whose action has frozen since we left it.

The second beacon inside television that stands out against the tide of dross is the documentary. At their best non-fiction films continue and develop from the tradition established more than fifty years ago. Editing plays a crucial role in this process, both in respecting the subjects of such films and in bringing structural coherence to the presentation of sometimes complex issues.

Meanwhile one hope for the future of fiction film is probably in the hands of those American directors who combine strong stories with a superior grasp of the craft. Two examples: John Sayles, whose *City of Hope* (1991) is shot and cut with the vigour of the best of Altman, and Lawrence Kasdan, whose *Grand Canyon* (1991) is similarly arresting in its content and editing style.

FORM AND CONTENT

In the application of technique to arrive at a satisfactory structure there are two cardinal rules. Never make a cut that calls attention to its own cleverness; in doing so you not only destroy your credibility as an editor, but you also break the link between the film and the audience. Such self-conscious cutting can be seen all too frequently in magazine programmes on television where perhaps appropriately the form is as superficial as the content.

Concomitantly, never divorce form from content. As Lindgren said in *The Art of the Film*: 'Form is itself a quality of content, and the more highly charged the content of a statement the more formal in character it is likely to be. To destroy the form of a line of poetry is to rob it of the most vital part of its content.'

In these days of formal anarchy, when the technology makes anything possible at the touch of a button, it is all too easy to use content as raw material for formal manipulation. The risk is, as Marshall Macluhan said thirty years ago, that before we know it 'the medium **is** the message'.

Sound in editing 6

My most vivid memory of a response to a film I had cut was from Edith Vogel, the late virtuoso pianist and teacher. After the screening she said: 'Very nice, but not enough silences.' It was a very important lesson. She also believed that musical performance was 90% technique and 10% inspiration. Perhaps that applies to film making too.

The greatest truths do seem to be paradoxes, and one is that sound creates silence. It even creates the **need** for silence. We have no trouble grasping the fact that visual composition consists of elements which are separated by space, by which we appreciate physical form and context, yet the natural equivalence in sound often escapes us.

Filling the silence is the worst approach imaginable to the creation of a soundtrack. Just as everything that appears in the visual frame should be in the right equilibrium of substance and shadow, so everything that is heard should exist in a balance of sound and silence.

There is a wonderful moment in the film of *The Unbearable Lightness of Being* when two characters are in a restaurant and the woman's request for the musak to be turned off is refused, so she climbs up and rips out the wires to the loudspeaker. Our society is obsessed with presentation rather than substance and our attitude to sound is part of the phenomenon. It is important that the makers of films restore the power and dignity of the aural dimension to the imagined world that we create.

Sound has the potential to contribute as much to narrative meaning as images, and no sound is neutral in its effect. All sound has its own rhythms and cadences that can prove intractable in relation both to images and to other sounds. This is obvious in the case of music but less apparent with the spoken word and effects. Yet rain on a window pane can sound everything from sad to threatening. Words, certainly in English, often depend for their precise meaning on emphasis, inflection and tone. As well as having certain innate qualities that we must learn to respect, sound has a degree of flexibility that is not available in the fixed images which are the raw material of editing.

Some directors, for example Robert Altman, have learned to layer their sound in a masterly fashion using changing perspective, sound beyond the frame and interwoven overlapping tracks. It is to this sophisticated level that we must aspire whilst remembering that elegant simplicity will always be more effective than clutter.

THE EFFECT OF EQUIPMENT

One of the benefits of the application of digital technology, both to the editing process and to track laying, is that there is no reason to be concerned whether you are hearing the sound well enough to judge its quality. With traditional cutting room equipment not only is it difficult to judge what you are hearing, but without careful use and maintenance, editing machinery has a tendency to damage soundtracks. This is why it is normal practice in features to replace the working track with a virgin transfer for the mixing process. After all, we wouldn't use the cutting copy or work print for presentation purposes.

Whatever equipment and techniques you are using the objective is the same: to end up in the dubbing suite or mixing studio with the best quality sound, well aware of its detailed characteristics. If for any reason you are anxious that the tracks you have laid may not work in the way you have designed them, I recommend that you fight your way into the studio and run the tracks in advance of the booking, so that you can adjust or replace anything that is revealed as unsatisfactory. This is far less necessary if you are working non-linear and can hear several elements at once, or if you have access to digital track laying systems and can review your sound under ideal conditions as you prepare it.

WORKING METHODS

It is important to establish the way your soundtrack should function during cutting. Editors' attitudes to sound vary enormously. There are those who follow the words in a scene as the pegs to hang the structure on. There are also those who orchestrate their soundtrack from the word go, never having only one track with which to review the cutting copy. There are even those who will cut dialogue scenes mute, having once digested the words and their rhythm.

This last is the common practice of Dede Allen, and it is worth pausing a moment to appreciate why she should prefer such an apparently perverse working method. The meaning behind the words is often conveyed in the body language and reactions of the actors. The mood and dynamic of the scene is best supported by matching the rhythm of the cutting to the psychological motivation. Whether we can all achieve this in editing without reference to the audible dialogue only experience will tell.

If you rely on the dialogue itself to dictate the structure of the cutting, opportunities to mould the scene in more flexible ways are unlikely to occur to you. If you watch the scenes where Gene Hackman visits the runaway girl's mother in *Night Moves*, and compare Dede Allen's version with the original script, you will see how she has used Arthur Penn's staging as her guide rather than Alan Sharp's dialogue. Dede has enhanced the mood and function of the scene by visual sleight of hand, rather than by sticking slavishly to the words.

Whatever machinery you are using to edit, even if it gives you the facility to work simultaneously with several sound elements, you must decide what is the dominant sound at any given moment and use that in the cutting track. Of course there are times when the layering of sound is imperative to a sequence before you can judge its effectiveness, or when voice-over or music have to be laid alongside the sync track, but often there is a temptation to lay a second track in the belief that it will transform something that is not working into a convincing scene. What actually happens is that the second sound element adds a certain concreteness, and thus appears to prove the validity of the scene.

This is especially true of music and is a dangerous and seductive way of obscuring the real problems in cutting. Indeed even scenes which are meant to be covered by music alone should be cut mute first: they will be all the stronger if the visuals have had to stand on their own before music is added, even though you are likely to adjust individual cuts for musical cadence. Obviously this does not apply in the same way if the music is sync or playback.

Working with one track in this way makes the most of flexibility in cutting. There is a psychological inhibition which works against altering more than one element of sound and this can discourage even the proper consideration of subsequent picture changes. Working with more than one track can also make projection very difficult, and nothing should discourage the practice of regular screenings to judge the true feeling of your work.

It is also true that to leave shots mute in the cutting of a sequence can be dangerous; judging the overall flow of a scene is made impossible by the sudden loss of sound. For instance, it may have been felt unnecessary to shoot a reaction shot in sync, but when the scene is cut you should try to use part of the sync track to cover the mute shot or insert a suitable wild track, or the rhythm will be lost. If you leave this until track laying you may get a rude shock at a time when picture changes are not a priority.

CATEGORIES OF SOUND

There are four main types of sound: dialogue, effects, narration or voice-over and music. The following chart gives an indication of the origins from which these sounds can be acquired (the more normal sources are asterisked):

	DIALOGUE	EFFECTS	VOICE-OVER	MUSIC
Sync	/*	/*	/	/*
Wild track	/	/*	/*	/
Post-sync	/*	/*	–	–
Playback	–	–	–	/*
Library	–	/*	/	/
Special recording	–	/	/*	/*

Perhaps the most interesting aspect of such a chart is that potentially all kinds of sound can be obtained from several sources. The way a final soundtrack is created for a film can vary enormously. In major feature film the profile is normally as follows:

Dialogue:	*Sync* and/or *Post-sync*
Effects:	*Wild track* and/or *Post-sync*
Voice-Over:	*Special recording*
Music:	*Playback* and/or *Special recording*

However, in a documentary that is attempting to convey the impression that the total film is built out of elements innate to the subject being filmed, **all** sound may be sync with perhaps occasional wild tracks recorded during the shooting.

The first task in the cutting room in relation to sound after synchronization is to check and catalogue all location and original studio recordings. There is no point in finding out after the picture editing is completed that even wild tracks are unusable. The earlier you know the sooner steps can be taken to obtain satisfactory replacements for essential material.

DIALOGUE

Nothing is more important than the spoken voice in the language of narrative film. Too often, both in the cinema and on television, the words are difficult to understand. There is no excuse for emerging from the final mix with less than perfect voice levels and comprehensibility, unless the clarity of the actors' speech has been compromised in the original recording.

There is still an approach to acting, blamed perhaps unjustifiably on the 'method' school, which seems to work on the assumption that mumbling is great acting. This was prevalent in the sixties when Hollywood heroes or anti-heroes were often characterized as inarticulate neurotics. Only the director can prevent such affectation from sabotaging the film.

Assuming that the words have been clearly enunciated, the editor must hope that the recording is good enough not to require post-synchronization. If there are minor problems with the original dialogue recordings it is always best to search through alternative takes that could be carefully fitted rather than resort to expensive and second-best post-sync. Not only is it possible to replace fluffs, but if there is a badly delivered phrase in an otherwise good speech, another take may well give you a satisfactory alternative.

POST-SYNCHRONIZATION (ADR)

If sections are totally unusable, or it is decided that a voice is to be replaced by that of another performer (a delicate matter at the best of times), then it is very important to make the decision early for two reasons. Firstly, the editing is made easier if the replacement tracks are available before the picture is fine cut, and secondly, if you delay there is the risk that the performer(s) concerned may not be available.

It is not advisable to post-sync the odd line or two from a scene, especially on exteriors, or even the lines of one character and not the others since this creates serious problems in matching the ambience and the background sound. The decision has to be whether you are happy with **all** of the voice tracks for a particular scene.

Over the years there have been a number of methods for post-synchronization, but the predominant system now is ADR or automatic dialogue replacement. Different studios will vary in some details but the basic system is common to all. The crucial factor is meticulous preparation, remembering that lost time in the dubbing studio is very costly, both in facilities and artists fees.

The process involves running the picture and guide track, if one exists, so that the actor or actress can match the new version to the existing rhythm. Since it can take many attempts to get a satisfactory replacement it may be advisable to order a 'slash dupe' from the laboratory, as the cutting copy may not survive persistent re-running.

Each scene has to be looked at by the editor to decide on manageable sections, or 'cues'. This is usually a compromise between how much the artist can be expected to cope with on each run and the need to keep a good rhythm in the performance.

Every word of the dialogue must be transcribed and broken down into these separate cues. The first modulation of each phrase or sentence is cued on the picture by a diagonal line which is drawn across the film for about a second before the start frame. A note is taken of the exact footage and frame of the beginning of each cue. The actor or actress hears three bleeps over headphones and speaks where a fourth bleep would come in the same rhythm.

Some sound editors prefer to cue the performer up to four frames in advance of the first modulation, assuming that they will always be late coming in, and then risk rushing the line to catch up, thus spoiling the rhythm. Remember the editor must expect to adjust each replacement line, even each word, when he or she gets back to the cutting room.

These days, when a great deal of drama is shot on 16mm, it is still often the practice to post-sync on 35mm, since by using triple or multi track facilities you can keep re-recording until you have several good versions to choose from. You can also be far more precise in laying up, since there are four perforations to the frame on 35mm. It is very important to keep accurate notes of preferred takes if you use this method.

If there is more than one artist the cue lines can be drawn running alternate ways across the film for clear differentiation. A new cue should be given every time there is a substantial gap in the dialogue; not just for each sentence.

The decision to post-synchronize artists together or separately should be considered carefully. It is common to assume that the risk of overlapping voices, giving less flexibility in the final track laying, makes it preferable to record each voice on its own. On the other hand if the artists have a good rapport from having performed together during the shooting, it may be best to trade on this familiarity.

You will find that post-synchronization highlights the existence of two very different kinds of actor: the 'classical' who decides on an interpretation of each role and proceeds to refine it marginally every time it is performed, and the 'intuitive' who is forever searching for new ways of expressing the words and actions of a character. The latter can be a very awkward customer at a post-sync session, especially, as I remember, if they have had what we euphemistically call a 'liquid' lunch.

The complexity of the artist's craft is put under considerable strain in ADR sessions. This is especially true in the re-recording of exterior scenes which require a dead acoustic to be convincing. This can only really be achieved if the actor or actress stands close to the microphone and avoids moving anything but their lips.

Unless the original scene was a quiet, unemotional situation with no physical movement, the actors are totally inhibited by the restrictions this artificial situation puts them under. Observe the average post-synchronized film and you will soon see the effect this has.

The worst situation that arises is when the images for a film have been compromised to get reasonable sound and the sound still turns out to be unusable. The only good reason for post-synchronization of dialogue, in my opinion, is if the imagery is absolutely wonderful, which is certainly the case with the work of Italian masters such as Fellini, Visconti and Pasolini.

EFFECTS

The value of good effects is often underestimated, which explains why they are called 'noise' in some quarters. All natural sound that is not dialogue should be very carefully considered for its potential benefit to the overall and particular effect of a scene.

Even if the sound recordist has provided good atmosphere tracks for each scene and wild tracks for any specific needs, it is still likely that the recording of additional effects will be useful. When this is done to picture in the studio it is called a 'Foley' session, after a man who was an acknowledged expert at this kind of work.

FOLEY

For this the first things to remember are facilities and props. The most common use of Foley sessions is to re-record footsteps. For this the studio must possess a variety of surfaces to match those in the film. Ideally asphalt, concrete, gravel, sand and wood should be available and troughed, so that each can be dampened to simulate wet conditions. Each trough should be a couple of yards long to avoid the impression of 'running on the spot'. Footwear should be similar to that used in the film. If you engage specialists they will bring with them a range of footwear and several suitcases full of other useful items. Most theatres possess a miniature door for replacing the false sound of studio doors, or even adding off-screen opening and shutting for dramatic effect. Unusual doors and gates should however be obtained or recorded from other sources. The noise of crockery, cutlery and chairs are often required and these must also be brought to the session.

All experienced sound editors will make their own analysis of effects requirements and where necessary endeavour to record those items which could be difficult to simulate in the studio. Indeed the modern 'sound designer' works with sophisticated technical apparatus to satisfy the exacting needs of directors. Gone are the days of primitive effects when, for instance, an axe cleaving a cabbage was common currency for the guillotine.

VOICE-OVER OR NARRATION

If this has to be specially recorded, it is best done to picture to ensure that length, positioning and effect are going to work. If possible, the effectiveness of narration should be tested by recording a guide track in advance of bringing in the narrator. It is in any case essential to test each section carefully against the picture. When recording to picture you should annotate the typescript with front and end footages to ensure correct timing. Without picture, timings should be supplied and a stop-watch used to check the lengths while recording. Words may have to be dropped or added if a reasonable change of pace fails to give a good fit on any particular section.

Choosing the right voice is not easy. If there are other voice-overs then there must be sufficient contrast to avoid confusion and to differentiate between the 'objective' narration and 'subjective' voices. It is easy to assume that an authoritative voice will lend that quality to an otherwise unconvincing film. In fact, such a voice may actually emphasize the less than convincing visuals. The best guide is to determine in your own mind the tone and mood of the piece. Deciding between male and female should be a matter of common sense, although subtle alterations in effect can be achieved by changing the sex of the speaker even though the words remain the same.

The most important decision, however, is whether to use narration at all and, if so, what purpose it serves. In these days when dramatic and documentary film are always borrowing elements from each other's styles, narration/voice-over/commentary are being used in a much more interesting way. The first-person voice-over adopted by a number of feature films as a natural extension of the Raymond Chandler or Dashiell Hammett private-eye, commenting on situations they are trying to deal with/get out of/run away from, is the traditional approach. All you need is Elliot Gould or, in a previous generation, Humphrey Bogart, seeming to be unable to control events that they accidentally or casually get involved in and the narration becomes a natural element. This allows the director to keep his audience in touch with things which are difficult (or expensive) to show, at the same time as conveying a feeling of identification with the thoughts of the protagonist. It also enables insights to be revealed that the visuals do not convey, thus layering the superficial with 'meaning', especially if the words are spare and ambivalent.

Narration used in this way will always function best if preconceived, so that the shooting incorporates and allows for its eventual addition. You can give your film a very particular flavour by deciding which character is going to tell the story on the soundtrack. The girl's narration in Robert Mulligan's *To Kill a Mockingbird* (1963) and Terence Malick's *Badlands* (1973) lend a deceptively innocent air to the way we view the events portrayed. Remember though that if you choose such a 'direct' method of letting the audience in on the story you will inevitably shut off certain options, and relying on voice-over to carry the plot may give the impression of cheating and avoiding visual exposition. However, like any good device, if it is integrated well into the fabric of your film, first-person voice-over can be a valuable asset.

The third-person narrator has now lost favour amongst film-makers. It is recognized as a literary device that does not transfer easily, least of all to dramatic film. It has a certain quaintness unless associated with events rather than emotions. War films can always be introduced with a voice-over statement of dates, places and deployment of forces, although a caption would do just as well. Documentary, especially in television, is still dominated by the 'Voice of God' technique. The words are what make the conventional documentary supposedly credible and also, incidentally, are usually the only cement holding together the disparate elements that make up the visuals. There is obviously much more to documentary use of narration or voice-over than this. Especially valuable is the use of wild-track description of events, or the background to them, by a participant or someone we know, from evidence in the film, to be privy to knowledge that is useful in understanding or appreciating the events portrayed.

Except for films that are strictly concerned with detailing a process and thus require an exact description in words and pictures of what goes on, voice-over should always be seen as an opportunity to say what cannot be shown, or to counterpoint the images with words that cast a new light on the pictures. Still, it is no coincidence that the traditional voice-over is the most frequently imitated or parodied element in film technique, producing some of the funniest cartoons, television sketches and feature sequences just by playing a commentary dead-pan. For, without discretion and conviction, even the most serious use of narration will become unintentionally funny and destroy rather than support your thesis or structure.

The worst kind of narration is where the pictures are shot subsequent to the 'expert' writing the voice track. This almost inevitably becomes the equivalent of a slide-show which has little or nothing to do with film-making. The best voice-over is spare, economic, allusory rather than direct, cathartic in its effect on the images, and questioning rather than answering. In this way it becomes a stimulus rather than a solution, and points rather than leads the audience.

It is worth comparing narration with captions doing the same job:

	VOICE-OVER	CAPTION
1	Gives tone and colour and emphasis to the words.	Allows neutral 'reading' but is cold and depersonalized.
2	Prevents the 'flow' of other voice tracks.	Requires superimposition or interruption of pictures.
3	Can be read at speed and in manner determined by director.	Must be kept on screen long enough for 'average' reader.
4	Allows positioning on shots to precise words.	Only relates directly to shots before and after.
5	Easy to record and place for fine cutting.	Needs shooting and/or optical dupe before effect can be judged.
6	Useful as links into and out of sync or wild statements which are not coherent in themselves.	If kept to factual background can add to credibility of film and its maker's attitude.

MUSIC

The use of music in film is often unsatisfactory. It is an easy – but dangerous – assumption that there are basic aspects of film and music which allow for a confluence of purpose and style so that the one may mesh with the other. Bresson has very strong views about the effect of music on film: 'It isolates your film from the life of your film (musical delectation). It is a powerful modifier and even destroyer of the real, like alcohol or dope.' He has also said: 'People flood a film with music. They are preventing us from seeing that there is nothing in those images.' His decision was to have 'no music as accompaniment, support or reinforcement'. (*Notes on Cinematography*, 1977.)

Music isolates your film from the life of your film. This isolation or separation can be emotional, stylistical, rhythmical or it can relate to pace. Music establishes its own existence just as soon as it takes shape between the composer's brain, the hand holding the pen and the manuscript paper. Music is a formal abstraction and as such has an inherent coherence which is stronger and more immediate (though not necessarily more superficial) than the other elements which make up narrative film. Unless you are able to give your visual construction and its attendant sound elements, especially dialogue and synchronous effects, the same metaphorical strength, music will dominate, indeed eclipse, the film. Since reducing your narrative to abstraction is self-defeating, the only real answer is for the music to remain unmusical in the sense of eschewing melody and the other elements of composition which make it discrete and self-sufficient. The ideal music for film has to be that which makes no sense played separately from the film of which it is supposed to be part.

In George Roy Hill's *Butch Cassidy and the Sundance Kid* (1969), the morning after Butch and the Kid have spent a night at Etta's place, Butch rides around the yard on a bike. This becomes a sequence cut to 'Raindrops are Falling on My Head'. Although this represents a happy interlude in the uneasy life of the outlaws, the song interrupts totally the flow of the film and effectively prevents the pursuance of a narrative line beyond the particular sequence. Another example was the song 'Bright Eyes' in *Watership Down* (1978) which did exactly the same disservice to the aesthetic of the film – the animators even changed the style of the cartoon just for that sequence. Commercially both songs probably helped the films but aesthetically they were mistakes.

The way music fails in film terms is much harder to demonstrate when we are talking of other than best-selling popular songs. Sometimes an existing piece of classical music is used as theme and background for a feature film in the belief that a priori Mozart, Brahms or Richard Strauss are bound to improve the films they are applied to. The music used in Bo Widerberg's *Elvira Madigan* (1967) and Stanley Kubrick's *2001 – A Space*

Odyssey (1968) are well-known examples of this practice. A shot of the Eiffel Tower and a few bars of accordion music are still used to signify Paris, although a television comedy series had the cheek to use a picture of Blackpool Tower instead. There is constant exploitation of the eminently available classical repertoire as easy pickings for the film-maker.

The reasons for this wrong-headed tendency are not too difficult to discern: laziness, ignorance, anxiety and, of course, poverty. The lazy director and editor think music of an accepted quality is an easy answer to covering any sequence which does not hang together on its own merits. The ignorant director and editor are not aware of either the deleterious effect of such music or the alternatives. The anxious director and editor need to support their material in a prestigious and snobbish way. The poor director and editor prefer to find a disc on which there are no royalties to pay, rather than to explore the possibilities of music composed and/or played especially for the film, or to make the film work without music.

You may be thinking by now that I am implacably against music in film. This is far from the truth – but only if music is used carefully. If music can be counterpoint to action; if it can support without taking over; if it can substitute for other sound (e.g. effects); if it can heighten where tension already exists, or quieten when silence has won; if it can emphasize its own absence by its presence – then music is to be encouraged. The composition of such music for films is a discrete art form, and should be encouraged by music schools everywhere. Only by such encouragement to understand the particular needs of film will we begin to break down this parasitical and irrelevant reliance on both the classics and derivations from the popular form. If Prokofiev can do it for Eisenstein, Britten for Grierson and, in the commercial idiom, Morricone for Leone, then it should be possible throughout film-making. After all Prokofiev, as Eisenstein acknowledged, had the ability to use music as a substitute for all other forms of sound. Are we still content to plagiarize and pirate our music for film?

Let us assume that you have decided to make use of specially composed music for at least part of your film. The first thing to realize is that you do not need a full symphony orchestra for effective accompaniment to your visuals and other sound. Indeed, a piano and percussion occasionally augmented by another particular instrument can be far more effective than an over-elaborate score which swamps the film. You should also not look for a melodic line that becomes a theme: any progression of notes which is catchy enough to hum after one or two hearings is again a distraction from the film itself.

Epic music for 'epic' films is usually expected to work with a formula usually containing three themes: one for the hero, one for the romantic couple and one for the 'cause' or the larger dramatic conflict. The contrast between this and, for instance, scores for Bergman's films is considerable. His scores have the integration lacking in epic films. He is a man much concerned with silence, indeed he is also on record as admiring Bresson. There are wonderful and terrible silences in his films, and it is sometimes possible to say that these are created by music.

At what point should it be decided whether to use music? Unless the music relates to the scene in some direct way, I would suggest that the decision should usually be taken at the fine cut. Not, that is, when everything is set in concrete, but at a point when the visual material has been made to work on its own, although of course with the support of dialogue and other sync sound. Never be reduced to thinking that a scene will be all right when the music is on it because it will not be if it is not 'all right' without the music.

Perhaps the best thing music does is to support or emphasize the mood or atmosphere of a scene, but the composer must pick up resonances in the film itself and carry them on, rather than let the music act as the clue for the audience. Georges Delerue did this very well in films such as Truffaut's *Jules et Jim* (1961), where there is a real partnership, which seems almost conscious, between the characters in the film and the music, as if the music represents the director. That is, **not** what the director wants the audience to think about a scene, but what the director thinks about it – a much more interesting point of view!

The challenge of making music an integral part of a film has led to some interesting solutions. Lindsay Anderson's *O Lucky Man!* (1972) starts with Alan Price being seen as a sort of chorus or troubadour commenting, in vision and as music-over, on the situations that the hero, Malcolm McDowell, finds himself in. Eventually McDowell meets up with Price and his group of musicians, gets a lift back to London and becomes friendly with Helen Mirren who is a sort of group mascot. In this way the use of the music is up-front, overt, direct. Price's lyrics and driving style are an objectivization of McDowell's personal experience. So the score is informative and also available to Anderson as a pacing device. It is not by accident that Anderson is seen at one point in the recording studio during a number.

Feelings which are impossible to express in words often get transmuted into musical communication, especially through one or other performer sitting down at the piano! People go to concerts, listen to records, hum tunes, whistle, all in the service of using music as an expressive device. Never ignore the value of a musical element being part of the scene rather than just a superimposed score.

If music is to be specially composed and recorded, careful preparations must be made. The composer should first be shown the whole film and given an indication of where music is desired. If he is any good he will have suggestions of his own about mood and instrumentation. Exact timings will be supplied in minutes and seconds (footages are no good to someone working away from footage counters) with the music 'cues' numbered and described. The procedure from here to the final recording of the music can

vary quite considerably. It is fairly certain that, given the time and opportunity, at least one more session will be held when the composer will go
over his suggestions with the aid of a piano or synthesizer, preferably in a
sound studio where the picture can be run.

Perhaps the most important thing to watch and listen for is duplication
of emphasis and effect. If a cut, a word, an action or reaction is achieving
the dramatic effect required, do not allow music to be wasted doing the
same job. This is not so simple as it sounds since such confluence of effect
seems superficially correct. If you remind yourself that the film is not meant
to be a melodrama, there is a good chance you will draw back from
unnecessary and unhelpful musical excesses. You should be looking to
music to supply the emotion or tension directly or by counterpoint that is
not present in the pictures or other sound, rather than to underline that
which is being shown or described by other means. In *Montage mon beau
souci* Godard refers to music as 'sounds which have the value of images –
I have never used music otherwise. It plays the same role as black in
Impressionist painting.'

Eventually a score is arrived at and the cutting room must prepare the
sections for projection. If possible music 'cues' should be looped as for
post-synchronization. Cue lines should be given for each start and for
important moments in the section. Some studios and composers like to
use what are called click tracks. These are a mechanical and precise
substitute for a metronome, providing a constant beat to allow the
composer/conductor to pace the recording.

Do not assume that music thus obtained will necessarily be appropriate.
It is often very hard for a composer to judge the director's intentions, but
he must settle for some interpretation in order to translate the drama into
musical terms. So at a recording it is imperative that the director and editor
are quick to point out if music is tending to change the emphasis in a way
that is undesirable.

Perhaps the hardest thing is to know where to start and finish a piece of
music to achieve the required effect. In film we can choose whether to signal
events, feelings, reaction, changes, either by visual or aural means or by
both. If we use both, they can be simultaneous or – better still – one can
precede the other. Not only this but by cutting **and** by using different kinds
and levels of sounds we can create a complex series of relationships
between the events and emotions being portrayed.

In documentary film you may sometimes acquire music as background
to actuality. The temptation here is to use it as a prop to your narrative line,
to include it as background before and after the scene it strictly applies to,
or to make a virtue of intercutting with differing perspectives on the music
track. Such techniques can be successful, but your starting point should be
the attitude that considers music discrete to its own context. In fact, one of
the most pleasing aspects of good use of music stems from the simple

technique of laying it to start 'late' and finish 'early', thus allowing a scene to establish itself without music and to conclude in the quiet after a period of harmonious support. Delerue was very good at this, but then he was a 'movie maniac' anyway, so saturated in film that it seemed right to him to let the scene be seen to be inspiring the music rather than being slave to it.

One further point on music: there is no virtue in cutting on the beat. Nor is there any principle worth expounding about how to avoid doing so. However, it is a similar problem to cutting on visual action. The answer to both can be ascertained by first deciding what you are cutting for, i.e. what 'action' or what 'phrase' you want to emphasize or avoid emphasizing by cutting. Then imagine what time is required to be conscious of the action or phrase. This is entirely subjective but has the useful effect of avoiding the impression that the music is pulling the visuals along, which will certainly appear to be the case if you cut on or, even worse, after the beat.

An editor I once knew had a simple solution to the problem of the beat. He started out by making his cuts on a music montage exactly to the beat. Then to help himself decide how many frames he should advance the picture, he invented a mental sliding scale with Bach at one end and Debussy at the other. He came into my cutting room one day looking very worried – someone had asked him to use Tchaikovsky's orchestral suite *Mozartiana* and he could not place it on his scale!

PLAYBACK

When music is being used in performance, either sung, played or for dance sequences, it is usual to pre-record the score and playback the track during shooting. On feature films and for special musical television films, the cutting room is usually required to prepare the tracks for these playback sessions. The music is recorded under optimum conditions on to a master ¼-in. tape with a sync reference. A copy is made in sync with the addition of countdown leaders for each section that is being shot. This involves the director and the choreographer or music director deciding in advance how the sequences are to be broken down into individual shots. So copies must be made from the music master for each section, always allowing slightly more music than is required. Although the technique can vary slightly the basic requirement is for a countdown and clap followed by a pause and a further countdown to the music start. So the tape might have at the beginning 3 – 2 – 1 CLAP – 3 – 2 – 1, then the music. It is also valuable to add 3 – 2 – 1 CLAP at the end for further sync reference. The countdown should be in the same rhythm as the music.

In shooting, the copy playback track is started with the camera locked in sync, the clapper is inserted in sync in vision and the whole is re-recorded as a guide track. Before cutting commences a transfer from the guide track and the master film copy are rubber-numbered in sync to enable precise laying up when the cutting is finished. In addition to the countdown, it is invaluable to identify each section in order, and even to announce the bars of music that the section covers. This numbering will coincide with a copy of the score that has been marked up bar by bar.

The advantages of playback are that it guarantees a high-quality, 'clean' recording and allows other sounds such as dialogue and effects to be obtained separately without being tied to exact and predetermined places in the score. It is possible to shoot dance sequences to a click track or metronome equivalent, but the artists then suffer from having to perform to a clinical rhythm rather than to the track which evokes the real atmosphere of the scene.

It is interesting that silent films were often shot with musicians playing appropriate music during the shooting to help the artists appreciate the mood. Even today it is not unknown for a director to use music on the set for sequences that demand a highly charged atmosphere. I well remember Stravinsky's *The Rite of Spring* being played back during the shooting of a particularly frenetic scene in Ken Russell's *The Devils* (1971). When the visuals had been shot the sound editor was allowed access to the performers for the recording of appropriate wild tracks. The actual music was, of course, composed and recorded later.

TRACKLAYING

Sound of all varieties is gathered together for one final objective: the mix. To this end, when the 'cut' has been approved the next job for the editor is tracklaying. This needs to be done meticulously. Failure to pay attention to detail and precision when tracklaying can cause chaos and disaster at the mixing session. Remember that you are dealing with the synchronous and asynchronous sounds that are meant finally to complement in all their richness the visuals of your film. It is possible to end up with upwards of a score of separate tracks, each with important sound elements to be meshed into the balanced whole. In a matter of a few hours, using the combined aural response of director, editor and mixer and the hands of the latter, one strip of magnetic track must be used to contain the right relative values of those myriad sounds. From this it can be seen that the objective of tracklaying is to provide the sounds in a form which maximizes the chance of getting the best mix. The ideal situation is to avoid the necessity of expecting the dubbing theatre, in advance, to come up with the answer to soundtrack problems.

For some, tracklaying is a chore, and it is true that on occasions its satisfactions are too subtle to be discernible. But not least of them is the pleasure of providing the raw material for a smooth and efficient mixing session. Given access to good-quality sound, a few simple procedural points will virtually guarantee good use of the dubbing theatre.

You must always be aware of the physical condition of your tracks. There are three aspects to watch: the joins, the perforations and wear of the oxide itself. Ideally all tracks should be pristine copies from master material. Since this entails considerable expense on stock and transfers, it is unlikely that you will experience such luxury except as a sound editor on feature films. This means that care of your tracks throughout the process of cutting is essential. To ensure that your tracks are in good condition when you reach the dubbing theatre it is important to observe the following points:

1. When synchronizing and viewing rushes check that the transfers are at the correct sound level. Low level tracks will inevitably lead to trouble with background noise in the mix.
2. Ensure that all joins and rejoins are well made with no excess tape and with no gap or overlap at the join.
3. Use only one joiner, otherwise you will probably find that recutting results in the creation of a gap or overlap because of variations in the alignment of the guillotine.
4. Do not clean the joiner with metal objects since it will easily become magnetized, resulting in 'clicks' or 'bumps' at the joins.
5. Avoid running on machines or projectors where the tension is too great as this will stretch the joins and eventually cause re-perforation of the stock.
6. Keep your sound heads clean and avoid getting chinagraph or other dirt on the track, otherwise the track will become worn and damaged causing deterioration of the signal and 'drop outs'.
7. It is advisable to cut your sound diagonally to ensure a smoother transition at the join.

If, having observed the above, you reach the point of tracklaying and need to replace pieces of track for some reason, take care to match them carefully, especially for sync, and always transfer slightly more than you need to allow overlaps.

DIALOGUE

Having set up the cutting copy and track on your synchronizer with at least one roll of spacing, the first job is to mark up your leaders with proper sync marks and to allow several feet on the head for lace up. Clearly identify the existing track and your roll of spacing as DIALOGUE 1 and 2. The function of this first operation is to split the dialogue into two tracks and to note at the same time all requirements for wild tracks and, if necessary, further dialogue tracks. You may have narration and post-sync dialogue already inserted, both of which should go on separate tracks. Whatever you do it is as well to deal with one aspect at a time, so if you are merely splitting dialogue your original track will still contain other sound elements to be split off later.

Splitting has the prime functions of allowing the mixer to balance the dialogue and also to permit creative use of the overlap. (Some editors prefer to split their dialogue last, using the cutting track as a guide for laying all other sound.) If your trims are properly filed, each junction of dialogue is an opportunity to provide a smooth transition. With coded sync material it is a simple task to find the next section of sound, both head and tail and, as you split, to add a few frames at either end, taking care to retain the original sync at the cut. Normally the addition will contain only the background atmosphere, giving the mixer the chance to match levels and equalize if necessary. However, there are some cases where the overlap can contribute considerably more to the final track. If you have cut dialogue very tight even the breath on the front can be useful. Sometimes footsteps or other effects are only audible on one of the two shots being intercut, and the overlap allows their insertion. Occasionally some lines are 'off-mike' in the section used and these can be replaced by 'on-mike' lines from another slate, even if this means splitting **within** a shot. If the dialogue is 'loose', removal of heavy background between phrases and replacement with specially recorded atmosphere or buzz track can heighten the feeling of a scene. There is a practice in feature films called 'stripping' where all sounds other than dialogue are removed and replaced by wild tracks obtained either at the time of shooting, by post-sync or recorded by the sound editor. Never assume that because you are dealing with intercut shots all recorded in the same situation, they do not require splitting. Mike positioning, closeness of shot, relation to background, level of recording, variation in voice intensity, all contribute differences that the mixer must deal with. Indeed, never make your splitting coterminous with picture cuts. Sometimes a conversation between two people has to be split even if covered in a two-shot, to allow the opportunity to balance the voices and their background levels. So the best attitude is never to assume that what seems like a smooth sound transition on the editing machine will also appear so in the dubbing theatre. For this reason a running of the film in the mixing studio prior to tracklaying can be of great value.

EFFECTS

If for any reason there are specific effects that have not been recorded during the shooting, these can be obtained from sound libraries and dubbing theatres. However, it is very dangerous to rely on these sources for adequate substitutes.

Effects should be dealt with in two distinct categories: atmospheres and specific or 'spot' effects ('spot' referring to the need for accurate placement when laying up). Atmospheres can be further divided into general and particular. Often the mistake is made of treating all atmospheres as general, and making loops to be run as background to the whole of a sequence. This can be a wasted opportunity and even a problem if the 'specifics' are not considered. Even country atmosphere or distant town traffic can contain variations that should be taken advantage of. Remember that any distinct sound in a loop will recur at regular intervals and seem artifical, even comical.

The best approach is to go through the film noting all effects required: not just the ones that are needed to match what is seen, but any pertinent sounds that might enliven the background track. You can overdo this: all effects must be used with discretion as some sounds are inevitably clichés. The cuckoo over springtime countryside is an obvious example. On the other hand, the dramatic opening of Losey's *Accident* (1967) depends upon sound effects culminating in a car crash off-screen. By careful orchestration and concentration on a 'neutral' visual of a house seen from the front gates we are impelled to listen for sound clues and subjected to an intense build-up of tension which is somehow 'relieved' by the crash. Furthermore the gap or silence before anyone emerges from the house as a response to the crash is effective because it makes the audience feel impotent in face of the inaction. An interesting comparison both visually and aurally can be made between this opening sequence and that of *Don't Look Now* (1973) by Nicolas Roeg. In this film parallel action between the parents working indoors and their little girl playing in the garden culminates in the father failing to save his daughter from drowning. The imagery is carefully controlled and sound is used as a very effective support to the tragedy without dialogue being resorted to. Both are masterly expositions of the event around which the film narrative is built. Neither opening scene as it turns out is the 'subject' of the film – indeed one is in fact a sort of resolution and the other 'merely' a starting point.

It is worth being extremely fussy with effects. Some people even categorize their sound into homogeneous varieties and use a separate track for each type. At the very least, it is important that you present the mixer with effects that are not a rag-bag intercut without sufficient gaps on the same track. Gun shots, bird calls, footsteps, doors slamming and bells ringing, to give a few examples, all have to be handled differently and therefore need enough space for proper handling.

When cutting in specific effects, be careful to remove all extraneous sound from before and after the effect itself. On the other hand, do not remove echo or reverberation and watch the way the background to the effect fits. Sometimes it may be preferable to keep the background running either side, especially if you can hear it behind the effect anyway. This care and attention is of course essential to all tracklaying. Common enough are the mistakes that arise from not examining a track carefully. For example, coughs, unwanted breathing and page turning are often forgotten on narration or voice-over, even though it is easy enough to check for these things. On studio recordings it is not unusual for the mixer's announcements to end up being at least partially recorded and, even if they are eliminated in the final mix, it is very irritating for the mixer to have to close his pots (sound faders) completely between each section to avoid re-recording extraneous sound.

As each section of track is added, you should be aware of the need for positive sync reference points to avoid problems of re-synching, especially when inserts are added to an already completed track. The ideal way is to quote on the soundtrack the last two digits of the code number opposite the frame on the picture. Use quick-drying felt-tip pen to avoid wax rubbing off on the oxide of the section which is going to be rolled tight against the mark. In this way the cutting copy need not be marked at all. Simply mark the sound frame in between the perforations. When the cutting copy is not coded, similar use can be made of key numbers if they are distinct enough for easy reference.

In all tracklaying you should follow the principle that no gaps should exist in sound of which the background atmosphere is a continuous complement to the visuals. If sections of the sync track have to be removed in the 'cleaning up' process always off-lay on another track a matching atmosphere or background overlapping with the sync sections, but **not** continuously across the existing sync. This allows the mixer to fade across with no noticeable change. With post-sync dialogue a continuous backing track may be valuable. Obviously, the availability of such background or buzz track depends upon the efficiency of the sound recordist.

It is tempting to attempt too much at once when laying soundtracks. Remember that if you fill all the available heads on the synchronizer, there will be no spare to allow for lining up each section without removing the spacing or whatever already exists on the synchronizer. Even for experienced sound editors this can make the operation very complicated as sync marks have to be made each time something is removed; it is obviously more efficient to allow for a second run through to deal with the extra track.

The mechanics of tracklaying are not complicated but it is as well to follow a few simple rules:

1. Always cut the track in on the **left** of the synchronizer to avoid loss of sync in the material already laid.
2. Make all necessary sync marks before cutting so that nothing has to be re-adjusted after laying.
3. Review each section at sync speed to ensure that the desired effect is achieved – effects are pointless if the sound is not entirely appropriate.

4. Keep all spacer with the cell or base side against the heads so that there is no danger of emulsion rubbing off and causing build-up when re-recording.
5. Make end sync marks on the protective spacer at the end of a completed track common to all tracks and a similar mark on the picture.
6. Rewind each track 'sync' to those marks and check that it is still in sync at the front.
7. Run at normal speed with picture – preferably with another relevant track to get a good indication of whether everything is working as expected.
8. Make sure there are no marks or accretions on the track surface and be careful to avoid bad joins.
9. Insert a frame of 1000 cycle tone opposite '3' on the leader of each track (some organizations use '4' instead of '3'). This sync plop is a more positive reference point than the sync mark, and will be used by the laboratory for lining up picture and sound for combined printing.
10. Ensure that the picture leader is the proper dubbing length. The standard is twelve 35mm feet from the sync mark which is usually a cross or 'envelope'. If this is not adhered to all your footages will be wrong.

If you are laying your tracks using one of the new digital systems rather than magnetic film, all the advice above still applies. Properly used the advantages of these devices are considerable, and we are moving rapidly towards an integrated digital, random access, picture and sound facility for **all** post-production.

With a system like Audiofile or Sound Station it is possible to lay up all forms of sound with the utmost precision. What gives it the advantage over traditional tracklaying is the ability to try alternatives and to shift, trim or extend any chosen sound at will without destroying the original cue, which remains available for further use.

Additionally, you are able to view the combination of sounds that are being laid down on the graphic display, which confirms the positioning of each section that is added. Since the sound is reproduced through a high quality system there should be no nasty surprises in mixing.

Ironically it is the picture quality which can leave much to be desired and it is essential that the copy you are replaying as you lay tracks is good enough to allow you to judge the combined effect of image and sound.

It is important to remember that the function of tracklaying is to prepare the best possible combination of all types of sound. For this reason it is very valuable if you can play the different groups of sound against the dialogue guide track, for instance; otherwise it is possible to treat the laying of effects as a mechanical task rather than part of the creative process. This can be especially true regarding effects and music, which should have an integral function.

ADR and Foley can also be achieved through digital recording systems with the commensurate advantages of flexibility, accuracy and speed. With all these pluses we should at the same time remember that the film that is meant for the big screen does need to be mixed in a large space or at least in an area that can be acoustically treated to respond to sound as if being reproduced in a cinema. Even then the relationship between sound and picture may be skewed if the process has occurred in front of a monitor rather than a big screen.

DUBBING CHARTS

It remains to tackle the dubbing chart. The formats vary in detail but the objective is always the same. Having laid your tracks efficiently it is imperative to convey the information that the mixer needs in a graphic and comprehensible form. It is to your advantage to make a rough chart as you lay each track. This avoids having to run all the tracks again for charting and allows you instantly to refer to other tracks already laid if you are in doubt about how to dovetail a certain element. It is fairly universal practice to dub to 35mm footages, as 16mm is too imprecise. Remember that one 35mm foot is ⅔ second at 24 frames, whereas one 16mm foot is 1⅔ seconds at 24 frames. Even so it is best to work to the nearest half a foot when charting, thus allowing accuracy of ⅓ second for each cue. An essential part of the chart is picture cues. These need not list each change of shot, but commonsense and experience will tell you when it is useful to know the footage at a cut, dissolve or fade.

In drawing up the chart it is essential to be clear, consistent and accurate. The example on p. 129 demonstrates the simple code and signs that ensure the necessary communication.

THE MIX

Although the prime objective of tracklaying and mixing is to achieve a balanced combination of all sound reduced to one track, for convenience this is often arrived at through one or more intermediary steps. If there are more than four or five tracks to start with, mixing them down to one in a single operation is asking a lot of the mixer. It is therefore normal to go for one or more 'pre-mixes', usually balancing the tracks which contain similar elements. The most likely approach is to achieve a good balance of music and effects and to add all voice tracks in a later runthrough. This music and effects mix, known as an M and E, is useful if foreign versions are contemplated, as it allows the replacement of voices by another language without having to re-mix from scratch. Of course if the music is the most important part of the film this should be added last, thus reducing the 'generations' gone through to a minimum.

Twickenham Film Studios Ltd.

ST MARGARETS · TWICKENHAM · MIDDLESEX · TW1 2AW

Telephone: 081 892 4477   Fax 081 891 0168

Title .... " MARY REILLY " ....

Action Cues	Ft.	Track Fx 1	Track Fx 2	Track Fx 3	Track Fx 4	Track Fx 5	Track Fx 6	Track Fx 7	Track Fx 8	Track Fx 9	Track Fx 10	Track Fx 11
EXTERIOR STREET SLAUGHTERHOUSE.	0	0 STEREO MARKET B/G CHATTER FOOTSTEPS TRADERS.	0 STEREO HORSE AND CARRIAGES B/KGROUND		0 LITTER ROOM B&L HORSE AND TRAP PASS IN B/G 27 39 C/RASH STEAM HISS	0 ROOM B&L HORSE AND TRAP PASS 12 53 B/MT MAN LAUGHING	0 C HORSE AND CARRIAGE UP & STOP AT CAMERA		15 C 23 HORSE SNORTS 25 C 23 HORSE SNORTS 28	11 LEFT CHICKENS 23	0 TOWN ORE BELL	0 HORSE NEIGH 4 25 HORSE NEIGH 30 38 39 NEIGH 44 C/S SPLASH 59
CUT TO STEPS MEAT MARKET.	39	39 Q LOW					39 COWS MOO	39 C WATER SPLASH 48	39 C WATER SPLASH FROM BUCKET. 63	50 C 46 WATER SPLASH AND RUN 64	
CUT INT MEAT HANGER.	64	64	64	64 STEREO BG INT SLAU/HOUSE (TRESPUISTIN)	64	60	64 STEREO PIGS SQUEAL 70 LOW	64 COWS BELLOW 71	64 L.C.R. COWS 84	75 R/MT COW MOO 81	81 METALLIC NOISES BACK'G.
			86 STEAM HISSES 180								
OPPERATING THEATRE.	171			171 @ LOW	171 HOSPITAL SICK ROOM	171 HOSPITAL SICK ROOM	171	171 WOMAN SOBBING B/G.	175 R BABY CRY B/G.	171 SLIDING DOORS.	81 R/MT OLD PUMP ENGINE 171Q
							194				
INT CARRIAGE.	212	212 STEREO INT CARRIAGE WITH HORSES HOOVES.	212 STEREO INT CARRIAGE RUMBLE AND MVS.	212	212	212		212	212	212	212

Figure 6.1 A sample dubbing chart from a pre-mix on *Mary Reilly*.

Pre-mixes have one drawback. They commit you to an existing balance between those sound components when you are adding others. It takes considerable experience to predict the overall value of particular sounds when some of them are not being mixed at any given stage. Nor is it just a matter of levels. It is also very easy to assume that perspectives that seem right in isolation will still seem right when placed alongside other elements. A simple example is conversation on a dance floor with an orchestra audible in the background. We have all witnessed the film where the music is noticeably lowered in level when speech has to be heard, with a resultant loss of credibility. Here as in other such cases much can depend upon the approach used in the original recording. If the couple having the conversation have to raise their voices in the shooting situation then, although the balance may still be controllable because either the music was playback and/or the dialogue is post-sync, the final combined sound can be mixed credibly without undue emphasis on the discrepancy in levels.

We have naturally and quite rightly returned to the importance of having the proper attitude to sound from the outset – and that means from the time of writing the script. Unless the film-maker treats sound with the respect it deserves through all stages of production it will be undervalued and underexploited as the partner in the audio-visual medium of film. Ironically it is a lack of understanding of the functions of sound which more often than not means that films have too much of it. Inevitably we are reminded again of Bresson: 'The soundtrack created silence.' Indeed, discretion is the better part of tracklaying. There is no inherent value in having more elements in your track than you need. It is much more important to ensure that each sound has a proper function and is serving that function well.

Completing the picture: from mix to screen

7

The path a project will follow after the sound has been mixed will depend on a number of factors. The first is the technical path that has been chosen: whether or not the shooting was on film or video and what system has been used for editing. Unless the intention is to show the finished product in the cinema there are now distinct advantages to completing post-production in the electronic mode. Titling, effects and all image manipulation are easier to achieve and to control electronically. However the overriding influence on the way completion is achieved may be neither technical nor indeed artistic; it may be merely commercial.

Before we consider the implications of the newer methodologies we must talk about the relationship between the editor and his or her main source of magic: the laboratory. The material that we call film is delicate. The chemistry of the emulsion that film carries is not only fragile, it also depends upon the observation of fairly tight limitations to function effectively. It is appropriate that a device for capturing and reproducing reality should require precise handling.

Indeed, before 'safety film' was invented, the tendency of nitrate film to self-combust could be interpreted as natural justice against the arrogant and presumptuous desire to store images of our existence. Yet the main-springs of our social and psychological life are left untouched by most essays in the media, perhaps because we are so concerned with the visceral that has immediate appeal to the superficial appetites of the audience. Just as beauty is skin deep so film reality is only emulsion deep.

There are those who wish that film stock and lenses had the same sensitivity as the optic nerve. However, since many of my favourite movies were made in black-and-white, I am not about to argue that the ability to make closer facsimiles of reality leads to better films. Indeed technical progress seems to produce a narrower spectrum of artistic possibilities, since efficiency and profit tend to be the overriding concern. Why else would it be so hard to get good black-and-white processing these days?

In this environment, it is even more important for editors to familiarize themselves with the laboratory and to be able to take maximum advantage of the expertise available there. The best laboratory technicians have always been able to contribute much more to films beyond the slavish interpretation of how your material matches up to some abstract standard.

THE 'CONTACT'

It is not accidental that the person most important to a film-maker at the laboratory is called the 'contact'. Usually there is a particular person who co-ordinates rushes and it is imperative that you make contact with him or her **before** starting to shoot. Informing the rushes person of your schedule, arrangements for sending in the exposed material and return of the rush print, and of any particular problems you foresee, can make a great deal of difference to the smoothness of this part of the operation. If, during shooting, there are doubts raised about the rushes, then instant contact must be made to ascertain if there is a problem and whether it is irredeemably built into the negative or if the laboratory can eliminate it for the purpose of later printing. I have already discussed this fully (p. 65) but the importance of vigilance and quick action bears restating.

Once the film is shot, responsibility for it almost invariably passes to the post-production contact who will see it through to at least the first acceptable show or release print. Subsequent copies are often handled by another person. This way liaison for reprints, opticals, titles, negative cutting, grading and printing are funnelled through the same individual. At any given point in the process it is difficult to resist the desire to talk directly to whoever is handling a particular aspect – this should always be possible, but to avoid confusion it is obviously best to make any arrangements through that one contact. It is also imperative that you avoid splitting responsibility for liaising with the laboratory between too many people. If director, editor, assistant editor and even cameraperson are giving conflicting information and instructions, the contact will not know whom to satisfy or even to whom to refer. So delegation of particular jobs in relation to the laboratory must be carefully handled.

REPRINTS AND DUPLICATION

The first likely requirements during cutting are reprints and duplication of stock or library footage, the latter only on compilation films or where a specific shot could not be obtained in the material shot especially for the film. Reprints may be required because the editor and/or director is not happy with the rush print and would like to confirm that a section is usable.

They may also be necessary if footage is damaged during editing and must be replaced in the cutting copy to confirm the effectiveness of a sequence. For the laboratory to supply such reprints it is essential to give them the key numbers of the start and end of the section required and also, if possible, the camera-sheet number, the roll number and shooting date. Not all this information may be necessary but, as with all requests to the laboratory, it is better to give too much data than too little. You may be able to facilitate speedy supply by telephoning a request, but it will always be best to back it up with a written order. So a reprint order might read:

PLEASE SUPPLY: 'TITLE'
    16mm COLOUR CORRECTED RUSH PRINT OF SECTION BK66869–943
    FROM EASTMANCOLOR NEGATIVE IN YOUR POSSESSION
    CAMERA SHEET: 04672
    SHOOTING DATE: 8 JUNE 1995
    ROLL NUMBER: 15

As with all orders it is as well to print in BLOCK CAPITALS the essential information. Note that the request is for **colour corrected** rush print. This is to help gauge the best possible result from the negative. You may well add special instructions, e.g. MATERIAL SHOT IN LOW LIGHT CONDITIONS – PLEASE PRINT UP FOR MAXIMUM DETAIL, or RUSH PRINT SHOWS NEGATIVE SCRATCHES PLEASE TREAT BEFORE PRINTING.

At this point I should sound a note of warning. Reprints are expensive, there is usually a minimum charge and in any case it is technically difficult for the laboratory to supply less than 50 feet. Where you merely desire to check on questionable material, it may be best to ask the contact to get the section in question examined and reported on. It is usually possible to find out whether scratches can be removed or polished out without going to the expense of a reprint. If you are forced to work in black-and-white on a colour film it is sometimes essential to have sections in colour to check on such things as exposure, focus and fogging. You should also bear in mind that every time the negative is handled there is some risk of damage or accretion of 'sparkle' (dirt) – not because laboratories are careless but merely because film is a fragile material. So always convince yourself that your reprint is essential.

Duplicating from library or stock footage has other problems. You must first be certain of the type of master material that is being 'duped'. It may be negative or reversal, it may be a master print. The gauge may be 35mm or 16mm. If it is 35mm the format may be other than Academy. Always remember that your objective is to obtain a negative or master and a rush print that will conform with your other material. The source of the stock footage will tell you in what form the laboratory can supply the shots you want duped, and you must be sure that your requirements are clear.

The most common complication in duping happens when you have shot material on negative and need stock shots from reversal material. The geometry is reversed between a contact print from negative and reversal masters or camera originals, so to see the image the right way round a contact print from negative is correct with the emulsion to the observer, whereas with reversal original the base is on the side of the observer. So an internegative made from a reversal original will be unusable for intercutting.

The shorthand method of referring to emulsion position is 'A' wind and 'B' wind. A wind refers to material that is correct when the **emulsion** is towards the observer and B wind refers to material that is correct when the **base** is towards the observer. So when ordering dupes it is best to specify the wind required, especially if you are mixing negative and reversal. Remember that both negative original and reversal original are B wind but internegative from reversal original is A wind.

This necessity to make all your material conform to the same geometry also applies to optical soundtracks, so a track for original negative or reversal must be B wind. If, however, your picture is an internegative the track must be A wind. If you have any doubts it is essential either to specify on the order to what your duplicate must conform, or to ask the laboratory for clarification.

The danger is that it is possible to join together material which has contrary geometry and even to be unaware that you have different emulsion positions at a cut. The loss of focus is marginal enough to be hardly discernible on an editing machine and you may therefore only become aware of the problem when the cutting copy is sent to the negative cutters. It can be a real disaster if the material you have duped from is hard to obtain again for re-duping when there may be pressure on completing the film – so get it right first time!

OPTICALS

Apart from reprints and duping there may be little contact between cutting room and laboratory before the fine cut is completed. The one important exception is the need for opticals. Because A and B printing allows for dissolves and fades to be part of the final printing process, it is quite common for the only optical requirement to be the superimposition of titles. You may decide to go for straight titles without superimposition, partly because of cost and partly because it is no longer believed that the mere existence of elaborate title sequences has anything to do with the quality of the film itself. If, however, superimpositions are desired, several factors must be remembered. The shots for title overlay should be considered carefully before shooting starts, since a suitable background is essential:

- The shots should be steady to avoid appearance of 'jiggle'.
- They should be low key if the lettering is to be the normal white (and high key if titles are black).
- You should decide in advance where in the frame the titles will be positioned, as no action or relevant background detail should be obscured by the titles. However, too much lettering will either be cramped if restricted to a small part of the frame or require a long period of superimposition.
- Avoid wide angle or shots where there is distortion of straight lines, either horizontal or vertical.
- Remember that the cost of your optical superimposition is related to the total length of the shot used as background, and not to the length of the title overlay itself. It is possible to cut in a dupe of just the section with the title but the result will almost certainly be unsatisfactory as the change to and from the section duped will not match the original quality.

So the ideal title background is static, on a tripod, using say a 50mm lens, of a relatively dark subject (for white titles) that does not include too much fussy detail.

You may, of course, opt for a roller caption instead of static titles – this demands accurate timing to ensure that you allow sufficient length in the shooting of the background shot. Whether the titles are static or rolling (or even if they are straight) several rules must be observed:

- The titles must be steady and accurately positioned.
- They must be shot on high contrast stock and properly exposed, otherwise they will 'bleed'.
- They must not be too tight to the edges of frame (for television the safe area is particularly restricted).
- The lettering should not be too fussy or too small – remember that if the type face is not easy to read in isolation it will be even harder when superimposed.

When you have the material for optical superimposition, the order to the laboratory must be very carefully prepared. Some laboratories will supply special order forms for this purpose, but in any case the information they require is always similar. Ideally you should submit both a written breakdown and a cutting-copy guide.

The breakdown needs to be something like this:

START BACKGROUND DUPE AT AC 241076 – 5 frames.
START 16 frame fade-in of 'MAIN TITLE' at AC 2410 81 + 6 frames.
END 16 frame fade-out of 'MAIN TITLE' at AC 2410 94 + 17 frames.
END BACKGROUND DUPE AT AC 2411 07 + 12 frames.

The boxed letters and numbers, e.g. $\boxed{\text{AC}}$ or $\boxed{81}$, refer to the particular frame from which the calculation is made. The plus or minus frames from this point take you to the actual frame for the desired effect to start or finish. If this frame is actually numbered you should write it thus: $\boxed{\text{AC}}$ 241076 ± 0 frames.

It is possible to use only plus signs, which is visually clearer, but if you are submitting a cutting-copy guide it makes sense to refer only to frames that are in that guide. Thus, in the example above, START BACKGROUND DUPE AT $\boxed{\text{AC}}$ 241076 – 5 frames, is better than AC 2410 $\boxed{75}$ + 13 frames, as that number will not occur in the guide.

The ordering of dissolves or other transitional effects is similar except that the centre point must be referred to. Thus, after noting the starting frame of the dupe, you must list the frames immediately each side of the middle of the effect (i.e. at the cut point in the cutting copy), e.g.

$$\text{CENTRE of 32 frame dissolve at } \frac{\text{DB } 1035\,\boxed{68} + 2 \text{ frames}}{\boxed{\text{XY}}\,794812 - 10 \text{ frames}}$$

and follow this with the end frame of the second shot.

To make a cutting-copy guide you remove the relevant background shot(s) from the work print and show the desired effects with standard markings. Perhaps the ideal form in which to supply such a guide is to insert white spacer in the synchronizer alongside the background shots and to mark up with felt-tip pen the equivalent effects and title information as appropriate. A simple superimposition would look like this:

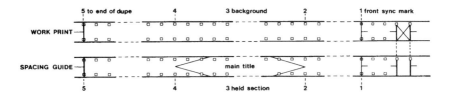

The above represents in schematic form: the start of the dupe (1); the point at which the superimposed title fades in over a specified number of frames from (2); the title is held for a specified number of frames (3); then faded out over a specified number of frames to (4); the background continues to its own cut point (5). The same sort of guide can be used for a whole series of superimpositions or indeed for other forms of optical. If opticals are ordered while you are still cutting, always insert the equivalent length of spacing to replace shots removed as guides.

As I said above, dissolves are obtainable in A and B printing so they are not normally required as opticals. However, such A and B effects are only available at specified length, usually the following:

8 frames	=	⅓ second	(at 24 frames)
16 frames	=	⅔ second	"
24 frames	=	1 second	"
32 frames	=	1⅓ seconds	"
48 frames	=	2 seconds	"
64 frames	=	2⅔ seconds	"
96 frames	=	4 seconds	"

There is one further limitation: such dissolves must be a certain number of frames apart since the printer cannot be cued instantaneously. It is as well to check with your laboratory if you suspect that the effects you want might be too close together. The minimum is at least 12 frames between the end of one dissolve and the start of the next, but it may be more.

Remember that all effects that demand an overlap of shots require you to be certain that the extra frames of each shot concerned are usable. In the cutting copy these overlap frames do not exist and, unless you check as you cut, it is imperative to look at the front or end trim when marking up for such effects.

The optical department is a source of much magic which results directly from the fact that film is made up of static images. The frame can be stopped or frozen; you can speed up the action or slow it down; blow-up the frame, making a close-up out of a medium shot; reverse the action; combine different actions; diffuse the image; even superimpose rain or fog! However, because obtaining these effects is labour-intensive and demands special film stock, the cost is very high. Unless you are prepared to budget in advance for such things, they must be a last resort and normally used only because a particular dramatic effect is unobtainable in any other way or because you are convinced that the optical in question is the best way of achieving that effect.

I am tending in this chapter to consider things on a purely technical level, but we should not forget that everything the laboratory contributes to the film is in the service of its style and content. If we are reduced to considering opticals, for example, as abstract effects, we have lost touch with the life of the film. Consider too for a moment why we should augment the language of a film with dissolves, fades and other opticals. It used to be true to assume that the dissolve merely conveyed a passage of time and that a fade-out was taken to mean the end of a scene and perhaps a more emphatic time lapse, combined sometimes with a change of location. We are now more willing to accept such changes of time and place on a simple cut, preferring perhaps to develop the way pacing and rhythm convey the logic of the narrative. This has released optical effects for a wider range of uses. Dissolving two shots, for instance, can emphasize connections between places and people that have their own continuum within the structure of the narrative. Such juxtapositions allow the film-maker to convey to the audience the thoughts of characters and the film-maker's own attitude to the drama, without the need for words. So a dancer sitting alone in the quiet of her dressing room is cued into the thought and emotion of a ballet by the music seeping into her, and therefore into our consciousness, so that the dissolve through to an earlier performance serves to emphasize and particularize that sensation. In this case the dissolve is an alternative to a straight cut and would be chosen as much because of the mood of the piece as out of consideration of the time/space relationship between the two scenes.

Sound is always an important element in the use of opticals and indeed can often be substituted for dissolves or fades. The effect of fading sound to a cut is sometimes more interesting than the visual equivalent. Of course, it is imperative to co-ordinate the use of opticals with the matching sound effects during the mixing of the film – it is no good having a smooth visual transition if the sound is an abrupt cut.

The one drawback of A and B opticals is that you do not see them until you receive an answer print from the cut negative. So you must be as certain as possible that the dissolves and fades will work as expected, especially in terms of the length you decide upon. If possible, insert both shots being dissolved in the gate of your editing machine. As long as neither shot is too dense you can get an indication of how the two shots will 'mesh'. Unless the density of both shots is very similar one or other will dominate the dissolve – a darker shot loses effectiveness quicker and a lighter shot is apparent sooner. You should also be very vigilant about movement and composition during the passage of dissolves. An awkward movement that starts during a dissolve is disconcerting and if, for instance, you are dissolving one face through to another face the positioning in frame will affect the design of the superimposed section.

One last point about fades – it is not a rigid rule that a fade-out and fade-in should always be used together. If, for instance, you want to leave a scene quietly but hit the next scene abruptly, there is nothing to stop you fading out and cutting in. Indeed it is possible to fade out, hold on black for a beat or two, then cut in. The reverse can also be effective – cutting to black and fading up after a pause.

Incorporating effects demands as much thought as each cut you make. Never assume that a particular junction of shots requires the use of an optical because of some hidebound logic of film grammar. Maybe the juxtaposition is wrong and you have perhaps wasted the opportunity of a pause or the insertion of an extra shot. It is sometimes the case, on the other hand, that both shots have been allowed to die at the cut, and should be shortened to make a more dynamic confluence. For the fact is that dissolves are often the easy way out of a problem caused by ineffective shooting. This is always a negative reason for using opticals, so be honest with yourself every time the idea of using such effects comes into your head!

NEGATIVE AND ORIGINAL CUTTING

Once cutting has been completed the cutting copy must be prepared for the negative cutters. To avoid confusion and the possibility of mistakes it must be carefully examined and marked clearly with standard indications that instruct the negative cutter of particular requirements. Each reel must have a standard leader to allow for lace up in projection, synchronization, protection from damage and identification – the last consisting of clear title and roll number markings on opaque leader or spacing. The standard markings used during cutting have already been described in full (p. 78). Those that must be retained at this stage are the marks indicating the unintended splice, build-up, extension, dissolve and fade.

All these must be clear and precise and any other marks not relevant to the negative cutter should be removed to avoid misinterpretation. You may have plastered the cutting copy with sync marks, cue marks for post-synchronization and any number of now irrelevant accretions. These must be excised before sending off the cutting copy. Remember also to add protective leader to the end of each reel, clearly marked so that it can be identified immediately even if tail out.

The most common form of negative cutting on 16mm is chequerboard. The joins are eliminated during printing by putting each shot on alternate rolls and lapping black spacer on the roll which is without a shot at any given point. This is an extension of A and B rolling where alternate rolls are used only when a fade or dissolve is required. It is a technique used because the 16mm frame line is far too narrow to allow for a join overlap. Some laboratories use an alternative to chequerboard to eliminate joins: 'zero cut' or auto-splice deletion which incorporates an overlap of frames at each cut either on two rolls as in A and B or in a single roll. A special shutter device is used to eliminate the extra frames and, although there may be a one-frame overlap of images at the cut, no join will be visible. If you are ordering chequerboard negative cutting the laboratory in question will inform you if they offer an alternative method.

Always remember that at least three or four frames are lost at each cut during negative cutting. Since tape joiners make it possible to cut without losing frames, this must be borne in mind especially when using a shot twice. Otherwise there will be no way of matching your cutting copy short of re-synchronizing and/or cutting the soundtrack.

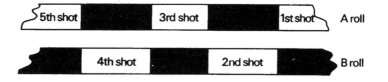

GRADING AND PRINTING

Once the negative has been cut to match your cutting copy the film is ready to be graded. Although your rush prints may have been largely acceptable in their rendition of the shot material, grading has to be related to matching the film shot by shot as cut. If, for instance, the reverse angles that you have intercut were not matched in their respective lighting set-ups, the discrepancy will be dramatized by cutting them together. It is irrelevant that shots may have looked all right in the rushes: grading is not a process of looking for the ideal rendering of each shot but of achieving an acceptable balance throughout each sequence and indeed throughout the whole film.

At the first stage of grading the procedure will vary depending upon your particular laboratory. Modern equipment allows for analysis of the cut negative by electronically 'reverse-phasing' the image so that it is seen as positive. The most sophisticated machinery of this kind can run both A and B rolls simultaneously and the cutting copy can be projected as a reference. The value of running the cutting copy is partly to compensate for the shortcomings of an electronic reading of a photographic image. As the grader watches the monitor, they can instantly rebalance the colour by reducing or increasing the amount of yellow, cyan and magenta components, i.e. the negative equivalents of the three primary colours. The grader will make extensive notes for the grading of the print, but basically each shot will end up with three numbers alongside it in the list, referring to the printer values for the three primary colour components.

It is natural for director and editor to wish to consult with the grader at this stage, at least to point out any shots or sequences that they feel need abnormal treatment. Ideally, if a viewing of the cutting copy and/or a session on the analyser can take place, it will allow the film-makers the opportunity to pre-empt any mistaken interpretations of colour and density. It will also allow the grader the chance to demonstrate what is possible and what limitations exist with regard to 'correction' of the image. However, such discussions depend upon the availability of time and facilities, both of which are often at a premium at the laboratory. Even so, the least that must be done before any prints are struck is for the editor to supply careful annotations of all potential problem areas in the film so that the grader is not working totally abstracted from the 'feel' of the film.

Even with thorough and exhaustive consultation it is unlikely that the first attempt or 'answer print' will be entirely satisfactory, and further corrections will then be made before another print is struck. When checking the answer print, always project it under optimum conditions, otherwise the colour balance and overall density will be misrepresented. Do not be surprised to find that there is a discernible variation between different projectors. The intensity of the lamp and its age, the lens on the projector, the length of 'throw' to the screen, the screen surface and the degree of darkness in the viewing room will all affect the appearance of the image and must be taken into account when estimating the quality of the print.

When this first attempt is being viewed, several other checks must be made in addition to those of colour balance and overall density:

- Is the print clean or has the negative acquired an unacceptable degree of 'sparkle or dirt during handling?
- Are there any scratches which need treating? Watch especially for dirt and scratches at the beginning and end of reels and also at joins.
- Is the soundtrack of acceptable quality and in sync with the picture? You will invariably be disappointed with a 16mm optical track, but the inevitable degradation compared with the master magnetic should only be marginal and another transfer should be ordered if it is totally unsatisfactory.
- Are the A and B opticals what you expected? Watch for jumps in fades and dissolves which may result from a fault in the cueing device. If dissolves or fades do not produce the required effect they can be shortened or eliminated, but remember any alterations to the cueing of the print will mean treating the next attempt as a new answer print at a higher cost than if it is termed a show copy or release print.

Assuming that no substantial problems exist with the answer print, there should now be further consultation with the grader to correct the unsatis- factory shots. Viewing the answer print with the grader is the best method of communicating requests for modifications, since you can discuss and clarify points which may be too subtle to reduce to a few words on paper. In addition, this is probably the first time the grader has heard the soundtrack and thus can get a proper sense of the atmosphere of the film. Grading is meant to complement the mood and this can only be conveyed when picture and sound are together.

If, however, you are reduced to a written report then the easiest system is to insert numbered pieces of paper in the print and to list your comments correspondingly. Perhaps the hardest part of communicating desired grad- ing corrections is to use a language or form of words that are least open to misinterpretation. You will mostly be dealing with pairs of words that suggest a range between some form of extremes. Do not be tempted to write an essay about the psychology or philosophy of the film as there is no way this can be translated into printer-lights by the grader. The following is the kind of information the grader will appreciate:

- Scenes are: too dark/too light
              high contrast/low contrast

too saturated/de-saturated (refers to colour intensity)
too warm/too cold
- References to colour bias that you want emphasized or removed.
- Perhaps the best method is to refer to a particular shot in a sequence as being the one to grade to. This can be done either in reference to the cutting copy or, if appropriate, the answer print. For example, a note saying 'Grade all shots in sequence between papers as per second shot (W/S dining room)' allows the grader the best possible chance of getting it right.

Grading can never compensate for an unsatisfactory negative. If you use material that is under- or over-exposed or insert a shot that contains the wrong colour balance compared to the rest of the sequence, you are taking a considerable risk. Recognizing such limitations is an inevitable part of being an editor and you should always be ready to weigh the value of a shot against its photographic shortcomings. A 'good' negative, that is, one that has received optimum exposure, is the only guarantee of flexibility in grading. If you have congratulated yourself on obtaining an incredible shot on the end of a 16mm zoom with the lens wide open you must be prepared to live with poor resolution and colour balance. Indeed, it cannot be emphasized too strongly that a lack of meticulous vetting of your cutting copy with grading potential in mind will inevitably lead to problems in the print. There must be a proper screening of the cutting copy before sending it to the laboratory for negative cutting. Often the odd frame that is fogged or damaged will escape your attention under the less than perfect conditions of the editing machine, and this is especially true at the beginning and end of shots. A dark rush print can hide embarrassing detail which will be made apparent when graded up. Never assume that familiarity with your material is the same as being aware of every detail.

Orders for negative cutting and printing must be as precise as those we discussed earlier for opticals. Never assume that information can be taken for granted. Always mention the following:

1 Title
2 Gauge
3 Original stock
4 What you are sending with the order
5 What is held by the laboratory
6 Your requirements

Every order describes one or more processes. In each case you are asking for a product to be supplied from existing raw material. Thus an order for negative cutting should read:

TITLE (1)

Please supply 16mm (2) chequerboard negative cutting (6) from Eastmancolor negative (3) in your possession (5) to match cutting copy herewith (4). Please hold for printing instructions.

To obtain the optical track the order should state:

TITLE (1)

Please supply 16mm (2) optical soundtrack (6) from 16mm magnetic master herewith (4). Track should be B wind to match Eastmancolor negative (3) in your possession (5). Sync plop on 3 of leader. Please hold developed negative for combined printing – order to follow.

For grading and printing you should state:

TITLE (1)

Please grade (6) 16mm Eastmancolor cut negative (3) in your possession (5) as discussed, and with reference to notes herewith (4), and make combined answer print (6) with optical soundtrack (plop on 3 of leader) advancing for printing sync, from optical sound negative in your possession (5). Please send print to the cutting room (address).

If you are synchronizing your soundtrack for printing you must know that the number of frames the soundtrack is advanced is as follows:

> 35mm optical – 20 frames.
> 16mm optical – 26 frames.
> 16mm magnetic stripe – 28 frames.

You must then inform the laboratory that you are supplying the track in PRINTING SYNC.

With regard to 16mm magnetic stripe, you should remember that while the quality can be better than 16mm optical it does restrict the showing of such prints to those projectors which have a magnetic replay head. When ordering 16mm stripe prints you must request that after making the mute print the laboratory should apply the stripe and transfer from the magnetic master on to the stripe again in printing sync with reference to the sync plop that you specify.

One further point about combined printing. If your film is being printed in more than one reel, which is normal on 35mm for anything over 20 minutes and on 16mm for anything over 50 minutes (although in the latter case each reel may be considerably shorter), you must specify the need for the recording of a sound overlap on the end of the first reel and any subsequent reels, including the penultimate one. This is to compensate for the fact that, when two reels are joined together, the sound advance on the second is cut off and must therefore appear on the end of the first one. So, in terms of 16mm optical, the first 26 frames of reel 2 sound must appear alongside the last 26 frames of reel 1 picture. This is not necessary if it is intended **always** to run the film with the reels separate.

If, however, you run the film in separate reels then each reel that is not the last must be cued for projection change-over. This can be done by the laboratory if requested, otherwise you need the use of a cue-dot marker. This device will apply a mark, which is normally circular, to four successive frames at two separate points near the end of the reel. These appear in the top right-hand corner of the frame, the first cue for 'striking up' the second projector and the second for the actual change-over. Since 16mm projectors can usually take up to 2000 feet of film, it is now unusual to need cue dots on that gauge. However, 35mm films of over 20 minutes would normally require at least one change-over. When applying cue dots you must know the number of frames from the end that they should appear (see Glossary). The easiest way is to mark up in the synchronizer, preferably with the use of a template already prepared on a length of spacer.

DUPLICATING THE MASTER

Once you have obtained an acceptable show copy or release print of the film there remains little for you as the editor to do. If it is expected that a considerable number of prints will be needed then you have to consider whether it is worth the expense of making a duplicate master from your negative to protect the original. As a general rule it is unwise to expect to obtain more than five prints without the danger of damage to the negative. Each time it is handled you run the risk of damage in the form of scratches or blemishes and not all marks can be successfully removed by cleaning and polishing. In any case you should specify that the negative must be cleaned whenever reordering after the initial prints.

Deciding to make a protection dupe is obviously better done early, otherwise you are shutting the door after the horse has bolted. These days there are two basic systems of duplicating from colour material. One is the C.R.I. or Colour Reversal Intermediate, which has the advantage of being one process. The other is to go through interpositive and internegative, which has the drawback of being two stages, but once you have a satisfactory interpositive, successive internegatives can be made from it and you are doubly protected from having to touch the original cut negative.

STORAGE AND RETENTION OF THE MASTER

Do not forget that arrangements must be made for storage of your master material. The cut negative and sound master will be held by the laboratory for a considerable time after completion. You should also keep the magnetic track master and any music and effects track that exists. The dubbing tracks and charts and the cutting copy should be retained until you are absolutely certain that no alternative versions of the film will be made. The rush print trims and magnetic track trims can usually be junked fairly soon, but the original ¼-in. tapes should be kept as protection. Any material that is retained should be stored under conditions that inhibit the natural process of deterioration, i.e. where temperature and humidity are neither too high, nor too low nor tend to fluctuate widely. Every can and box should be clearly labelled and properly secured.

THE DIGITAL ALTERNATIVE

The vast majority of editors are ignorant of the details of electronic technology, even those who were already video-wise. Until recently there has been widespread scepticism regarding the potential for creating a system that has the flexibility of the traditional film method. Digital systems have overcome these doubts to the extent that random access provides the equivalent potential for editors to mould their material in unlimited forms.

Although random access is the most fundamental breakthrough in digital systems, it also allows the editor to experiment in other ways. During editing the soundtrack can be developed and augmented by introducing additional elements, thus allowing the chance to judge the relationship between image and sound as the cut is refined. It is now possible to envisage the situation where, whatever the origination, once the rushes have been digitized, one person and one machine can produce the final presentation copy of the production. This is not only true of the soundtrack but just as feasible in picture post-production. All visual effects and image manipulation can be tested and incorporated once you are convinced that the result is what you need: a distinct advantage over the film optical house method both in predictability and cost.

As I have said elsewhere, the only problem at the moment is the quality of final image, which is just good enough for television broadcast but nowhere near the resolution required for large screen presentation, so we are likely to revert to photographic presentation in cinemas for some time to come. This is a simple process when time-code facilities are incorporated into cine cameras.

For all production that is not intended for the cinema we can already envisage the option of individual production, shot on systems like Hi-8, edited through a personal computer at a fraction of the industrial cost that we are used to.

One way or another, the craft of editing has to be applied, whatever the technology. Different systems are more or less editor-friendly, depending to some extent on how much real editors have been involved in the development. All electronic systems involve a display which combines actual images with graphic symbols to represent the process. The trick is to use the particular methodology to provide you with the maximum control over your material.

The biggest danger with the new technology is analogous to the effect felt when tape joiners were introduced. At that time the editors who had worked all their careers with the finality of cement joins warned that the option of reassembling and trying alternative cuts would make for sloppy editing. Certainly a lack of commitment to the cut can lead to unfocused editing. If you can review several options, the risk is that you choose on the basis of form rather than meaning.

There is, nevertheless, no contest between even the best organized cutting room with the most efficient assistant, and any random access system in offering virtually immediate opportunities to make and compare alternative cuts. With the discipline of good craft no editor is going to turn down this revolution in his or her working environment.

In the end what the audience sees should not be better or worse because of the technology used in post-production. We have come a long way since the days of light boxes and cutting in the hand. All aspiring editors would do well to look at early classics: once you get past the quality of the print there is much to admire. It is an easy self-deception to assume that better editing is related to the latest tools for the job. 'It ain't necessarily so', as the song says. We do well to remember this as we sit in front of our very expensive electronic wizardry.

CONCLUSION

The temptation to behave as if you are in possession of a magician's power when editing is not only dangerous when faced with poor material, it is even more hazardous when the footage is fine. Interfering with the innate rhythm of performance, for instance, is especially dangerous. Satisfying your egotistical needs by ruining the delicate balance achieved by writer, director, photographer, designer and performers is not going to make you a major contributor to the future of audio-visual media.

Editors are not originators, although the effect of their work can be cathartic; they do not provide the thesis for a film but the synthesis they produce is crucial; they are seldom in at the conception, but preside over the confinement and birth. More often than not they must re-motivate the director, for whom the shooting has inevitably been less than ideal.

It is a job for which there is no close analogy, but it has the satisfactions inherent in close collaboration, even if the spotlight is elsewhere, and like all worthwhile occupations, it rewards in proportion to the degree to which you refuse to abuse the power it gives you.

A final warning: if editing gets in your blood it will stay there. There is no cure except more of it, but it will never cease to provide the kind of satisfactions only available to those involved in a few such privileged positions.

The elusive art: some editors and their work   8

It is no accident that less than a handful of editors have been referred to by name in the pages of this book on editing. If this were a book about camerawork or design, much of the text would refer to the individuals who have contributed to the development of their particular craft, but in the case of editing credit has invariably accrued to the directors for innovation and development in the cutting room.

To some degree this is justified by the fact that the best structures and rhythms are achieved by applying ideas about editing to the whole process of mise-en-scène. The editor's contribution depends then on being sensitive to the style determined in the shooting.

One logic suggests that the best person to judge the way editing should be applied on a picture is the director. Kurosawa stated that shooting was only valuable in so far as it gave him something to edit. He was in the habit of shutting himself away, on his own, for weeks at a time, until he was satisfied with a cut. Meanwhile food was passed through a hatch.

Orson Welles was just as obsessive. In an interview with André Bazin he said: 'The one place where I exercise absolute control is in the editing room; it is only then that the director has the power of the true artist . . . I search for the precise rhythm between one-shot and the next. It's a question of the ear: editing is the moment when the film involves a sense of hearing . . . I work very slowly at the editing table . . . I don't know why it takes me so long; I could work forever at the editing of a film . . . The essential thing is the duration of each image, what follows each image; it's the whole eloquence of cinema that one is putting together in the editing room.'

Although directors are not always eager to give credit for the editor's work, most good directors will prefer to use the same editor time and time again once a good relationship has been established.

Even when film became a world industry and each function acquired a separate status, few editors were known by name outside of the studios. Robert Wise, who cut for Welles, only became recognized once he became a director. The same was true of David Lean, and after him Tony Harvey.

MARGARET BOOTH

In Hollywood the first editor to emerge from anonymity was the legendary Margaret Booth, who was so trusted by MGM that she was made post-production supervisor, often overseeing the editing on several films at once. She began her career as a negative cutter in D. W. Griffith's laboratory as a teenager in 1915. A remarkably modest woman, she said in an interview some years ago: 'I was lucky, because I started very young, and I was lucky enough to get with John Stahl. At that time he was one of the top directors in the industry. He taught me a lot. I used to just stand and hand him the film, and he put my name on the screen as editor. Those were silent pictures. When you worked in the silent days you learned about rhythm, and you learned to cut film like poetry. I think that's one of the great accomplishments. Just to learn to cut from sound you can become choppy.'

Margaret Booth was at Goldwyn before Mayer joined to make it MGM in 1924. In her early career she used to assist during the day and make her own versions of sequences from the out-takes at night. Her editor knew that she did this. One day he couldn't get a particular scene to work to his satisfaction. He asked Margaret if she had made her own version. In trepidation she showed him, and he incorporated it in the film without alteration. She never looked back.

She received an Academy Award nomination for the 1936 version of *Mutiny on the Bounty*. She was most proud of that and *Camille* with Greta Garbo, which she cut for George Cukor. Late in her career she was supervising editor on films directed by, amongst others, Sydney Pollack and John Huston.

WILLIAM HORNBECK

If Margaret Booth was the mother of Hollywood editors, then the father was William Hornbeck. His mother, who ran a hotel in Los Angeles, was asked for advice by some people who were looking to build a studio. She told them that the best place was where the Hornbeck family lived, and eventually this led to young William being engaged winding film, in the Mack Sennett Studios laboratory, at the age of fourteen.

Hornbeck learnt his trade through total immersion, cutting 37 films for Sennett between 1926 and 1929! He worked with both Alexander and Zoltan Korda in England in the thirties, and his cutting for Frank Capra on the *Why We Fight* series during the Second World War led to him being the editor on Capra's *It's a Wonderful Life* in 1946. In 1951 he cut *A Place in the*

Sun for George Stevens, for which he received an Academy Award. Subsequently he worked on *Shane* and *Giant* with the same director.

In an interview with Kevin Brownlow for his book *The Parade's Gone By*, Hornbeck had this to say about being an editor: 'Of course, you can't teach anyone how to edit. You can only pass on advice and tips they should follow. These tips are not rules; if you had rules for editing, why, you could put it in a book and anyone could become an editor.' (!)

Margaret Booth was one in a long line of brilliant women editors in America starting with Anne Bauchens who cut forty films for Cecil B. De Mille! The list has included Adrienne Fazan, Verna Fields, Dede Allen, Thelma Schoonmaker and Carol Littleton.

ADRIENNE FAZAN

Adrienne Fazan matched Hornbeck for 'total immersion', cutting 38 shorts at MGM between 1939 and 1944. She was much in demand post war, especially for the musicals which were the staple fare at MGM. Stanley Donen, Vincente Minelli and Gene Kelly relied on her cutting for all their work, and her credits are a roll call of the best of that genre. From *An American in Paris* (1951) to *Gigi* (1958) she gleaned a dozen musical credits in just a few years. You only have to watch *Singin' in the Rain* (1952) to gauge the superb quality of her craft.

VERNA FIELDS

Verna Fields reached the zenith of her editing career when she won an Academy Award for her editing of *Jaws* in 1975, but years before she had become the 'mother cutter' for a generation of young Hollywood directors. Haskell Wexler, Peter Bogdanovich and George Lucas had by then all benefited from her expertise.

Steven Spielberg once said: 'I can give Verna three adjectives to express my meaning about how a scene should feel, and she'll put it into a rough-cut assembly and suddenly it's four adjectives – my three plus hers.'

At the beginning of her career in the forties, Verna concentrated on sound editing. Even when she began to cut picture she alternated for some years between the two, doing sound on *El Cid*, for instance, in the sixties. Quite rightly she considers sound to be important and undervalued. She once said: 'Frankly, if I am a good editor, it is largely due to the years I spent as a sound editor, a very unappreciated job. I think that's where I learned about rhythm and pace because sound is all rhythm and pace – you become terribly conscious of them.'

Universal Pictures recognized Verna's value to them by making her Vice President in charge of post-production. Since then many directors and editors have benefited from her advice.

DEDE ALLEN

The career of Dede Allen is full of beautifully crafted work, even when the film itself has been disappointing. Directors have often gone out of their way to give proper credit for her contribution, including Elia Kazan, Arthur Penn and Sidney Lumet.

We have already discussed in some detail Dede's craft as applied in *Night Moves*, but perhaps her most outstanding achievement was for Warren Beatty on *Reds*, his epic dramatization of John Reed's *Ten Days That Shook the World*, an eyewitness account of the first days of the Russian Revolution. Dede's credit as executive producer confirms that her contribution was highly significant. She and Beatty had met, I believe, when Dede cut *Bonnie and Clyde*, and all the years that he was nursing the idea of the project there was only one editor that he ever contemplated.

Reds is a highly complex combination of documentary interviews, sophisticated political argument, intense personal moments and epic action. It shouldn't work. The fact that it does owes much to Dede's consummate skill, despite Beatty's lack of experience as a director and combining that with playing the leading role himself. Dede's strong

Figure 8.1 Dede Allen.

commitment must have been the salve to Beatty's nervous energy. It took more than two years of her life; such was her dedication to the project.

In effect Dede was at the head of a small army for the post-production of this film. Craig Mckay, who is credited as co-editor, reports that there were 64 employed on post-production, including several associate editors. The interviews of 'witnesses', for instance, were the responsibility of Kathy Wenning, another well established editor.

Observing Dede at work on this film, I was reminded very forcibly that she had begun her career in sound editing, and put great store in the function of the track alongside the images. Whilst I was there a sequence was run in the preview theatre, which had been through a dozen cuts and as many crash mixes. It was a clear lesson that no cut should be locked unless the interrelationship of sound and image has been demonstrated meticulously.

More than that, I felt very humble in the realization that, like all great crafts people, the secret of Dede's success was in the infinite capacity for taking pains to hone the work to perfection. Orson Welles once said that he did not value a piece of work unless it had the smell of sweat. No amount of talent will achieve quality without hard work. But then if you love the work it becomes a labour of love.

THELMA SCHOONMAKER

Thelma Schoonmaker first made her mark with the editing of *Woodstock*, that epic documentary of the famous pop festival, for which she received an Oscar nomination. She has worked with Martin Scorsese on numerous occasions. If *Raging Bull* has obvious editing gymnastics, the more recent *Age of Innocence* demonstrates a surprising range for the director but an even more convincing case for the supreme talent of Thelma.

This period melodrama is realized with a skill that outshines the many examples of this genre that are an indigenous part of British cinema and television. Above all else the economy of narrative expression is cleverly achieved. The use of the dissolve is especially skilful, reaching a level of sparkling bravura in sequences like the honeymoon montage that combines paintings of the period with short pithy scenes that conjure a mood in seconds. Here, as throughout the film, the editing is skilfully complemented by Elmer Bernstein's score; elegant but never intrusive.

Earlier in the film, Thelma is not happy with the speed of a tilt down from the face of Daniel Day Lewis to his hands, clipping the end of a cigar, so a short dissolve is incorporated to shorten the movement and achieve the right pace to punctuate the moment. The most poignant use of dissolves comes at the end of a scene between Ellen (Michelle Pfeiffer) and Newland (Daniel Day Lewis) as she leaves him in a restaurant: first she is dissolved out of the shot and then he 'disappears' leaving the emptiness to express their sorry plight. The use of a plaintive melody, Marble Halls, over a slow

Figure 8.2 Thelma Schoonmaker.

motion shot of businessmen demonstrates the creative courage that all special films need from their editors. Ms Schoonmaker would modestly credit Mr Scorsese for much of the above, but who would wish to detract from the individual contribution to such collaboration?

ANNE COATES

It is not only in the States that women have been prominent amongst the best of editors. In England the prime example is Anne V. Coates, who had only been an editor for eight years when she was chosen by David Lean to cut *Lawrence of Arabia*. Due to a chance encounter with his Assistant Director she learnt that Lean was testing Albert Finney for Lawrence. With a little pushing Anne got to cut the test and Lean chose her on that evidence saying: 'That's the first piece of film I've ever seen cut exactly the way I would have done it.'

Since *Lawrence* in 1962, for which Anne received an Oscar, she has cut a multitude of large and small features, and although she is proud of her contribution to epics she prefers the little films where she can find the heart of a story: 'I think editors don't get a lot written about them because it's not easy to explain what we do. It's what we feel. An instinct. You have that flair and instinct – I guess you're born with it.'

'I like a well run editing room and well trained assistants, but once it's running smoothly I like a pleasant atmosphere . . . Of course you worry, we all worry, but you should enjoy the work.'

These remarks of Anne Coates are from the book *First Cut . . . Conversations with Film Editors* by Gabriella Oldham, where Anne is the sole non-American since she has worked a great deal in the States. However she appreciates some of the British practices, like having the sound editor on board from the start of editing and working together, as picture and sound interact with each other in the process. She cites the importance of this on a film like *Greystoke, The Legend of Tarzan*, where creating convincing ape noises and orchestrating the natural sounds of the jungle were an essential part of the editing. Certainly the rhythm and flow of this film are clear evidence of the special instinct that Anne Coates has for cutting.

CAROL LITTLETON

Yet another eminent female editor is Carol Littleton, who has cut for Lawrence Kasdan ever since *Body Heat* in 1981. She also cut *E.T.: The Extraterrestrial* for Steven Spielberg. As a music student in Paris during the New Wave, Carol discovered cinema. It was Pontecorvo's *Battle of Algiers* that convinced her that she wanted to be involved in movies, recognizing the special impact that somehow combined the qualities that she enjoyed in music and literature.

There is a particular quality about the way Carol cuts dialogue scenes, especially what you might call domestic interiors. It is as if we are watching the performance of chamber music, where the score is carefully constructed to emphasize the interplay of harmony and discord. Watch the group of friends in *The Big Chill* or the strange family of Geena Davis in *The Accidental Tourist* or the family meal at the beginning of *E.T.* Of course much is a given of the direction, but Carol controls the musicality in a way that is as impressive as the work of Dede Allen. Although we often denigrate such dialogue scenes as uncinematic or merely expositional, the truth is that the emotional heart of a good film is often centred in such scenes, and very few editors have the skill to deliver the dramatic pulse with conviction.

ROBERTO PERPIGNANI

It is possible to discern a European feel in Carol Littleton's work; partly, perhaps, as a result of the time she spent studying in Paris and partly her background in music. Music figures in the lives of most good editors, whether or not they can play an instrument. You can sense the musicality in Roberto Perpignani, for instance, the man who has worked many times

Figure 8.3 Roberto Perpignani.

with the Taviani brothers. Perhaps his studies of fine art were even more formative for Roberto; certainly this would have provided the basis for an understanding with Bernardo Bertolucci, that most painterly of directors, with whom he worked in his early career as an editor. Bertolucci has said: 'Perpignani was forever looking for the freedom one might find in poetry . . . he tended to let himself be completely overtaken by the material. We hit it off perfectly from the word go and carried on working together for ages bouncing ideas off one another all the time.'

Perpignani began his love affair with cinema by insinuating himself into the cutting room of Orson Welles when the latter was editing his film of Kafka's *The Trial*. From then on there was only going to be one career for Roberto.

After the period with Bertolucci, Perpignani began his most productive collaboration which continues to this day, that as editor for the Taviani brothers. When he cut their first masterpiece, *Padre Padrone*, Roberto had already edited three films for them. Since then *The Night of San Lorenzo, Kaos, Good Morning Babylon* and *Night Sun* have all given this enviable editor remarkable opportunities to demonstrate his skill.

As with all good editors, the art conceals art, a fact in this case which I was lucky enough to have confirmed directly when Roberto gave a workshop at the Poitiers Festival a few years ago, during which he showed the rushes from part of *The Night of San Lorenzo* alongside his first and final cuts. The energy of the original material allowed Roberto to create a rhythm that disguised continuity problems and overcame spatial and narrative shortcomings. It was not that the material was poor, more that the editor needed imagination and skill to construct an effective realization of the action.

Although Roberto has worked with many famous directors, including Bellochio, Bolognini, Jancso and Patroni Griffi, it is the work with Paolo and Vittorio Taviani that has established him amongst the most respected editors in Europe.

Incidentally, Bertolucci's current editor is Gabriella Cristiani, who made the transition from cutting on film to working with random access technology. She, and a number of other traditionalists, are like converts to a new faith: wishing it had been invented years ago.

LOU LOMBARDO

But of course technology is only a means to an end. As Lou Lombardo puts it: 'I don't give a damn if he can work the machine, can he cut the film? . . . Equipment will change but talent is going to be the same.' This from the man who cut *The Wild Bunch* for Sam Peckinpah and many films for Robert Altman including the ground-breaking *Brewster McCloud*, *McCabe and Mrs Miller*, *The Long Goodbye* and *California Split*.

Lou is an instinctive editor: 'You run it, you feel it and you mark it. With me it's all touch and feel. It is all emotion with me. If it demands lots of cuts, then that's what I do, or if the emotion is there in one set-up, I'll let that play. The film talks to you, it tells you.'

Of course Mr Lombardo, like all good editors, has the film running in his head 24 hours a day: 'I might be home eating dinner and I say to myself, "Goddamn, that's it, that's what will work!" I'm thinking about it and I've solved a problem.'

For *The Wild Bunch* Lou even directed the second unit material of the Bunch being shot at, since Peckinpah had not covered it, except in wide shot. He then constructed a cut of the main gunfight sequence that lasted for 21 minutes. 'It's a ballet' said Lou, who stretched or truncated real time to suit the feel of each moment; this by a combination of slowing down or speeding up individual shots, and by artificially extending movement through intercutting and returning to a shot almost at the frame that he cut from previously. The final cut of this sequence is 4 minutes, but it retains this balletic and extended feel. There are 3642 cuts in *The Wild Bunch*, still believed to be a record.

If his work with Peckinpah broke new ground in manipulation of the image, then the films that Lou Lombardo cut for Altman certainly explored new territory in the use of sound. Reading between the lines, Altman may have had the novel ideas, but it was Lou who had to make them work in practice. The concept that Altman had, that the audience should be presented with all conversations in a room and tune in to those lines which they choose to hear, had to be modified so that there was a balance that favoured the key speakers. 'What Bob forgot, or wouldn't accept, is that you are a human being. A machine can't do that, you hear it all.'

Yet there is no doubt, as I have mentioned elsewhere, that the questions Altman asked about the function of sound encouraged a radical approach to the use of dialogue and indeed other sound, both in and beyond the frame. Lou Lombardo must have played a major part in making the ideas work.

ANTONY GIBBS

The generation of American editors of which Dede Allen is a part have given considerable credit for the inspiration for their work to Antony Gibbs, the English editor of films directed by, amongst others, Tony Richardson, Nicolas Roeg and Richard Lester.

There is a daring and energetic quality to Tony Gibbs' work, especially in some sequences in *The Loneliness of the Long Distance Runner*, *Tom Jones*, *The Knack* and *Performance*, which must have given a shot of adrenalin to aspiring editors on both sides of the Atlantic at the time.

Dede ascribes her work on *Bonnie and Clyde* directly to the influence of Tony Gibbs. It may be culturally surprising, but stylistically it seems entirely apposite that Gibbs and Lombardo should co-edit *In Country* for Norman Jewison in 1989. The cinema of Peckinpah and Roeg are not a million miles from each other.

A whole chapter could be written about the apprentices who have been with Dede Allen and made it big. Dede herself gives much of the credit to the likes of Arthur Penn who gave a solid base to feature film editing at the time in New York. Craig Mckay was mentioned earlier, and amongst other former assistants are Stephen Rotter and Jerry Greenberg.

RICHARD MARKS

Perhaps the outstanding graduate of the Dede Allen Academy is Richard Marks. After only a few credits he became co-editor on *The Godfather, Part II* and a few years later Coppola made him supervising editor on *Apocalypse Now!*, a job which was to occupy him for nearly three years. This was a test of stamina as well as skill, but Richard was up to it. He says that confidence is very important and cites the example that Dede proposed him to Alan Pakula for *Klute* when he was only 24. He decided to turn it down because he didn't feel ready for it.

On the other hand, he remembers Dede giving him a sequence to cut on *Little Big Man* whilst she was away on location in Montana. He sweated over that 'little' sequence (with 30 000 feet of rushes) for nearly three weeks before she returned. When Dede saw it her comments were so positive it did wonders for his confidence, and when she later proposed that he be the second editor he knew his career was duly launched. 'Dede is one of the greatest teachers I have ever known.'

Richard Marks acknowledges a debt to Francis Ford Coppola both in terms of the experiments with form that had to be tried on both *Godfather* and *Apocalypse*, and because of Coppola's impatience with technology which makes him buy it, build it or invent it if a new device will help with the process.

In contrast to the high-tech and sophisticated post-production of the modern large scale feature film, the work of the documentary editor has always been a cottage industry. Indeed the early documentary film-makers often did without the services of the specialist editor.

HELEN VAN DONGEN

Helen van Dongen first worked with Robert Flaherty on *The Land*, which was a process of jumping in the deep end with an initial 70 000 feet of rushes, later to become much more. Helen had begun working with Joris Ivens in Holland in 1929. It was a wonderful apprenticeship on films like *The Bridge*, *Borinage* and *The New Earth*. Later she followed Ivens to the USA and came to Flaherty's notice. However she was not prepared for the lack of precise instructions from Flaherty, who had no idea what form his material might take and was incapable of putting his thoughts into words.

By the time they worked on *Louisiana Story* Helen knew how to interpret his every gesture: 'What he did not say in a discussion was written all over his face during a screening. The way he put his hand through his hair, or smoked his eternal cigarette, or shuffled his chair, spoke more than a torrent of words.' Fortunately we have Helen van Dongen's analysis of the editing of *Louisiana Story* in Karel Reisz's *Technique of Film Editing*.

STEWART McALLISTER

It is not usual for the editor of documentaries to have the luxury of working on location, as Helen van Dongen did with Flaherty, but another editor whose collaboration with his director allowed him to influence the shooting was Stewart McAllister, whose work, including that with Humphrey Jennings, is celebrated in Dai Vaughan's book *Portrait of an Invisible Man*.

McAllister studied fine art before getting into films, and there must have been considerable common ground to share with Jennings, who never gave up his primary desire to be a real artist, and for whom film was a way of earning a living rather than a calling.

If they were 'amateurs' in the true sense of loving what they did, the films they did together are perhaps a salutary lesson to set beside the crass 'professionalism' that surrounds us today. At least in Dai Vaughan's own editing that spirit lives on and many a director has reason to be grateful for the special qualities that Dai has brought to the editing of their documentaries.

Figure 8.4 Stewart McAllister.

Much work could be done to unravel the contribution of other editors to the quality of good films. What, for instance, did Henri Colpi bring to the complex form of Resnais' work, especially *Hiroshima mon Amour* and *Last Year in Marienbad*? How symbiotic is the working relationship between John Schlesinger and his editor Jim Clark, who often work together from the script stage? Does Tony Lawson encourage Nic Roeg in complex and often disturbing story structures?

There are very particular qualities which made Ernest Walter not only a favourite with the likes of George Cukor, Robert Wise and Billy Wilder, but also gained him the respect of his peers amongst editors; just as he still gains the affection of each new generation of students at the National Film and Television School in England.

Part of the difficulty in analysing the real contribution of editors is their modesty. Much of their value is destined to remain hidden, but in an age when speed is becoming more valued than craft, it is important that editors themselves show a visible pride in their work, so that the next generation realizes the potential value of editing to the art of film.

Glossary

A and B cutting The practice of conforming original material (either reversal master or negative) on two separate rolls so that optical effects can be made by double printing. Thus dissolves are assembled to include the overlaps of the two shots to allow cross-fading during printing. Not to be confused with **Chequerboard** cutting.

A and B wind The alternative modes of winding film that has single perforations. Important when related to duping material from different sources and for indicating the form required when ordering optical sound transfers.

Academy standards Standards established by the American Academy of Motion Picture Arts and Sciences and recognized by manufacturers of equipment and film stock, e.g. the gap or pitch between perforations on stock and the corresponding alignment of sprocket wheels in editing machinery and projectors is standardized, as is the relationship between camera and projector apertures.

Acetate The base material used to 'carry' film emulsion. Its value lies in being 'slow burning' which makes it much safer than the old nitrate base.

Action 1 The picture material as opposed to the separate soundtrack used in cutting.
2 The word used by the director to cue the start of a take.
3 The activity being filmed.

Action cutting (or cutting on action) The practice of using movement as the bridging mechanism at a cut, to allow a smooth change of angle and/or size of the subject in the shot. Also used to convey continuity of movement when the subject enters and exits the frame. This technique is only valid where the motivation for the cut is seen to coincide with such movement.

ADR (Automatic Dialogue Replacement) The common acronym for the process of re-recording dialogue which was not of an acceptable quality in the original synchronous recording. (*See* **Post-synchronization**.) Still some-times referred to as looping because of the earlier method of preparing sections of the track as loops.

Ambient sound   The general background sound to any shooting situation, without which the dialogue or other specific sound seems to exist in a vacuum. Effective sound recording takes this into account and may require the use of a separate microphone to convey a sense of the 'space' in which the scene is occurring. In tracklaying separate background tracks may be required to compensate for a sync recording that has used only close perspective directional microphones.

American cut (or concertina cut)   The practice of cutting together two shots of different size on the same camera axis. Such cuts are very effectively used by Akira Kurosawa; *see* description of use in *Sanjuro* and *The Seven Samurai* in Chapter 2.

Answer print (or trial print)   The print that represents the first attempt to grade (or 'time') the cut film correctly. The laboratory may make several tries at this before submitting such an 'answer' for approval. Its function is to allow for discussion of detailed corrections of colour balance, density and matching for the making of the show or release prints. It is also an essential stage before the making of a master dupe positive or colour reversal inter-mediate when a considerable number of copies are known to be required.

Aspect ratio (or frame format)   The dimensions of the film frame in a ratio of height to width. In 16mm 1:1·33 is normal. Wide-screen formats are 1:1·66 or 1:1·85, and, by squeezing the image, anamorphic processes provide ratios that include 1:2, 1:2·2 and 1:2·35. Since High Definition Television is now established as a ratio of 1:7·5 this is likely to become the dominant shooting aspect ratio for the future in both film and tape. It is imperative that cutting takes place under conditions that imitate the intended ratio, otherwise pacing of action in and out of frame and the elimination of unwanted areas can provide problems, especially where the picture has been shot without a mask in the camera, giving excess image which will not be seen in the final print.

Assembly   The first stage in cutting after synchronizing the rushes. Usu-ally taken to mean the joining together of chosen takes in script order, or in documentary the usable material, in shooting or chronological order.

Asynchronous sound   All sound which is relevant to the circumstances of a shot but which is not synchronized to the action.

Atmosphere   Usually applied to the sound that is appropriate to the background of a scene. The more general it is the less use it has. 'Atmos' should be specially recorded as a wild track to enable precise use in tracklaying. When an atmosphere contains specific references to the picture it is bad practice to rely on library recordings to substitute for the real thing. Water sounds, for instance, have an infinite variation which relate to distance, intensity and quality.

Back projection (or rear projection) The technique of using pre-photographed images as background to the action. Preparation of such material may involve the editor. The print to be used for such projection must be obtained on double-perforation stock with negative perforations to ensure steadiness. In the electronic mode Blue Screen or 'Chroma-key' is used to achieve similar control over the relationship between foreground and background elements in the image. With sophisticated post-production tools the most complex combining of action and background can be achieved. The actors need never leave the studio; only the cameraperson has to go to the Caribbean island demanded by the script!

Background action The action in a shot that is not intended to be the focus of attention but that requires careful matching if it is relevant to intercut material.

Background music This can be the bane of an editor's life. Where a scene is shot that includes music being performed or reproduced in the background, the intercutting of the relevant action may be inhibited by the effect on such music. In fiction films it is often the practice to shoot scenes with a source of music visible but not actually playing and adding the music in the final mixing of the film.

Big close-up (B.C.U.) A shot of less than the complete head of the subject or a detail of an object.

Black Video tape that has been prepared for use by recording a signal that produces a black image when replayed as opposed to the 'snow' visible when you play a blank or virgin tape. For most purposes video tape must be blacked and time-coded before use in editing.

Bleed, Bleeding Fuzziness around the edges of an element in the film image. A term most frequently applied to unclear superimposed titles and matted shots.

Blimp The soundproof cover on a camera which prevents the noise of the camera mechanism being audible on the recorded sync soundtrack. Modern cameras are mostly self-blimped although this does not necessarily make them soundproof if the camera is excessively noisy or the acoustics for the recording are bad.

Bloop, Blooping The technique of covering or removing a V-shaped section of the soundtrack area to avoid a bump or click, especially at joins. This can be done by applying an opaque piece of paper or inking across the relevant section of optical track. With magnetic track it is usually achieved either by cutting out a V-section or by removing the oxide with acid. Whichever method is used, extreme care is required to avoid either damaging the track or obliterating wanted sound.

Blow-up Converting 16mm to 35mm by laboratory process (can be applied to a similar process with 8mm). The term is also used where the frame is optically enlarged so that the image is made to correspond to a closer shot. This is sometimes done where it is realized that the original shot is too inclusive. The resultant degradation in quality may not be worth the cost.

Bridging shot The kind of shot that allows a smoother or more acceptable transition than a direct cut. Sometimes useful in pacing the junction between sequences but it can be an excuse for a badly conceived structure.

Build-up Dramatic cutting leading to a climax in the action. The term is also used colloquially in the cutting room for the insertion of frames to designate a missing section or shot in the cutting copy or work print.

Butt splice A join between two pieces of film without an overlap – facilitated by the application of tape across the end frame of each section.

Buzz track Sound that represents the 'presence' in a room or space in which a recording usually of a voice or voices has been made. Most commonly obtained to allow insertion or bridging when laying up dialogue or narration.

Camera sheet (or negative report) The information on a standard form that describes the precise technical details of shooting for laboratory reference, including film emulsion, day or night, good and bad takes, footages etc.

Caption Title, descriptive text or translation placed between shots or superimposed on them.

Caption generator Electronic means of inserting or overlaying captions on a video image. Most useful for sub-titling foreign dialogue.

Cell-side The opposite side to the emulsion on a piece of film, usually recognizable because it is shiny and reflective.

Cement joiner (or cement splicer) Allows for joining of pieces of film by overlapping, and the application of a form of glue or cement. Now super-seded in cutting rooms but still predominant in negative and original cutting. Also used for repairs by projectionists since it gives a longer lasting and more reliable join. It involves the removal of frames from the shots to be joined.

Centre track The standard position of the audio signal on magnetic film. *See* **Edge track**.

Change-over The co-ordination of the start of a new reel of film with the end of the previous one during projection (facilitated by reference to **Cue dots**), so that the film appears to run continuously.

Cheat The repositioning of a character or object in a way convenient for taking a shot that is not consistent with the positioning in other shots. Allows for reverse angles and better visibility of facial expressions, etc. It may be made necessary by shooting in restricted space and/or the limits presented by the angle of view of the lens.

Chequerboard Method of conforming original or negative to cutting copy or work print whereby **every** shot is put on to alternate rolls with spacing in the other roll. Primarily used to eliminate splices in printing. Also allows for fades and dissolves during printing. *See* **A and B cutting**.

Chrominance The colour characteristic of a video signal relating to both hue and saturation (*see* **Luminance**).

Cinching, Cinch marks The result of a roll of film being pulled tight on a core or spool. The friction in the roll causes scratches where dust or abrasive particles are present.

Cinéma-Vérité (or Ciné-Vérité) A style of film-making begun in Europe in the 1950s, in which the use of light-weight cameras and recorders encouraged a direct approach to the capturing of 'reality'. Now taken to mean an unstructured approach to the filming of documentary material with little or no attempt to influence the events being filmed.

Cinex-strip (or Cinex) The printing of a few frames of each shot in a camera roll as reference for grading or timing the material, thus determining the optimum printer-light.

Circled takes The practice of circling the preferred takes listed on the **Camera sheet**, to indicate to the laboratory which ones should be printed.

Clapperboard (or slate) The device to aid synchronization, filmed at the beginning or end of each take. The 'clapping' of the hinged section provides an exact visual and aural reference point. It also gives slate and take numbers.

Click track A substitute for a metronome in the form of a soundtrack with regular clicks inserted, enabling the conductor to retain the correct tempo in recording music to the cut film.

Close-up (C.U.) Taken to mean the complete head of a person. M.C.U., B.C.U. and E.C.U. are tighter versions of the basic C.U. shot. With a small object a C.U. would mean that the object fills the frame. Applied to a large object it can refer to the most significant detail filling that frame.

Code numbers (edge numbers or rubber-numbers) A method of numbering film and/or magnetic stock to provide a reference for logging purposes and corresponding sync. Usually consists of 6 or 8 letters and numbers which progress at 1-foot intervals by a digit at a time. On 16mm, coding machines can give numbering at 6-inch intervals.

Colour correction The process by which film is adjusted for correct colour balance in the printing. It must be specifically requested when sending exposed material to the laboratories since colour rush prints are normally supplied at a mean printer-light without attempts being made to rectify variations in exposure and colour values.

C.R.I. (Colour Reversal Intermediate) This is made when a dupe is required either for optical work or protection of master material. It eliminates the need for the interpositive/internegative process although this may still be the preferred method.

Combined print (composite print or married print) A print that combines the matching picture and sound of a completed film.

Compilation film A film edited from material gathered from a number of sources on the same subject, possibly including specially shot film but also consisting of library footage and material duplicated from other films. The coherence of such films usually depends upon a linking narration or voice-over. Prime examples are documentaries on war and obituaries.

Complementary angles Shots that are matched between two or more subjects in the same scene and are calculated to cut together.

Component video A video signal that keeps the red, green and blue components separate for high quality recording, each colour having its own cable.

Composite print *see* **Combined print**

Composite video A video signal that combines the three colours that make up the whole picture, encoding them at the camera and decoding them at the recorder. As this system only requires one cable it is far more common than component video.

Compression The squeezing or reducing of data, for instance digital video images, for storage and easy manipulation.

Concertina cut *see* **American cut**

Conforming Process of cutting master or original negative to match the cutting copy or work print in preparation for printing.

Contact-printer Machine for printing material where the negative or original is kept in contact with the raw stock. 'Continuous contact-printers' are used for printing rushes at high speed.

Continuity Usually describes the effort to maintain consistency in the details of the staging of scenes for the camera. This includes continuity of movement and of the relationship between action and dialogue, and details of dress and any placing or use of objects. The continuity person is charged specifically with scrupulously observing such detail, pointing out any deficiency and recording the details of each take, including deviations, in the continuity notes. A really observant continuity person will also pick up problems of matching between shots (angles, eyelines, etc.) and even problematical variations in lighting. The value of this function in the filming of drama cannot be overestimated.

Continuity cutting The editing of sequences so that the action and progression of the scene matches the natural flow captured in the various shots, thus avoiding a disjointed effect. Where a scene is shot in a variety of set-ups this may entail judicious shortening of dialogue and/or action whilst maintaining the desired smoothness and plausibility.

Contrast Photographically, contrast is the ratio between the most dense and least dense areas expressed in terms of **Gamma**. Contrast can vary between 'flat' where there is little range of tones, and **High contrast** ('contrasty') where there is only very slight gradation between the lightest and darkest areas of the image. Printing can vary the contrast range, but only within the limits established by the original material.

Core (or bobbin) A plastic centre on which film is wound. In most cases the core has an indentation for engaging with the 'tooth' on the take-up mechanism and is designated as female. Exceptionally, 'male' cores may be necessary where the mechanism being used incorporates the indentation or slot.

Cover The collection of shots taken for each particular sequence. Conventional cover includes everything from wide shots to matching close-ups.

Crab shot A shot that covers lateral movement from the side. The camera faces the action but moves in a crab-like fashion.

Crane shot Literally a shot that incorporates a vertical movement obtained by mounting the camera on a crane. This facilitates elevation from ground level to a height above the action.

Credits The titles on a film which 'credit' crew and cast involved in the production.

Crosscut The method of **Intercutting** the primary elements in dramatic sequences, especially where the action is leading to a dramatic climax, e.g. crosscutting between the participants in a gun fight.

Cue Each section that is broken out of the cutting copy for post-synchronization. In the notes that are prepared each cue will have a number corresponding to that marked on the film. Also used electronically to describe the process of preparing an edit.

Cue dots The marks, usually appearing in the top right-hand corner of the frame, that allow the projectionist to change over between reels. A cue-dot marker normally removes a circular area of the emulsion over four frames. These cue dots are placed at two set points towards the end of a reel, to allow for both starting the projector and changing over the lamp. The standard position is for the first set of dots to start at 192 frames from the end of the reel and for the second set to start at 24 frames.

Cue line The line that is drawn on the cutting copy to provide a visual cue for post-synchronization.

Cue sheet The various forms of detailed and enumerated information sheets, used as reference for different stages in the post-production sound-recording processes. Thus cue sheets are used for post-sync, music recording and for the final mixing of the film.

Cutaway The much maligned – perhaps justifiably – kind of shot which, as its name implies, shows a person or object that requires cutting away from the dominant focus of a scene. It is used to bridge shots that do not cut together and to allow for editing/shortening of the action in a continuous shot. A form of 'cheating' that some film-makers consider dishonest.

Cutting copy The **Work print** of a film or, more specifically, the progressively evolving structured visuals of a film.

Cutting on action *see* **Action cutting**

Dailies *see* **Rushes**

DAT (Digital Audio Tape) As its name implies, a miniaturized high quality recording medium; an alternative to the traditional ¼-inch tape.

Day for Night (D/N)   The shooting of scenes which, by control of exposure, use of filters and specified processing requirements, gives the effect of night despite being shot during daylight. The editor must be aware of such material both in assessing the rushes and in controlling any subsequent printing.

Definition   The quality of an image as it is affected by variations in focus, exposure and lighting. The term is also used in relation to the clarity of sound. The definition of picture and sound can also be affected by the circumstances of projection or reproduction.

Degausser   A device which erases recordings or demagnetizes tape, film or sound heads. Also used on tape joiners which have become magnetized.

Density   The variable degree of light-stopping power in a photographic image.

Desaturation   The reduction of the degree of colour in a film image resulting eventually in a monochromatic effect.

Develop   The process which renders the latent image on film into a permanent image by use of a chemical reaction.

Diagonal cut   The method used on magnetic film to reduce the noise at a splice, facilitated by a guillotine on the splicer which is set at an oblique angle to the frame.

Dialogue   Speech that is obviously or apparently emanating from the person or persons visible in the scene. It is either seen in sync or heard over other characters involved in the scene.

Digital/Digitize   A technology and technique which records and stores for subsequent reproduction and manipulation, audio and video information by a system of sampling the basic components, e.g. the pixel in an image. By compression, a sufficient amount of material can be digitized to allow for convenient editing.

Direct Cinema   The type of film that depends on pictures and sound indigenous to the situations being filmed. The film 'speaks for itself' without the superimposing, by voice-over or other means, of the attitude of the film-maker. Direct Cinema also puts severe limitations on the way the material can be manipulated in the cutting room. It implies a more disciplined approach than its immediate precursor **Cinéma-Vérité**.

Discontinuity   A fault in the **Continuity** during the filming of a scene.

Dissolve (or mix)   The effect produced by the fading out at the end of a shot overlapping with the fading in of the next (*see* **Fades**). Can be produced in the camera but now almost exclusively created by optical dupe or in A and B printing. Originally used to mean change of time and/or place, but it has developed into a general facet of film language that complements the pacing or mood of a film. Dissolves can vary in length from less than a second upwards. However, A and B dissolves can only be obtained at specific lengths usually ranging from 8 to 96 frames (⅓ second to 4 seconds).

Dolly A platform with wheels on which the camera is mounted to allow smooth movement.

Double-head projection Running the film in the cutting room or on a projector with the soundtrack separate from the picture.

Drop-shadow Used in titling to improve definition of lettering, especially when titles are superimposed over live action backgrounds. Provides a darker area below and to the side of the titles.

Dub The process of re-recording sound, specifically to replace dialogue or effects. The term is a source of some confusion, since in England dubbing is coterminous with mixing (*see* **Mix**), while in the USA it refers only to post-synchronization (particularly in the making of foreign language versions).

Dubbing cue sheet The written information that acts as a guide for the sound mixer. It is known in the USA as the mixing cue sheet because of the variations in terminology referred to above.

Dubbing session Specifically a dialogue-replacement recording session in the USA. The term is used more generally in England to describe the processes involved in mixing the sound on a film.

Dupe, Duping To make or the making of duplicate material from an existing negative, print or reversal master.

Dye-transfer A system of printing that involves the production of three colour separation positives (yellow, cyan and magenta). These dyed images or matrices are then transferred to blank film and allow for the printing of large numbers of release prints without further use of the original negative. This is a Technicolor process which has now unfortunately been discontinued.

Echo chamber/plate A source of reverberation attached to a sound-recording studio, connected to the mixing desk to facilitate instant and variable use when required.

EDL (Edit Decision List) A computerized listing, or printout of the same, of the edits (otherwise known as events) in a sequence or of a whole film or video. This is essential for efficient on-lining.

Edge numbers *see* **Code numbers, Key numbers**

Edge stripe A magnetic stripe used to carry sound as an alternative to optical sound, usually in **Combined prints**.

Edge track The standard position in the USA for the magnetic sound. *See* **Centre track**.

Editing bench (or sync-bench) The table that normally carries the synchronizer and rewinds when such are incorporated in the cutting process.

Effects (F.X.) *see* **Sound effects**

Emulsion The coating that is carried by the film base. In its unexposed form it is light-sensitive and has chemical properties which allow the development of the latent image during processing. In its printed form, the emulsion gives form to the photographed image both in terms of density and variations in colour.

Emulsion position   This refers to the geometry of the film image. The image is correctly viewed either through the base or with the emulsion to the eye.

Equalization   The alteration of sound frequencies to achieve a better balance, or even to remove unwanted signals from existing recordings. It is especially valuable in improving the clarity of voice tracks.

Establishing shot   The wide shot of a location or set that presents the full context of a scene to the viewer, thus allowing subsequent fragments of the scene to be perceived within this totality. In editing it is often more effective to refrain from showing this until it is relevant dramatically.

E.C.U.   Extreme close-up.

E.L.S.   Extreme long shot.

Exposition   The early scenes in a film which lay the foundations of situation and characters in the plot.

Fades   Visual or aural gradual revelation or obliteration of the image or sound: thus fade-in and fade-out. These effects are often used coterminously on both picture and sound but should also be considered useful when treated separately. Most conventionally, fades indicate the beginning and end of scenes.

Filter   Device used in shooting, usually in front of the camera lens, to accentuate or reduce specific aspects of the image to be photographed, e.g. colour and density. Also the device which alters the reproduction of selected frequencies in sound recording.

Final mix   The combination of various soundtracks into one composite master, often after the intermediate stage of pre-mixing.

Fine cut   The later stages of picture editing (after the **Rough-cut**) when only minor adjustments are being contemplated before the final cut is agreed upon.

Fine grain   The term is applied to emulsion that provides a high definition and resolution of the image by incorporating extra-fine particles of silver. It is consequently used in making master duplicate material especially for optical work. More appropriately applied to black-and-white film.

Flashback   Shots or sequences that convey events or information which precede the time established as the present in a film.

Flop-over   Reversing the image laterally. It can be valuable for restoring 'eyelines' or continuity of movement to the correct left-to-right appearance. Achieved by optical process in the laboratory.

Focus   The definition of an image, both as photographed and in projection. Loss of focus or differential focus in the image can have a crucial effect on the usability of material when editing.

Foley   Common term for the process of post-synchronization of sound effects, often incorporating the use of a Foley artist who specializes in this work.

Footage The accumulated material for a film. Also the measurement of film and the precise reading at a given point in a reel indicated on a **Footage counter**.

Footage counter A mechanical or electronic device that indicates the progressive number of feet in a reel of film being run on an editing device or projector.

Frame format *see* **Aspect ratio**

Freeze-frame The repeated printing of a single frame for a predetermined number of times, thus 'freezing' the action. Can be used in conjunction with or separate from part of the action before or after the particular frame by including part of the original shot in the dupe.

Front projection Inclusion of separate material as background to the action of a scene by projecting it from in front of the scene being filmed. Usually incorporates a special screen behind the action and supplementary lighting on the foreground subjects.

Gamma A way of measuring photographic contrast. It equals the density increase in an image divided by the log of the exposure increase over a specified range.

Gate Generally the section in a camera or projector mechanism where the film passes behind the lens. More exactly the hinged section that carries the pressure plate.

Gauge A convenient reference to film size by measurement of its width. Thus 8mm, 16mm, 35mm and 70mm.

Generations Each time video is copied it is referred to as 'going down a generation'. There is an inevitable deterioration in image quality through successive generations.

Gradation The variation in tonal values in a photographic image.

Grading (or timing) The work done by the grader or (in the USA) timer in selecting the colour balance and intensity and the overall density to be applied to film when preparing for printing. In practice the grader aims at a programme of values which are cued automatically in the consecutive exposure of scenes on the printer.

Graininess, Grainy The apparently distinguishable particles in an image where poor **Resolution** has caused the silver particles to group together in a way that provides an unsatisfactory rendition of the original scene. It can be caused by sub-standard lenses, slow stock or inadequate exposure or lighting.

Hardware Machinery or equipment, usually related to electronic, specifically computer-based technology. As opposed to Software.

Head The start or front of a roll of film. Also the device which enables sound to be picked up from a track passing in front of or over it.

Headphones (or head-set) Small sound receivers which fit over the head and are adjustable to the position of the ears of the user. Used by recordists as a monitoring device and also valuable for artists and conductors when recording post-sync and music.

High contrast Applied to photographic images that do not exhibit a gradual range from dark to light. Also applied to stock that is designed specifically to exhibit this lack of gradation. Especially suited to the shooting of titles and optical sound.

High key Images that exhibit a tendency to lighter tones. Also lighting that is calculated to achieve such an effect.

HDTV (High Definition Television) A wide-screen high-resolution video system, with more than double the lines of normal television. Now taken over by the digital revolution which maximizes the potential for image (and sound) quality.

Hold Takes that may be printed later but are not required for immediate use. Also the static section at the beginning and end of camera movement which is invaluable in cutting.

Horse The device on an **Editing bench** that is designed for mounting rolls of film by the insertion of rods through apertures in vertical sections. Especially valuable when working with many short sections of film.

Hot splicer (or heat splicer) A joiner that incorporates a heating device in the elements. These are clamped together to increase the efficiency of the cement that is bonding the two sections of film.

In sync The state of picture and sound material when they are in correct relationship to each other with regard to synchronization.

In the can A colloquial expression to describe completion of shooting either of a shot, a sequence or the whole film.

Inching The process of moving the film frame by frame through a transport mechanism for close examination.

Incoming shot The shot **after** any cut as opposed to the previous or outgoing shot.

Insert A shot that is designed to be cut into the body of another shot or sequence that focuses attention on a particular aspect or detail of the scene.

Intercut Editing by juxtaposition of elements that are related by time, place or action or where the establishment of such a relationship depends on such juxtaposition.

Intermediate A process in the laboratory that is necessary or valuable in proceeding from the original form of the material to some required duplicate – thus 'internegative' and 'interpositive'.

Intermittent movement The frame-by-frame movement in a camera, projector or printer that allows the recording or reproduction of images which, when combined, give the illusion of continuous movement when such movement proceeds above the speed at which the eye can perceive the individual static frames.

Iris An adjustable device that controls the amount of light passing through a lens. Also the effect gained by obscuring the outer area of the frame both in the camera or in printing. Used as a substitute for fades although this practice was more common in the silent era.

Jack   A convenient plug device for connecting into sockets during sound recording and reproduction.

Jog   Video equivalent of inching in film, i.e. viewing frame by frame, forwards or backwards.

Join   The splicing of two sections of film at a cut.

Joiner   *see* **Cement joiner; Tape joiner**

Jump cut   Strictly speaking the effect obtained by removing a section from the middle of a shot and joining the remaining head and tail of the shot, thus provoking a jump in the action. Loosely applied to any such abrupt change that implies a missing part of the original visual continuity.

Key numbers (or edge numbers)   Numbers that are exposed on to film stock at regular intervals, and that progress by one digit each time. Printed on to copies they provide a co-ordinating reference for matching. On 16mm they usually occur each 6 inches or 20 frames, and on 35mm every foot or 16 frames. When checking work or rush prints, it is important to ensure that these numbers have been duplicated. Where no code numbers have been applied, key numbers can provide an alternative for logging.

Kuleshov effect   Named after experiments conducted by Lev Kuleshov in Russia in the 1920s. In general this term describes the effects obtained through juxtaposition in editing – most notably Kuleshov proved that the interpretation of human facial expressions can be changed by altering the shots with which they are intercut. So he showed that 'meaning' is not dependent on a shot alone but also on the shot or shots placed around it.

Latent image   The image formed on photographic emulsion by exposure to light. It is made visible by developing the film.

Laying tracks   *see* **Tracklaying**

Leader   Extra film placed at the front or end of material which acts as protection to the body of the film and also functions as identification and for threading through editing machines and projectors. It can be spacer marked up with sync reference and details of the contents of the roll or it can be a standard leader with count-down markings, etc. Sync leaders should be of a specified length for projection purposes (*see* **Projection leader**).

Level sync   The relationship between separate picture and sound material that is sync-marked in parallel. Necessary for distinguishing from **Printing sync** where the sound has to be advanced by a specific number of frames for composite or married printing.

Library shots   Visuals available from stock footage for duplication and insertion into the body of specially shot material. Thus the Eiffel Tower to establish Paris where the scene is a studio set – although much more subtle use can be made of good library material.

Library sound   Stock music and effects available for use on films either from tape or disc. These can be transferred to film for tracklaying or played in from source during mixing.

Lip sync Speech that is coincidental with the image of the speaker.

Liquid gate A printer gate that immerses the film in liquid. It eliminates scratches by filling them in and prevents refractions during exposure. Not to be confused with **Wet gate**.

Live action Applied to the shooting of living things as opposed to abstract or animation filming.

Log (or Log sheet) The written catalogue of film material, usually cross-referencing **Key** or **Code numbers** with **Slate** and **Take** numbers, with additional shorthand notes of the nature of each shot.

L.S. Long shot.

Loops, Looping In editing, loops are made of sections of film and/or sound for two purposes. Firstly, for post-synchronization of dialogue or effects and, secondly, for use as continuous background effects during mixing to avoid laying up a long continuous length. The loop is joined head to tail for continuous running on projectors or sound reproducers. The length of loops must be carefully determined to allow for easy running and convenient use. This method is now largely replaced by ADR.

Low angle A shot taken from below the subject, i.e. any shot of a human being which is markedly below eye level. Usually chosen for dramatic emphasis.

Low key Lighting to produce an image that is dominated by darker tones, or picture that demonstrates this quality.

Luminance A measure of the brightness of a video signal from black through to white, thus defining the make-up of the image.

Magnetic head A sound component that acts in contact with magnetic film or tape to record, reproduce or erase sound.

Magnetic master The soundtrack that carries the final mixed sound to be used for transfer to the optical or **Magnetic stripe** which is combined with the picture for show or release copies. Also used for **Double-head projection**, although it is safer to run a copy.

Magnetic sound film Film that uses iron oxide as the coating on which sound is recorded and reproduced. *See* **Optical sound**.

Magnetic stripe The strip of iron oxide placed on film in the normal soundtrack position, usually as an alternative to **Optical sound** for release prints.

Magnetic tape ¼-in. sound tape.

Magnetic track Usually applied to magnetic sound film carrying various kinds of sound for use in the cutting process or laid up for mixing. (Note: the word magnetic in all its uses is commonly abbreviated to mag.)

Married print *see* **Combined print**

Mask A device used mostly in cameras and printers to limit the area of the frame that is exposed to light. Thus a mask can alter the **Aspect ratio** and it can facilitate split-screen filming by alternately covering matching parts of the frame.

Master Applies to both picture and sound. With picture it can refer to the printed camera original from reversal film and also to a timed, graded or corrected print (master positive) from which duplicates can be made. In sound, master refers to the final mixed track or the original recording or tape or sound film of any important component, e.g. music master or sync master.

Master shot The shot that covers a whole scene both in terms of duration and in containing all relevant action. It is conventionally shot first so that all **Cover** can be subsequently filmed to match.

Match(ing) action Cutting that uses the process of any movement as a device for providing a smooth transition between cuts. Although cutting on action is a useful technique it is not a substitute for proper analysis of the motivation for a cut.

Matrix *see* **Dye-transfer**

Matte A device for limiting the area of the frame to be exposed either on the camera or on a separate strip of film in the printer. In the latter case the shape and position of the matte can be altered frame by frame to match the area to be 'matted' – it is thus called 'travelling matte'.

M.C.U. Medium close-up shot.

M.L.S. Medium long shot.

M.S. Medium shot.

Mise-en-scène (or staging) The manipulation of all the elements which contribute to the filming of a scene. Primarily the setting, props, costumes, lighting and action and the way they relate to the camera. Proper consideration of mise-en-scène includes an awareness of the contribution envisaged in the editing.

Mix Applied to sound, this describes the process of combining two or more sound sources into a single recording. As a noun it refers to the resultant soundtrack. With regard to picture, *see* **Dissolve**.

Mixer The person who performs or co-ordinates the process of mixing.

Modulation Variations in a sound signal, either as heard or as it exists in a recording.

Montage The term was originally used to describe creative editing by the Russians in the 1920s; it was then applied to quick cutting often with the use of opticals exhibited in Hollywood films of the 1930s, usually for sequences that provided shorthand descriptions of events or narrative progression. The French use the term to describe editing *per se*. Nowadays montage is most usually taken to mean any cutting that assembles a number of shots in an impressionistic fashion so as to achieve an overall effect not inherent in the separate elements. It is often backed by a dense soundtrack which normally includes music.

Mood music Music used to complement or support the atmosphere and emotional content of a scene.

M.O.S. An American term applied to shots made without sound. It is said to be derived from a Germanic/English rendering of 'without sound' as 'mit-out sound'. Elsewhere such shots are described as **Mute**.

M and E track Music and effects track. Usually arrived at in pre-mixing or, in any case, as a separate part of the mixing process. Invaluable for alternative versions of a final soundtrack as it allows for foreign dialogue to be used to replace the original version without recourse to all the original tracks. It also simplifies the balancing of the voice tracks against the other sound.

Mute Shots without sound. *See* **M.O.S.**

Narration (commentary or voice-over) Words spoken over the film either by an anonymous person or by a person or actor who figures in the film. Can be first-person or third-person in style. The words are not related to the synchronous dialogue.

Negative cutting Conforming the camera negative to the cutting copy or work print in preparation for printing.

Negative report *see* **Camera sheet**

N.G. takes Takes that are no good and therefore not worth using in the cutting. In practice N.G. takes may be developed with the rest of the material but not printed.

Noddy A colloquial term describing a shot of an interviewer nodding, obtained for use as a **Cutaway** during editing.

Non-linear Refers to editing that is flexible and infinitely changeable, usually implying fast access to source material and easy manipulation of elements. Facilitated by digital storage and random access through computer technology.

Obligatory scene The scene in most narrative films without which the crux of the dramatic action is not established. It is conventionally placed between exposition and the development of the specific focus of the plot. In scripting shooting and cutting it therefore requires particular care and attention.

Off-camera Beyond the margins of the frame.

Off-laying The process of splitting soundtracks, especially dialogue, to allow for balancing and equalization during the mix.

Off-line editing The normal process of video editing using copies of original tapes with burnt in time-code for reference and subsequent matching in the on-line process. Little or no effects are attempted in the off-line and the final product is an EDL.

Off-mike Sound that is not picked up by the microphone at a usable level, e.g. feed lines from a character out of shot. Such dialogue must be replaced if it exists within the body of a shot as cut. It is usually available from the track of a complementary shot.

Off-scale Beyond the limits of the series of printer-lights. Applied to material that is either so under-exposed or over-exposed that a usable rendition of the scene is impossible.

Off-screen (O.S.) Action not seen by the camera but often pertinent. Sometimes conveyed by sound such as voice or effects.

O.K. takes Designation on **Camera sheets** and continuity sheets of shots which are good enough to be printed. Does not necessarily imply satisfaction with performance, but is an indication that both the camera operator and the sound recordist are satisfied.

One-light print A print in which all the scenes in a roll are made at the same printer-light setting. The setting is determined by analysing the range of exposure and striking an average which will provide a reasonable print of all the shots, assuming the range is not too extreme.

On-line editing In a way this is the equivalent of negative cutting in film. In the on-line situation the operator/editor uses the E.D.L. to match the decisions taken in the off-line, but at the same time is able to add special effects, where required, and titling. On-lining can also be used to sweeten the soundtrack, though this is now more likely to be achieved through separate facilities.

Optical effects (or opticals) The penumbra of effects obtainable by use of the optical printer at the laboratory. Includes **Dissolves**, **Fades** and **Wipes**.

Optical print The print that is produced by involving the process available through an optical printer.

Optical printer The device that, by projecting the original images and re-photographing them, can facilitate various alterations in the nature of those images, including enlargement, reduction, speeding up, slowing down, freezing and many special effects.

Optical sound A photographic means of recording and reproducing sound. Now almost exclusively of the variable area variety, although previously also available in a variable density form. Optical sound is still the predominant system for **Release printing** but has been superseded by **Magnetic sound** for shooting and cutting purposes.

Original Specifically the material on which the images have been photographed (also applied similarly to sound), i.e. original negative and reversal original.

Orthochromatic film (Ortho) Black-and-white film that is not red-sensitive, i.e. does not reproduce the red part of the spectrum properly.

Out of sync Any situation where the picture and soundtrack are misaligned when it is intended that they should be In sync.

Outgoing shot The shot before a cut as opposed to the next or **Incoming shot**.

Out-takes (or outs) Those takes that are not selected for use either after shooting or when cutting. Not to be confused with **Spares**.

Overlap The shooting of part of a scene so that it occurs in two or more shots to provide choice in cutting points. Also the carrying of sound from one shot over the beginning or end of the one adjacent to it.

Overlapping dialogue The overlap of the speech of one character with that of another. This can be a nuisance if it occurs in the shooting at a point that is valuable for cutting but, on the other hand, it can be manufactured in cutting to provide the sense of interruption or to increase the pace of a scene.

Over-the-shoulder shot (O.S.S.) Any shot framed with a character's shoulder and/or part of his head on one side of the frame, with his back to the camera, usually looking at another character.

Pan A shot that moves laterally from a static camera position (as opposed to **Tracking**). Can involve following the movement of the action in the shot. Also used for movement between two characters not contained within the camera frame. If there is variation from the original vertical point of view of the shot it is described as pan-and-tilt.

Panchromatic film Black-and-white film that is sensitive to the whole spectrum.

Parallel action The shooting and cutting of two or more sequences of events so as to convey the impression of their occurring at the same time. Usually – although not necessarily – reaching a conclusion by the two sequences merging into the same space. Most effective when it is implied that there is a positive connection between the separate events. Edwin S. Porter's *The Great Train Robbery* (1903) is usually cited as the first sophisticated use of this technique.

Persistence of vision The phenomenon without which the 'moving picture' could not exist: the retention of an image by the eye beyond the time at which it is 'visible'. The eye does not register a flicker between the static frames of film so long as the separate images are photographed and shown at a speed above 16 frames per second assuming the normal viewing conditions for film.

Pick-up shot An additional shot taken of a section in a scene which it is felt has been inadequately covered by the other shots. It is taken either at the end of the shooting for a particular scene or after the material has been processed and viewed.

Pixel Short for picture element. Describes the smallest unit of visual information in a recorded image. Storage of images in a digital system is achieved by sampling the pixels in the source material.

Playback The playing of previously recorded sound, both for reference or simply to check its quality.

Playback track A soundtrack specifically recorded for playing back during the shooting of the relevant scene. Most commonly vocal music for singers to mime to, although also used extensively for instrumental and dance sequences.

P.O.V. (point of view) Shots taken from the established view of a person or persons in a scene, usually to be intercut with shots of that person or persons watching the scene shown in the P.O.V.

Post-synchronization The process of replacing dialogue and/or effects by re-recording with reference to the original picture and (if available) the sync sound. Requires precise handling to match the appropriate visual details, especially with lip movement in dialogue. Also describes the dubbing of foreign language voices for overseas versions of a film.

Pre-mix   To mix some elements of the sound for a film as an intermediary process towards the final mix. Where there are many tracks it is often necessary to pre-mix each element, e.g. dialogue, music and effects. The most common pre-mix, however, is of music and effects before adding the dialogue and/or narration.

Presence   The background sound that conveys the sense of an identifiable space. Without room presence all other sound seems artificial.

Printer-light   The source of illumination in a printer. Also the range of illumination levels that allows for variation in printing to compensate for variable exposure.

Printing sync   The specific sound advance required for printing picture and sound together. For 35mm optical sound the advance is 20 frames, for 16mm optical 26 frames and for 16mm magnetic it is 28 frames. *See* **Level sync**.

Print-through   The undesirable recording of an audio signal on to the layer of magnetic tape adjacent to the one on which it is meant to register.

Projection leader   A section of film joined to the front of a reel with standard markings which act as reference for the projectionist in lacing up and in changing over between reels.

Protection shot   An admission of failure or insecurity. This is a shot that provides the editor with a convenient bridging device to cover bad continuity or mismatching of angles.

Quarter-inch tape   The usual vehicle for original sound recordings when filming.

Random access   This term is now used to imply instant access to any part of source or cut material which is only truly possible in a very powerful digital system. The advantage is that there is no inhibition on the editor's work process; the disadvantage is that real thinking time has to be created to avoid superficial use of the craft.

RAM (Random Access Memory)   It is the ability of computer systems to hold and manipulate considerable amounts of information that makes them suitable technology for the highly manipulative craft of editing. In a sense RAM provides you with a controlled work space for creating the form that is required in an edit. Once a section has been saved to disk it is always possible to bring it back into RAM for further editing, just as you can take a sequence off the shelf in the cutting room. The advantage with the computer environment is the ability to save successive versions for comparison.

Reaction shot   Any shot or part of a shot that is taken or used to show the reaction of one or more characters to action and/or sound that precedes it.

Rear projection *see* **Back projection**

Reduction printing The process of duplicating a film on to stock of a narrower gauge, e.g. 35mm reduced to 16mm.

Reel The spool that carries film or the roll of film that is so carried.

Release print Any print of a film that is made for distribution and exhibition.

Resolution The ability of a lens or emulsion to render fine detail in a photographic image.

Reversal film Film that combines the function of negative and positive thus producing a print without an intermediary process. Thus, when reversal original is used for shooting, the same stock becomes a print after processing. In practice a reversal work print is made to protect this original master.

Reverse angle Any shooting position or shot that is the reverse perspective to a shot already taken. In practice reverse angles are seldom at 180° to each other since film grammar demands that shots which must be intercut are framed **within** an arc of less than 180°.

Rewind The mechanism for and the act of rewinding film.

Roll Any section of film that is wound on itself or on a spool or core (bobbin).

Rough-cut The stage in cutting between **Assembly** of the rushes and a **Fine cut**. Used to establish the chronology of scenes but does not involve any attempt to refine specific cuts. Only valuable if there are problems about the overall structure which need to be faced before fine cutting commences.

Rubber numbers *see* **Code numbers**

Run-up To run a section of film prior to the shot or sequence being worked on or viewed, either over a previous sequence or a leader.

Rushes (or dailies) The unedited picture and sound material of any shoot which are made ready for synchronization and viewing as soon as possible after shooting, and from which the film is cut.

Saturation The degree of colour in film material. Useful when discussing the **Grading** of a particular shot, sequence or film – thus de-saturated, highly saturated.

Scene Each coherent but separate unit of dramatic action in the script or finished film.

Scratch print (or slash dupe) Usually a one-light reversal print made from the cutting copy or work print either to allow simultaneous processes to occur during the final stages of post-production, e.g. negative cutting alongside mixing, or made necessary by deterioration of the cutting copy to a point where further projection or other use is impossible.

Screen direction The way movement or the positioning of subjects within the frame is controlled to make sense in terms of film grammar. Continuity of screen direction must be maintained during shooting and cutting to avoid disorientating the audience. Thus, two characters in a simple scene must retain the same relationship in all shots unless a new position is established either by camera movement or by showing the characters themselves changing their position.

Set-up Any particular camera position. Several shots can be taken from the same set-up, even if they are separated in terms of the script. A set-up usually implies continuity of lighting.

Shooting ratio A measure of the amount of film shot compared with the length of the finished film. Thus 5:1 indicates that five times the footage of the completed film was shot. Especially useful as a way of estimating the stock needed to shoot a film, by multiplying the timed script by the expected ratio. This budgeted ratio compared to an analysis of the actual ratio as shooting progresses is a device much used by producers and film accountants to judge the variance and to estimate overage.

Shot list A more or less elaborate listing of shots usually including slate numbers and an abbreviated description, either of the action in dramatic films or of the subject for documentary purposes.

Sibilance Refers to the hiss created in speaking and recording of words that contain an emphatic 'S' sound. Can result in problems if the resulting sound is unattractive. Sometimes caused by positioning the speaker too close to the microphone.

Signal-to-noise ratio The relationship between the specific sounds required in a recording and the level of noise present in the background. Thus the lower the ratio is in decibels the more likely it is that the required sound will lack clarity.

Slash dupe *see* **Scratch print**

Slate The term for, or the device and process of, denoting a shot during filming.

Slug A section of spacing, leader or junk film used as **Build-up**.

Smart slate A clapperboard or clap sticks that incorporate time-code which is fed in lock to the audio tape to facilitate immediate synchronization in transferring to video.

S.M.P.T.E. (Society of Motion Picture and Television Engineers) A professional body in the USA that has established a number of standards and procedures with regard to film and television techniques. These have gained virtually universal acceptance.

Soft cut A very short dissolve conveying the effect of a merging of two images but without implying passage of time or change of scene.

Soft focus Either a deliberate or accidental effect where the image exhibits a slight lack of sharpness. Used deliberately especially on close-ups of female stars to enhance their appearance. As an accidental effect this can ruin a shot by spoiling a part or whole of the image.

Software Usually refers to the programme carrier or disks for use in computers or electronic hardware.

Sound advance The number of frames between any picture and its appropriate sound as positioned for **Printing sync**.

Sound effects Any sound other than dialogue, narration or music that exists in or is added to the soundtracks.

Sound head The optical or magnetic device that picks up sound during recording or playback.

Sound loop A section of sound (usually of effects) that is joined head to tail for continuous running during mixing, normally for use as additional background sound when required.

Sound report The sound equivalent of the **Camera sheet**, giving details of all recording and commenting on the quality of each take.

Sound speed The rate at which sound film is run through equipment – either 24 or 25 frames per second. Established at a time when it was necessary to regulate filming speed so as to provide consistency in the reproduction of sound. Such consistency was, of course, not an absolute prerequisite in the days of silent films.

Spacer Blank leader or gash film that is used as such in building up soundtracks.

Spares Takes that are usable but not yet incorporated in the cutting copy. These are filed separately for easy access.

Special effects Shots or the shooting of film that include abnormal photographic techniques. Also applied to explosions and other shooting using special devices.

Splice The process of joining pieces of film together or the resultant joins.

Splicer Any device used for joining film. *See* **Cement joiner**; **Tape joiner**.

Spool A reel for holding wound-up film, either solid or of the split variety. The latter is more useful in editing since it allows for easier handling.

Spot effects Sound effects that require precise 'spotting' in tracklaying and mixing, e.g. gun shots, door slams and footsteps.

Squawk box A derogatory term describing the kind of loudspeaker once prevalent in cutting rooms, referring to the poor quality of sound reproduction obtained from them. Higher fidelity equipment is now more normal.

Staging *see* **Mise-en-scène**

Start-mark The mark on a frame that provides a reference for projection and/or synchronized running of separate picture and sound rolls.

Static Marks caused by a discharge of static electricity during the photographic process. They result from friction between the stock and the machinery through which it is being run. They cannot be removed from the film and thus may cause rejection of the affected material.

Step printer/printing The machine or process that prints film by holding each frame still during exposure, thus allowing for special treatment of each individual frame.

Stock footage (or stock shots) Film that is held for use in films requiring material other than that specially shot. May be of an exotic or unrepeatable nature but can also be general establishing material.

Straight cut Used to differentiate the normal joining together of shots from those involving optical effects.

Stripping The process of removing all extraneous sound from dialogue tracks to assist in the creation of clean recordings during mixing.

Subjective camera, Subjective shooting Filming from an angle that is meant to imitate the point of view of a character in the film, or positioning the camera so as to give the audience the experience of direct involvement with the scene. The action is sometimes staged as if the camera is the focus of attention in the scene, whether or not we identify with another character's point of view.

Sub-title Words superimposed on the picture area, usually in the bottom half of the frame, either as translation of dialogue or to give information about the place, time or action.

Superimposition (super) The placing of one image over another, usually in printing. Thus superimposed titles.

Sweetening The post-production of audio for video, incorporating tape machines with up to 24-track facility.

Swish-pan *see* **Whip-pan**

Sync-bench *see* **Editing bench**

Sync effects Sound effects that are part of the synchronous recording.

Sync mark The mark placed on picture and sound as a level sync reference; either on the head of a roll or on the individual sync point at each slate.

Sync plop One frame of tone (usually 1000 Hz) that provides a sync reference opposite a predetermined frame on the leader. Usually placed opposite or parallel to the '3' on the picture leader.

Synching up The process of putting picture and sound material into synchronization.

Synchronizer The mechanical device most commonly used for preparing sync material and for conforming the negative or original to the cutting copy or work print.

Tail, Tail(s) out The end of a roll of film or the fact that it is wound-up end out.

Take The individual attempts to obtain a shot, differentiated by sequential numbering on the clapperboard and the corresponding announcement.

Take-up Any mechanism on which the film is accumulated after running through a camera, editing machine or projector.

Tape joiner (or tape splicer) A device that uses adhesive tape to make the join, usually incorporating a cutting device.

Telecine A machine for transferring film to videotape. Can incorporate separate sound in synchronization and can also accommodate the recording on to video of negative film by reverse phasing.

TV cut-off The area of the frame that is actually visible in television transmission. Important for such things as positioning of titles.

Tilt A shot that uses vertical movement of the camera without changing the horizontal level of the camera body.

Time-base corrector A device used in video, especially when making special effects, to avoid image deformation by balancing the vertical and horizontal signals.

Time-code The system for identifying each video frame with its own code, based on the fact that video records at 30 frames per second (actually 29.97). By the use of devices that can 'read' this time-code, individual frames can be recalled and edited, thus allowing accurate editing and the making of edit decision lists for on-lining.

Timing *see* **Grading**

Tracking Any shot made by moving the camera and its support, usually on wheels, along a pre-laid track.

Tracklaying (or laying tracks) In editing, the process of assembling sound film of all kinds in a form that allows for efficient manipulation during mixing.

Transfer The process of re-recording sound, e.g. from tape to film or film to film. Also the sound thus re-recorded.

Trial print *see* **Answer print**

Trim A short section of any shot or soundtrack that has been removed from the take as assembled or cut into the film. Where a shot is used once there will be both a front and end trim to be refiled.

Trim bin The device in which trims are hung or clipped while the material for a sequence is being cut. It should be cleared constantly during editing and the trims refiled to avoid the problem of not having immediate access to any piece of film.

Ultrasonic A method of cleaning dirt from film by the use of high frequency sound waves.

Undershot A sequence or a whole film that is inadequately covered in the shooting and thus makes editing unnecessarily difficult.

Virgin loops Mint sound film that is looped for the purposes of recording especially during post-synchronization.

Virtual editing Simulating the editing process, as in digital systems. The form thus created exists only as a display within the system and requires the use of an E.D.L. to produce the real equivalence from the source material.

Voice-over *see* **Narration**

Wet gate (or wet printing) Printing that incorporates a small tank of liquid through which the stock passes before reaching the point of exposure. *See* **Liquid gate**.

Whip-pan (zip-pan or swish-pan) Fast movement of camera during shooting or the shot that is thus produced which blurs the image between two points in a pan.

Wild track Sound that is recorded in the same situation as any shooting for a film but is not obtained as sync.

Wipe All optical effects that convey the impression of one shot being removed by the appearance of another. In its simplest form a hard-edged line travels across the screen simultaneously removing the outgoing shot whilst revealing the incoming one.

Work print The positive copy of the film that is used by the editor in the process of cutting, from which the **Cutting copy** is produced.

Wow A disturbance in sound that gives the effect of spasmodic changes in pitch, usually resulting from variations in the speed of the transport mechanism in a recorder.

Zero frame The first frame of a roll of picture.

Zip-pan *see* **Whip-pan**

Zoom The act of enlarging or reducing the image in the frame by means of a zoom lens.

Suggested further reading

Andrew, Dudley (1978) *André Bazin*, Oxford University Press. A stimulating biography.

Andrew, Geoff (1989) *The Film Handbook,* Longman. A concise if idiosyncratic guide to most important directors and their work.

Barry, Iris (1965) *D. W. Griffith: American Film Master,* Museum of Modern Art, New York. Delineates the development of Griffith's use of editing.

Bazin, André (1974) *Jean Renoir,* W. H. Allen. A wonderful companion to Renoir's own book.

Bazin, André (1978) *Orson Welles: A Critical View,* Elm Tree. Highly readable examination of Welles' career.

Bazin, André (1967) *What is Cinema?,* University of California Press. A collection of essays which represent the vital perceptions of the man who inspired the New Wave.

Bergman, Ingmar (1988) *The Magic Lantern,* Hamish Hamilton. An autobiography which provides considerable insight into his approach to film.

Bresson, Robert (1977) *Notes on Cinematography.* For Bresson, cinematography is art created with the camera, as opposed to what he calls 'filmed theatre'.

Brownlow, Kevin (1968) *The Parade's Gone By,* Secker and Warburg. A living memorial to the silent cinema in Hollywood. Includes interviews with many veterans, including editors.

Burch, Noel (1979) *To the Distant Observer: Form and Meaning in the Japanese Cinema,* Scolar Press. A refreshing analysis which encourages a different perception of cinema.

Dancyger, Ken (1993) *The Technique of Film and Video Editing*, Focal Press. Supplements the contribution made by the Reisz and Millar book in delineating the aesthetics of cinema.

Eisenstein, Sergei. Various writings available on theory and practice, plus a very readable volume of memoirs.

Godard, Jean-Luc (1972) *Godard on Godard* (translated by Tom Milne), Secker and Warburg. Includes a perceptive piece on editing: 'Montage My Fine Care'.

Happe, Bernard (1974) *Your Film and the Laboratory*, Focal Press. An excellent graphic guide and still relevant despite changes in technology.

Jackson, Kevin (ed.) (1993) *The Humphrey Jennings Reader*, Carcanet. Scripts, diaries, letters, talks, poetry, etc.

Lindgren, Ernest (1948) *The Art of the Film*, Allen and Unwin.
Lobrutto, Vincent (1991) *Selected Takes: Film Editors on Editing*, Praeger. A revealing series of in-depth interviews.

MacGowan, Kenneth (1965) *Behind the Screen: The History and Techniques of the Motion Picture*, Dell Publishing. An engaging and revealing analysis from a well respected Hollywood professional and film teacher.

Nizhny, Vladimir (1962) *Lessons with Eisenstein* (translated by Ivor Montague and Jay Leyda), George Allen and Unwin. Brings alive the mind and teaching methods behind the theories.

Oldham, Gabriella (1992) *First Cut . . . Conversations with Film Editors*, Cambridge University Press. Adds substantially to the recorded experiences of editors.

Ranvaud, Don (1988) *Bertolucci on Bertolucci*, Plexus. A lavishly illustrated book which is based on conversations with the director.
Reisz, Karel and Millar, Gavin (1953) *The Technique of Film Editing*, Focal Press. Still the most thorough examination of the aesthetics of cutting.
Renoir, Jean (1974) *My Life and My Films*, Collins. As life enhancing as any canvas painted by his father.
Richie, Donald (1971) *The Films of Akira Kurosawa*, University of California Press. Many references to his editing methods, especially in relation to mise-en-scène.
Rosenbloom, Ralph (1979) *When the Shooting Stops, the Cutting Begins*, Da Capo. A feature editor's perspective on his contribution.
Rubin, Michael (1991) *Non-linear: A Guide to Electronic Film and Video Editing*, Triad Publishing. An understanding of the new technology for the layman.

Sadoul, Georges (1948) *British Creators of Film Technique*, British Film Institute.
Schrader, Paul (1972) *Transcendental Style in Film*, University of California Press. The spiritual dimension of Ozu, Dreyer and Bresson.

Tarkovsky, Andrei (1986) *Sculpting in Time*, The Bodley Head. A profound insight into the thoughts of a very special film-maker.
Truffaut, François (1968) *Hitchcock*, Paladin. The perspective of one film-maker on the work of another; mutually revealing.

Vaughan, Dai (1983) *Portrait of an Invisible Man*, British Film Institute. The life and work of Stewart MacAllister. One superb editor's celebration of another. As close to capturing the ineffable as you could get.

Vigo, Jean (1983) *The Complete Jean Vigo*, Lorimar. Scripts, speeches and other writing.

Walter, Ernest (1969) *The Technique of the Film Cutting Room*, Focal Press. An excellent insight into the practice of feature film editing.

Wright, Basil (1974) *The Long View: An International History of Cinema*, Paladin. Affectionate and insightful; placing cinema alongside the other arts and historical events.

Index

Page numbers in **bold** refer to illustrations.

A Propos de Nice 19
A wind 134
Accident 38, 125
Accidental Tourist, The 154
Ackerman, Chantal 33
ADR (post synchronization) 112–13, 128
Adventures of Dolly 2
After Many Years 2
Age d'Or, L' 9
Age of Innocence 152
All that Jazz 105
Allen, Dede 57, 99–100, 109, 151, **151**, 152, 154, 157
Allen, Woody 103
Altman, Robert 36, 102, 109, 156
American Academy of Motion Picture Arts and Sciences 59
American in Paris, An 150
Anderson, Lindsay 20, 119
Andrew, Geoff 24
Angle 43–4
Année Dernière à Marienbad, L' 28
Answer print 140, 141
Antonioni, Michaelangelo 26, 41
Apocalypse Now! 157
Arcalli, Franco 32
Argent, L' 97
Arrangement, The 29
Art of the Film, The 2–3, 107

Astaire, Fred 61, 105
Atalante, L' 19, 20, **20**
Au hasard Balthasar 97
Auden, W.H. 17
Audiofile 127
Avid Technology Europe Ltd **80**
Aventura, L' 26

B wind 134
Badlands 115
Balance 84
    colour 141, 142
Barraqué, Martine 82
Barry, Iris 2, 4
Bartholemew Fair (1825) ix, x
Battle of Algiers 154
Battleship Potemkin 5
Bauchens, Anne 150
Bazin, André 9, 14, 15, 25, 148
Beatty, Warren 151
Behind the Motion Picture Screen 13, **55**, 56
Belmondo, Jean-Paul 97
Ben Hur 15
Bergman, Ingmar *frontispiece*, 36, 93, 94
Bernstein, Elmer 152
Bertolucci, Bernardo 32, 36, 155
Bicycle Thieves 23, **23**
Big Chill, The 154
Big Country, The 15

Birth of a Nation 4
Bitter Tears of Petra von Kant, The 45
Bitzer, Billy 2, 36
Blackmail 13
Body Heat 154
Bogarde, Dirk 30
Bogart, Humphrey 115
Bogdanovich, Peter 150
Bonnie and Clyde 100, 151, 157
Booth, Margaret 149, 150
Borinage 158
Bresson, Robert 22, 33, 38, 39, 95–7, **96**, 130
Brewster McCloud 156
Bridge, The 158
Brief Encounter 24
British Creators of Film Technique 1
Britten, Benjamin 17
Brooks, Louise 11, 31
Brown, Joe E. 105
Brownlow, Kevin x, 24, 54, 83, 150
Buñuel, Luis 9–10, 36, **94**, 94–5
Butch Cassidy and the Sundance Kid 117

Cacoyannis, Michael 36
Cahiers du Cinéma 25, 35
California Split 156
Camera positions 41
Camera sheet 52
Camille 149
Campbell, Cheryl **106**
Capra, Frank 149
Captions 116
Carné, Marcel 23
Casablanca 25
Cayrol, Jean 28
Cement joiners 58
Certaine tendance du cinéma français, Une (article) 26
Chabrol, Claude 24
Chandler, Raymond 36, 103, 115
Chaplin, Charles 10, 103
Chequerboard 139
Chien Andalou, Un 9
Children's Hour, The 14
Chinatown 38, 100–102, **101**
Choreography 105
Christie, Agatha 103
Cinemascope 29, 30
Citizen Kane 15, 16, 22, 24

City of Hope 107
Clapperboard 40, 67
Clark, Jim 159
Clark, Susan 99
Coates, Anne V. 153–4
Coding the rushes 71
Collins, Alfred 1
Colour 140
Colour balance 141, 142
Colour Reversal Intermediate (C.R.I.) 144
Colpi, Henri 159
Comedy 103, 104
Commentary 115
Compeditor 58, 59
Computer screen display 62
Conformist, The 32
Confrontation, The 45
Contact 132
Content 107
Contes Moraux 98
Continuity 41
Continuity notes 52
Continuity report 51
Conversation, The 38
Coppola, Francis Ford 38, 158
Cost of reprints 60
Coup de Torchon 34
Coutard, Raoul 36
Cowie, Peter 93
C.R.I. (Colour Reversal Intermediate) 144
Cries and Whispers 93
Crime and Punishment 7
Cristiani, Gabriella 32, 155
Cue-dot marker 144
Cukor, George 149, 159
Curtis, Tony **104**, 104
Cutting process 64, 76–7, 139
    dramatic emphasis 90–91
    junctions between scenes 90
    overcoming problems by 88–90
    reasons for 87–90
    standard markings **78**
Cutting room **55**, 57, 59, 60, 146
    consumables 60
    general requirements 60
    technology 54–63

Dali, Salvador 9

Dances with Wolves 105
Daniels, Bebe 54
Dean, James 29
Death in Venice 30
Death on the Nile 103
Decae, Henri 36
Delerue, Georges 119
De Mille, Cecil B. 150
Density 140, 141
de Palma, Brian 5
Depth of field 14
de Sica, Vittorio 23, **23**
Devils, The 122
Dialogue 43, 111–12, 154
    tracklaying 123–4
    unconvincing 90
Diamond, I.A.L. 104
Diary of a Lost Girl 12
Dietrich, Marlene **16**
Digi-slate 78
Digital sound 62, 63
Digital technology 109, 145–6
Digitized material 62
Digitized rushes 54
Direction of movement 43
Director–editor relationship 81–2
Directors of Photography (DOPs) 36
Dirty Harry 26
Discreet charm of the bourgeoisie, The 94–5
Dissolves 138, 152
Distance 43–4
Documentaries 8, 17, 27, 37, 45–9, 58, 65, 71, 72, 76, 107, 115, 116, 120, 151, 152, 158
Donen, Stanley 150
Don't Look Now 125
Dostoyevsky, Fydor M. 7
Dovzhenko, Alexander 7, 8
Dreyer, Carl T. 22
Dubbing charts 128, **129**
Dunnaway, Faye 101
Duplicate master 144
Duplication 132–4, 144
Duras, Marguerite 27
Dymytryk, Edward 36
Dynamic axis 84–5

Earth 7
East of Eden 29

Eastwood, Clint 25
Edit Decision List (EDL) 78
Editing
    early days of 54
    evolution 1–35
    examples 91–102, 148–59
    language of 83
    machinery 109
    materials checklist 65–7
    non-linear 54, 61, 62, 63, 79
    process 64–82
    random access 54, 79, 145, 146
    sound in 108–30
    technology 56
    see also Digital technology
Editor–director relationship 81–2
EDL (Edit Decision List) systems 61
Effects 111, 114, 128, 137, 138
    tracklaying 124–8
Eight-and-a-Half 28
Eisenstein, Sergei 5–8, **6**, 12
El Cid 150
Elvira Madigan 117
Emphasis 84
Emulsion position 134
Enfants du Paradis, Les 23
Epic music 118
E.T.: The Extraterrestrial 154
Evolution of the Language of Cinema, The 14
Eyelines 42

Fades 138
Family Portrait **18**
Fanny and Alexander Frontispiece, x, 93
Farewell My Lovely 36
Fassbinder, Rainer Werner 45
Faure, Elie 97
Fazan, Adrienne 150
Fellini, Federico 28
Femme Douce, Une 95–7
Fields, Verna 150
Film
    breaking down 75–6
    checklist 65–7
    footage/time conversion chart 60
    processing 131–2
    recording 60
Films of Akira Kurosawa, The 86
Finney, Albert 153

First Cut ... Conversations with Film Editors 154
Flaherty, Robert **8**, 8–9, 17, 158
Flaherty, Mrs Robert **8**
Flat-bed machine 57, 58
Flexibility 110
Foley 114, 128
For Love of Gold 2
Form 107
Fosse, Bob 105
Fuller, Samuel 26

Gance, Abel 29
Garbo, Greta 149
Garr, Teri 38
Giant 150
Gibbs, Antony 157
Gigi 150
Gish, Lillian 3
Godard, Jean-Luc 24, **27**, 86, 97–8
Godfather, Part II, The 157
Good Morning Babylon 155
Gould, Elliot 115
GPO Film Unit 17
Grading 140–44
Grand Canyon 107
Great Expectations 24
Great Train Robbery, The 2
Greenberg, Jerry 157
Greystoke, The Legend of Tarzan 154
Grierson, John 17
Griffith, D.W. 1–4, **3**, 149
Groundhog Day 105

Hackman, Gene 38, 99, 110
Hammett, Dashiell 115
Harvey, Tony 149
Hawks, Howard 57
Heavyworks One **80**
Heim, Alan 105
Hellman, Lillian 14
Hepworth, Cecil 1
High Definition Television (HDTV) 63
Hill, George Roy 117
Hiroshima mon Amour 28, 159
Histoire de l'Art 97
Hitchcock, Alfred 13, 24
Home Sweet Home 2
Hornbeck, William 149–50
Horror films 106

Hoskins, Bob **106**
Howe, James Wong 36
Huston, John 101, 149

Identification 39–45
In Country 157
Ingemarson, Sylvia x
Internegatives 144
Interpositives 144
Intolerance 4
It's a Wonderful Life 149
Ivens, Joris 158

Jancso, Miklos 45
Jaws 150
Jeanne Dielman 33, 34
Jennings, Humphrey 17–19, **18**, 158
Jewison, Norman 157
Journal d'une Femme de Chambre, Le 36
Jules et Jim **25**, 26, 119
Juxtaposition 5

Kafka, Franz 155
Kaos 155
Karina, Anna **27**
Kärré, Marianne 94
Kasdan, Lawrence 107, 154
Kaufman, Boris 19
Kazan, Elia 29, 150
Keaton, Buster 10, **11**, 103
Kelly, Gene 105, 150
Kieslowski, Krzysztof 34
King, Dave 50
Klute 157
Knack, The 157
Korda, Alexander 149
Korda, Zoltan 149
Kubrick, Stanley 117
Kuleshov, Lev 5
Kurosawa, Akira 36, 86, 91–3, **92**, 148

Laboratory 60, 131–2, 135, 140, 143, 144
Laboratory rushes report 65
Land, The 157
Lang, Fritz 13
Language 34
Lantern slides 1–2
Lasally, Walter 36
Last of the Mohicans, The 105
Last Tango in Paris 32

Last Year in Marienbad 159
Lawrence of Arabia 24, 153
Lawson, Tony 82, 159
Leacock, Richard **8**
Leaders 59
Lean, David 24, 149, 153
Lemmon, Jack **104**, 104
Lenin, V.I. 4, 7
Lescarboura, Austin C. **55**, 56
Lessons with Eisenstein 7
Lester, Richard 157
Lewis, Daniel Day 152
Life of an American Fireman, The 2
Lightworks Editing Systems Ltd. **80**
Lindgren, Ernest 2, 4, 107
Line 41, **42**
Linear nature of film and video 13
Listen to Britain 18
Little Big Man 157
Little Foxes, The 15
Littleton, Carol 150, 154
Logging 71, **72**
Lombardo, Lou 156–7
Lonedale Operator, The 2
Loneliness of the Long Distance Runner,
   The 157
Lonely Villa, The 2
Long Goodbye, The 36, 102, 156
Long View, The 21
Lorentz, Pare 17
Losey, Joseph 38, 125
Louisiana Story **8**, 9, 158
Love in the Afternoon 98–9
Lucas, George 150
Lumet, Sidney 151
Lumière brothers 1, 33

M 13
McAllister, Stewart 18, 19, 158–9, **159**
McCabe and Mrs Miller 156
McDowell, Malcolm 119
MacGowan, Kenneth 13
McGuire, Kathryn **11**
Mack Sennett Studios 149
Mckay, Craig 152, 157
McKechnie, Samuel ix
Macluhan, Marshall 107
Magnificent Ambersons, The 22, 24
Magnificent Seven, The 36
Malick, Terence 115

Malkovitz, John 32
Man with a Movie Camera, The 7
Mankiewicz, Herman J. 16
Marking up the script 53, 72
Marks, Richard 157
Mary Reilly **52**, **73**, **74**, **129**
Massacre, The 2
Master material, storage of 144–5
Media Composer **80**
Méliès, Georges 1, 103
MGM 149, 150
Millar, Gavin 29
Minelli, Vincente 150
Mirabeau, Octave 36
Mirren, Helen 119
Mirror 32
Mismatched action 89
Missouri Breaks, The 100
Mixing 128
Monroe, Marilyn 104, **104**
Montage 5, 7
Montage mon beau souci (article) 86, 97
Montage non-linear editing set-up **81**
Moscow Film School 4, 7
Mosjoukine, Ivan 5
Motivation 85
Mouchette 97
Movement, lack of static before or
   after 89
Moviola 12–13, 54, 56–9, 61, 67, 76, 79
Mulligan, Robert 115
Muriel 28
Murray, Bill 105
Music 110, 111, 117–21, 154
Music and effects mix (M and E) 128
Musicals 105, 150
Mute rushes 65
Mute tableaux 2
Mutiny on the Bounty 149

Nanook of the North 8, 9
Napoleon 29
Narration 114–16
Narrative 152
Nashville 102
National Film and Television School
   159
Navigator, The **11**
Negative cutting 139, 142
Neo-realism 23–4

New Earth, The 158
New Wave 24–9, 36
Nicholson, Jack 38, 101, **101**
Night Mail 17
Night Moves 99–100, 102, 106, 110, 151
Night of San Lorenzo, The 155
Night Sun 155
Nizhny, Vladimir 7
Non-linear 54
Non-linear editing 54, 61, 62, 63, 79
Nostalghia 32
Nuit et Brouillard 27
Nykvist, Sven 36

O Lucky Man! 119
Odessa Steps sequence 5
Off-line machine 61
Oldham, Gabriella 154
Optical sound 58
Opticals 134–8, 141
Outrage, The 36
Overlap 44–5, 137
Ozu, Yasujiro **21**, 21–2, 34

Pabst, Georg W. 12
Pace of movement 43
Pacing 86
    discrepancies in 89
Padre Padrone 155
Pakula, Alan 157
Pandora's Box 12
Paperwork 50–53, 65
Parade's Gone By, The x, 54, 83, 150
Parallel action 86
Partie de Campagne **15**
Passage to India, A 24
Passion de Jeanne d'Arc, Le **96**
Paul, R.W. 1
Peckinpah, Sam 156
Penn, Arthur 99–100, 150, 157
Pennies from Heaven **106**, 107
Performance 157
Perpignani, Roberto 32, 154, 154–5, **155**
Persistence of vision 12
Persona 93, 94
Pfeiffer, Michelle 152
Phantom of the liberty **94**, 94–5
Pic-sync 58, 59
Pierrot le Fou 26, 97–8
Place in the Sun, A 149–50

Playback 121–2
Plough that Broke the Plains, The 17
Point of focus 85
Poitiers Festival 155
Polanski, Roman 38, 100–102, **101**
Pollack, Sydney 149
Pontecorvo, Gillo 154
Popular Entertainment through the Ages
    ix
Porter, Edwin S. 2
Portrait of an Invisible Man 158
Post-synchronization (ADR) 112–13,
    138
Potter, Dennis **106**, 107
Powell, Michael 35
Pre-mixes 128, 130
Printing 140–44
Printing sync 143
Private-eye genre 102–7
Projection change-over 144
Pudovkin, V.I. 5, 12

Raging Bull 152
Ramis, Harold 105
Ramona 2
Random access editing 54, 79, 145, 146
Rashomon 36, 91–3, **92**
Red Beard 86
Reds 151–2
Reed, John 151
Reflexive options 13
Reisz, Karel 29, 158
Rendez-vous d'Anna, Les 33
Renoir, Jean 14, **15**, 36
Reprints 132–4
Resnais, Alain 27, **28**
Reverse-phasing 140
Rhythm 86
Richardson, Tony 157
Riefenstahl, Leni 19
Ritchie, Donald 86
Ritt, Martin 36
Roaring Twenties, The 25
Robbe-Grillet, Alain 27
Robe, The 29
Roeg, Nicolas 82, 125, 157, 159
Rohmer, Eric 98–9
Roma 28
Rome, Open City 23
Rosemary's Baby 100

Rossellini, Roberto 23
Rotter, Stephen 157
Round-up, The 45
Rubin, Michael 54
Russell, Ken 50, 122

Sacrifice, The 32
Sadoul, Georges 1
Sandrelli, Stefania 32
Sanjuro 44
Sayles, John 107
Schlesinger, John 159
Schoonmaker, Thelma 82, 150, 152–3, **153**
Schrader, Paul 22, 97
Scorsese, Martin 82, 97, 152–3
Screening 142
Script
    marking up 53, 72
    shooting 37
Sculpting in Time 32
Selection process 83–4
Sequencing 85
Serurier, Iwan 56
Servant, The 38
Set discipline 44
Seven Samurai, The 36, 44
Seventh Seal, The 93
Seyrig, Delphine 34
Shane 150
Sharp, Alan 99
Sheltering Sky, The 32
Shooting process 37–9
Shooting script 37
Shootist, The 26
Short-cuts 102
Shot lists 37, 52
Siegel, Don 25, 26
Silence 108
Silent comedians 10–12
Silent pictures 149
Singin' in the Rain 11, 39, 150
Singing Detective, The 107
Situation comedy 103
Smart Slate 78
Smith, G.A. 1
Some Like it Hot 104, **104**
Song of Ceylon 17
Song of Summer 50
Sound 10, 138

categories of 111
development of 12
equipment 109
in editing 108–30
pioneers of 13
quality 49–50, 109
stereophonic 30
synchronous 49
Sound of Music, The 24
Sound–picture matching 89–90
Sound report 52
Sound Station 127
Soundtracks 62, 78, 89–90, 109, 141, 143, 145
working methods 109–10
Soviet Union 4–5
Spacer 59
Spielberg, Steven 150, 154
Splitting 124
Stahl, John 149
Stalker 32
Stararo, Vittorio 36
Steenbeck machine 57, **57**, 62, 67, 79
Stereophonic sound 30
Stevens, George 150
Storage of master material 144–5
Stravinsky, Igor F. 122
Stripping 124
Structuring process 84
Sturges, John 36
Summer with Monika 93
Sunday in the Country 34
Superimposition 136
Surrealism 9–10
Sync-bench 59, 60
Sync-locked material 62
Sync rushes 67–71
    viewing 72–5
Synchronization 39–45, 59, 78
Synchronizer 58, 76, 144
Synchronous sound 49

Tape joiners 58
Tarantino, Quentin 57
Tarkovsky, Andrei 32, **33**
Tavernier, Bertrand 34
Taviani brothers 34, 155, 156
Technique of Film Editing, The 29, 158
Television 29–31, 58, 61, 63, 65, 103, 106, 107, 116

Ten Days That Shook the World (John Reid) 151
Thrillers 106
Time-code 61, 78
Time/space relationship 138
Title cards 2
To Kill a Mockingbird 115
Tokyo Story **21**
Toland, Greg 16, 36
Tom Jones 157
Touch of Evil **16**
Towne, Robert 38, 100
Tracklaying 122–8
   dialogue 123–4
   effects 124–8
   function of 127
   mechanics of 126–7
Transcendental Style in Film 22
Transcribing or marking up the script 53, 72
Transfer to magnetic film 67
Trial, The 155
Trim bin 59
Trintignant, Jean Louis 32
Triumph of the Will 19
Truffaut, François 24, **25**, 26, 82, 119
2001 – A Space Odyssey 117–18

Unbearable Lightness of Being, The 108
Unconvincing action 89
Universal Pictures 150
Untouchables, The 5

van Dongen, Helen **8**, 158
van Fleet, Jo 29
Vaughan, Dai 158
Vertov, Dziga 5, 7
Video editing 61, 62, 65, 78
Video masters 60
Video recording 60
Vie et Rien d'Autre, La 34
Viewing machine 67
Viewing the sync rushes 72–5

Vigo, Jean 19–20, **20**
Visconti, Luchino 23, 30
Vision, persistence of 12
Visualization 62
Vogel, Edith 108
'Voice of God' technique 116
Voice-over 111, 114–16
Voice selection 115
Voyage to the Moon 103

Walter, Ernest 159
War films 106
War of the Worlds, The 15
Warner Brothers 25
Watership Down 117
Weekend 98
Welles, Orson 14–16, **16**, 22, 148, 152, 155
Wenning, Kathy 152
West Side Story 24
Westerns 105
Wexler, Haskell 150
What is Cinema? 9
Why We Fight 149
Wide-screen 29–30
Wide-screen television 63
Widerberg, Bo 117
Wild Bunch, The 156
Wild River 29
Wild sound 49–50
Wild Strawberries 93
Wild tracks 50
Wilder, Billy 104, **104**, 159
Williamson, James 1
Winger, Debra 32
Wise, Robert 24, 149, 159
Woodstock 152
Wright, Basil 17, 21, 24
Wyler, William 14–16

Yankee Doodle Dandy 25

Zéro de Conduite 19, 20